The New Germany Votes

GERMAN STUDIES SERIES

The New Germany Votes

Unification and the Creation of the New German Party System

Edited by

Russell J. Dalton

BERG

Providence / Oxford

Published in 1993 by

Berg Publishers Inc.

Editorial offices:
221 Waterman Street, Providence, RI 02906 U.S.A.
150 Cowley Road, Oxford OX4 1JJ, UK

**A CIP catalogue record for this book is available
from the British Library.**

Library of Congress Cataloging-in-Publication Data

The New Germany votes : Unification and the creation of a German
party system / edited by Russell J. Dalton.
        p.   cm. — (German studies series)
    Includes bibliographical references and index.
    ISBN 0–85496–314–6. — ISBN 0–85496–386–3 (pbk.)
    1. Political parties—Germany. 2. Elections—Germany.
3. Germany—History—Unification, 1990.   I. Dalton, Russell J.
II. Series
JN3972.A979N48   1993
324.943'0879—dc20   93–18013
                                                              CIP

Printed in the United States by Edwards Brothers, Ann Arbor, MI.

In memory of our Friend and Colleague

Donald Schoonmaker

Contents

Contents

List of Tables

List of Figures

Acronyms

BFD	League of Free Democrats (Coalition of Eastern liberal parties in March 1990 election)
CDU	Christian Democratic Union
CSU	Christian Social Union
DA	Democratic Awakening
DBD	Democratic Farmers' Party of Germany (East German Farmers' party)
DFP	German Forum Party
DKP	German Communist Party (communist party in Federal Republic)
DSU	German Social Union
DVU	German People's Union
FDP	Free Democratic Party
FRG	Federal Republic of Germany
GDR	German Democratic Republic (East Germany)
LDP	Liberal Democratic Party (East German Liberals in 1990)
LDPD	Liberal Democratic Party of Germany (East German Liberals until 1990)
NDPD	National Democratic Party of Germany (East German conservative party)
PDS	Party of Democratic Socialism
REP	Republicans
SED	Socialist Unity Party (East German communist party)
SPD	Social Democratic Party

Preface

When East Germans went to the polls in March 1990, they were participating in an election like no other in their lives. For the vast majority of Easterners, this was their first real involvement in democratic electoral politics. Moreover, this election was to decide the nation's fate, not just in the rhetorical terms of election campaigns, but in *Realpolitik* terms of whether Germany should reunite and thus change the course of European history. There were tears of joy in many eyes as they voted for the parties that promised an end to the communist state, rapid unification with the West, and the creation of a new Germany.

This book describes the elections of 1990 and how they provided the basis for Eastern Germany's peaceful democratic revolution. The March 1990 *Volkskammer* elections were a de facto referendum on German union and a celebration of the end of communist rule. The results accelerated the race toward unification that had begun earlier in 1990. The local elections in May, and then the state elections in October, formalized the transfer of power to new democratic institutions and new political elites. Finally, the all-German elections in December 1990 elected a new parliament for the new nation, and provided a popular ratification by Easterners and Westerners of German unification.

There are many elements of the unification process that are important to study – we focus on the role of political parties and elections in this process. In part, this reflects the importance we attribute to political parties as actors in the German political process. The citizen protests in Leipzig and East Berlin in late 1989 were crucial in stimulating the peaceful revolution, but it was the actions of party leaders (East and West) that brought the revolution to completion. Furthermore, the future political course of the new Germany remains uncertain in many areas. We believe that the actions of the parties, and the public's choice among party options, will have a major influence in choosing which course the new Germany will follow. Thus our examination of partisan and political change extends beyond the elections of 1990 to the post-election challenges facing Germany.

This book also continues the venerable series of electoral studies edited by Karl Cerny (the *Germany at the Polls* series). We continue the documentation of German electoral history this series began with the 1976 Bundestagswahl, now extended to the new Germany. Several of the contributors to this volume participated in earlier *At the Polls* editions; all of us are proud to carry on Karl's tradition.

Finally, I would like to close with a note of thanks to those who helped in the development of this volume. The Center for German and European Studies at the University of California provided generous support for the collection of German survey data, the analyses of these materials, and the preparation of this manuscript; additional support for Alexandra Cole assisted in the preparation of Chapter 1. The Alexander von Humboldt Stiftung and the University of California, Irvine have supported the collaborative study of the German party system by Wilhelm Bürklin and me that is represented in Chapter 10. Many of the authors draw upon the public opinion data collected by the Forschungsgruppe Wahlen in Mannheim as part of the Politibarometer series of the Second German Television network (ZDF). The Forschungsgruppe and its directors – Manfred Berger, Wolfgang Gibowski, and Dieter Roth – have been extremely generous in sharing their data with scholars, and this has provided an unrivaled resource for electoral research. (These studies are available through the Zentralarchiv für empirische Sozialforschung, University of Cologne.) Several contributors would like to thank Inter Nationnes and the German Academic Exchange Service for hosting them on a study visit of the 1990 campaign.

We also acknowledge Eva Kolinsky's and Marion Berghahn's enthusiasm for this project, and their willingness to include this book in Berg's German politics series. Robert Riddell and Keith Fleming provided valuable assistance in the preparation and production of the manuscript.

German unification has closed a door on the nation's past, and opened a new door into the future. We hope this book both describes this transition, and provides our readers with a view of what lies ahead for the new Germany.

RUSSELL J. DALTON
Irvine, CA

I. Introduction

1
The Peaceful Revolution and German Electoral Politics

Russell J. Dalton and Alexandra Cole

IN THE SPRING OF 1989 both the Federal Republic of Germany and the German Democratic Republic were preparing for the fortieth anniversary of the founding of each state. In the West, Helmut Kohl and his governing coalition were celebrating the success of the postwar economic miracle (*Wirtschaftswunder*) and the Federal Republic's stature in the international community. In the East, the success of "real existing socialism" was announced with even bolder proclamations. Some media stories raised the question of whether the two Germanies would ever be unified, but these speculations were quickly discounted. One leading Social Democratic figure opined that unification would not come in his lifetime; the leader of East Germany, Erich Honecker, assured East Germans that the Berlin Wall would stand for another 100 years; and a Soviet government spokesperson said that talk about German union was an issue for the next century.

Yet within barely a year the seemingly impossible goal of national union became a reality. The collapse of the Berlin Wall in November 1989 and the subsequent withering away of the East German government amazed most political analysts and filled the world with awe. In a series of elections through 1990, the Germans – both East and West – began deciding their future. The East German parliamentary (*Volkskammer*) election in March 1990 produced a popular mandate for German union, and the all-German Bundestag elections in December confirmed the decision.

We have witnessed a revolution. It, as the East Germans proudly note, was a peaceful revolution where the seemingly omnipotent communist state was forced from office by the power of citizens willing to stand up for individual rights and the democratic process.

This book chronicles the process of German unification from the perspective of parties, the voters, and the German party system. We emphasize the partisan perspective because Germany is widely regarded as a "party state" (*Parteienstaat*), in which political parties are the key actors in the political process (Dalton, 1993, chap. 9; Dyson, 1982; Wildenmann, 1987). And, indeed, political parties have played a central role in the on-going process of unification. The policies of Helmut Kohl and the Christian Democratic party (CDU) have affected the unification process and the party's own electoral fortunes. The Green party and reformed Communist party (Party for Democratic Socialism [PDS]) have been the focal points for opposition to the unification process.

The reunification process is also affecting the German party system and the political parties themselves in fundamental ways. The incorporation of 8 million new voters would present a challenge for any party system, creating problems of political assimilation and the accommodation of opposition groups. The success of German union may be dependent on the extent to which the Federal Republic's party system can repeat its postwar accomplishment of integrating new voters into the norms and procedures of democratic politics. At the same time, unification has generated new lines of voting support that cut across traditional party alignments. For example, the Christian Democrats normally draw disproportionate support from middle-class voters in the West; they drew more working-class supporters in the East in the 1990 elections (Dalton, 1992). The established parties are thus attempting both to address the problems of German union as a policy goal, and to deal with the internal party changes produced by German union.

Research on political parties provides a vantage point for examining how political elites have addressed the issues of unification. It also provides a method for examining how unification is transforming the political and social divisions within the electorate of the new united Germany.

This book examines this interaction between the German party system and the process of German union. We begin our inquiry at approximately the time of the June 1989 Europarliament elections, and then track party actions and reactions to the events of German union. This book primarily focuses on the elections of 1990, in the grand tradition of the *Germany at the Polls* series

(Cerny, 1978; 1990). In addition to describing party actions, we explain the motivations that generated these behaviors. We also want to look forward and thus will track the evolution of the party system after the 1990 elections, discussing the implications of these trends for the future of the parties, the voters, and the German party system. The results can, we believe, help us to understand German union and therefore where this process may lead the nation, as well as to provide uniquely valuable evidence on the development of a new party system from the ruins of the prior communist political order.

This chapter begins by describing the events of the unification process as an introduction to the more extensive analyses of the following chapters.

The Lull before the Storm

The storm of political change that would hit both East and West Germany in 1989 gave little advance warning. The West Berlin *Land* election in January 1989 signaled potential problems for the government, but it came from another direction. The major story of the election was the rise in the fortunes of a small party, the Republicans (*Republikaner* [REP]). Located on the radical right of the political spectrum, the Republicans campaigned on themes of law, order, and cleanliness, with somewhat racist tendencies to the party's rhetoric (Stöss, 1991). At the outset of the election, analysts assumed that the Republicans might attract a few protest votes away from the major parties. To the surprise of these observers (and all the established parties), the Republicans siphoned off enough votes from the Christian Democratic Union (CDU) to force the CDU out of government (a Social Democratic/Green coalition took their place).

The success of the Republicans was then repeated a few weeks later in the local elections in the state of Hesse, where a revived National Democratic party (NPD) made strong showings and won entry into several local *Rathauser*. Government representatives tried to discount this right-wing surge as a simple protest vote against specific policy problems. In Berlin, for instance, Republican support was tied to negative reactions to the influx of ethnic Germans from Eastern Europe (*Aussiedler*) and asylum-seekers (*Asylanten*) who were straining the social and housing resources of the city (Roth, 1990). The Hesse elections, however, suggested that the base of the right-wing vote might be broader.

The Europarliament election planned for June thus provided an important test of support for the Christian Democrats; there were also simultaneous local elections in Rhineland-Palatinate and the Saarland. National public opinion polls showed the CDU was trailing the Social Democratic party (SPD), and the Republicans were attracting significant popular support (see Figure 1.1 below). A significant loss in votes for the CDU would weaken Kohl's stature and perhaps strengthen intra-party opposition to the chancellor. The SPD, expecting its fortunes to rise, was in a quandary about a potential ruling coalition: should the party ally itself with the Free Democratic party (FDP) or the Greens to form a new ruling coalition in Bonn?

Table 1.1. European Parliament Results, 1984–1989

	1984	1989
Christian Democratic Union (CDU/CSU)	46.0	37.8
Social Democrats (SPD)	37.4	37.3
Greens	8.2	8.4
Republicans (REP)	—	7.1
Free Democrats (FDP)	4.8	5.6
Other	3.6	3.8
Total	**100.0%**	**100.0%**

The Europarliament election results represented a stunning loss for the Christian Democrats (Table 1.1). The CDU lost 8 percent of the vote compared to the 1984 Europarliament election, and the upstart Republican party gained 7 percent. In local elections in Rhineland-Palatinate and the Saarland held the same day, the CDU vote share also decreased sharply. The only good news for the Bonn government was that the FDP managed to surmount the 5 percent hurdle and win representation in the Europarliament. The Social Democrats could console themselves that they had not lost votes since the 1984 Europarliament election, still they also had not gained. More ominous for the Federal

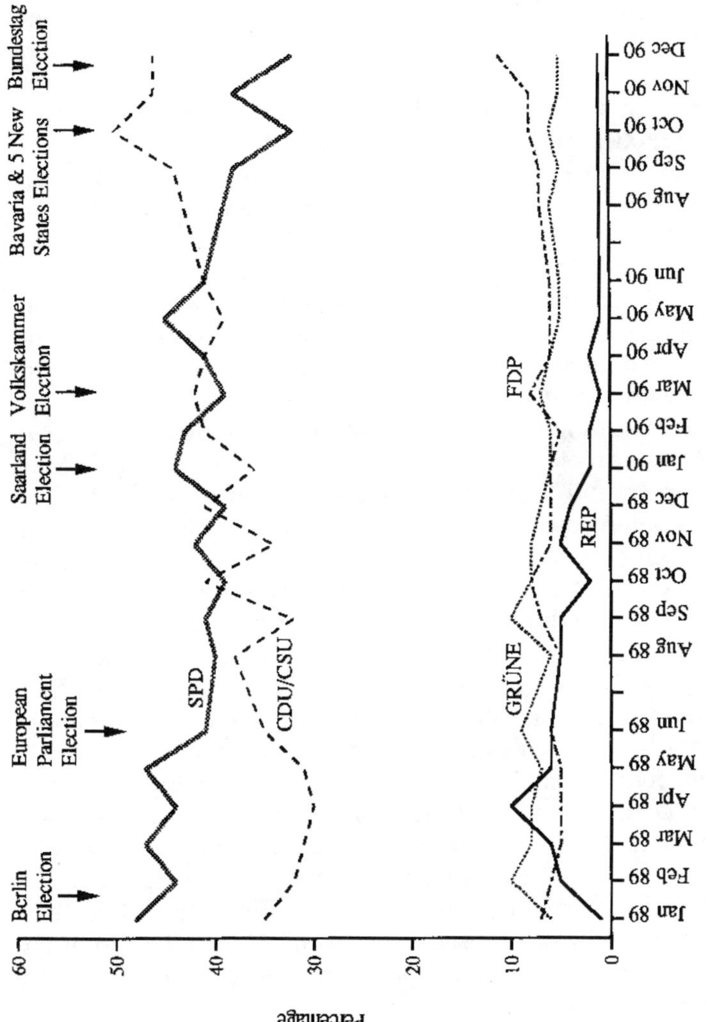

Figure 1.1. Party Support in the Western German Public, Jan. 1989–Dec. 1990.

SOURCE: Forschungsgruppe Wahlen Monthly Surveys.

Republic, if the Europarliament election results were repeated in the next Bundestagswahl, there would be no natural governing majority. The current governing parties, CDU/CSU and FDP, lacked a majority based on the Europarliament totals. Similarly, a Leftist coalition of SPD and Greens lacked a majority. The growth of the Republicans had changed the arithmetic of government formation.

In the German Democratic Republic, election results were also unsettling to the government (Glaeßner, 1992; Merkl, 1993). The first signs of the approaching storm began on the 70th anniversary of the assassination of Rosa Luxembourg and Karl Liebknecht (15 January 1989). Several hundred protestors demonstrated in Leipzig, calling for freedom of speech and freedom of assembly. Such demonstrations were not unknown in the German Democratic Republic, but they were not tolerated by the regime. The demonstration was broken up and more than 80 participants were arrested.

The arrests invigorated the opposition movement within the GDR. With local elections (*Kommunalwahlen*) set to occur in May of 1989, an ominous tone ran through the country as "many East Germans believed that if people voted as they actually felt, the Party would suffer a resounding defeat" (Gleye, 1991: 79). As in previous elections, East Germans would be presented a list of National Front candidates assembled by the ruling Socialist Unity party (SED), which voters could either accept or reject. To approve the candidate list, voters simply dropped their unmarked list into the ballot box. Voters who actually went into a voting booth, whether or not they approved or rejected the list, were perceived by the monitoring officials as not approving the list. To reject the list and vote against the government, voters had to cross off methodically each of the candidates' names on the list. An alternative means of voting against the government would be not to vote at all. Abstention was often difficult to accomplish, however, since party representatives went door to door in order to "encourage" people to vote and employees of a firm often voted together en masse.

Nevertheless, many East Germans intended to stay home for the May 1989 election. The public's frustration with the government over its lack of reform and the worsening economic conditions was tangible; the election was closely watched to see if this frustration manifested itself in widespread abstention and rejection of candidate lists. There was an informally organized effort by citizen groups and dissidents to observe the vote at polling places and so determine if there was a falsification of the vote count. The day after the election, when the official state newspaper *Neues Deutschland* reported that 98.85 percent of the electorate voted for the National Front's slate of candidates, election observers and the citizenry in general were stunned. What the poll watchers had counted and what was officially presented as the result had little to do with one another and suggested future unrest.

At the time, however, the GDR government seemed prepared to endure the growing winds of political change that were sweeping across Central and Eastern Europe. The government seemed willing to suppress opposition by force, and *Neues Deutschland* officially supported the Chinese suppression of the Tiananmen Square massacre in June. The GDR looked forward to celebrating its fortieth anniversary in late 1989 as the model of "real existing socialism" at work. The GDR seemed to be the bulwark of communism in Eastern Europe. Indeed, the stimulus for political change in the GDR primarily came not from within, but from events in the rest of Eastern Europe.

The Wall Falls

GDR officials were disturbed by the winds of change that were blowing from the East and fanning these flames of discontent in East Germany. The foundation of the East German system was its loyalty to the Soviet Union and its commitment to communist orthodoxy. Mikhail Gorbachev's ascendance to the leadership of the Soviet Union in 1985 introduced a reformist style of politics that was sharply at odds with the traditions of East German communism. Gorbachev's policies of *perestroika* and *glasnost* seemed to undermine the pillars on which the East German system was built. At one point, for example, *Neues Deutschland* even censored political reports from the Soviet Union to downplay the extent of Gorbachev's reforms. Similarly, an issue of the Soviet news magazine, *Sputnik*, was banned in the GDR because of its sympathetic discussion of Gorbachev's reforms.

Beginning in early 1989 the first cracks in the communist

fortress of Eastern Europe began to appear. In April the outlawed Polish Solidarity trade union was legalized, followed by partially competitive elections that Solidarity candidates won overwhelmingly. Poland soon became the first East European nation to have a non-communist head of government, and the Russians did not object.

The Hungarian communist party also was endorsing the idea of free democratic elections and the introduction of market forces into the economy. The liberalization in Hungary proved to be a decisive factor when it led to the dismantling of its border with neutral Austria in the spring of 1989. Because Hungary was one of the few countries East Germans were allowed to travel to without a visa, hundreds of vacationing East Germans used the opportunity to escape to the West when the barbed wire was removed. This flow quickly developed into a steady stream of emigrating East Germans, swelling to a flood when the Hungarians removed all border restrictions in September. East Germans were finally voting – with their feet.

As September came to a close, and the 7 October anniversary of the founding of the GDR drew near, the emigration problem was still growing. Relations with Hungary were deteriorating as more than fifty thousand East Germans had fled to the West across the Hungarian boarder.[1] Refugees from the GDR also sought sanctuary in the Federal Republic's embassies in East Berlin and Prague in order to gain asylum in the West.

The growing exodus stimulated public demonstrations within East Germany against the regime. Gorbachev was slated to take part in the anniversary celebration of the GDR on 7 October; East German authorities struggled with the problem of potential unrest and with the embarrassment of East Germans still seeking sanctuary at the Federal Republic's embassies. The GDR government allowed special trains to transport refugees from the FRG embassies through East Germany and to the West by maintaining that these refugees were being expelled from the state. Six thousand refugees left on 1 October and another eleven thousand left on 5 October. The spectacle of the closed trains passing through

1. Simply adjusted for the larger size of the United States' population, this would be as if more than 750,000 American emigrated in a six month period, drawn disproportionately from the young and well-trained members of the economy.

10

the GDR – seen by Easterners who watched FRG television news broadcasts – further weakened the GDR regime.

When Gorbachev arrived on 6 October for the anniversary celebration, he came to a land that had long been considered one of the most stable in the Socialist bloc but was now filled with frustration and public discontent. During the actual celebration on the seventh there were large-scale demonstrations in East Berlin (and several other cities) in support of Gorbachev's reform orientation and in opposition to the GDR's communist orthodoxy. Eventually, state security forces intervened and violently suppressed the protests.

A key turning point occurred two days later when over a hundred thousand people took to the streets in Leipzig, filling the air with their chant: We are the people! At this demonstration, the people feared that the state would violently crack down on the protesters, as had occurred in Berlin. Troops were in place as the peaceful demonstration began, but amazingly they were not called into action. From that moment on it was clear that the government would not repress the demonstrations by force (Darnton, 1991: 11; Glaeßner, 1992). Like the old German *Märchen*, the people finally realized that the emperor was standing naked before them.

The GDR government struggled to deal with this situation, and Gorbachev played a crucial role in directing the flow of events. He first signaled the Soviets' willingness to see Honecker replaced as head of state. Gorbachev informed the East German leadership that Soviet assistance would not be available to suppress the demonstrations (as it had in 1953), and encouraged them to undertake a process of internal reform with the cautious advice that "life itself punishes those who delay."

On 18 October Egon Krenz replaced the ailing Honecker as General Secretary of the Communist party. Krenz was considered a "moderate" by East German standards, but his appointment signaled the unwillingness of the old regime to undertake fundamental reforms. Although Krenz promised reform, his credentials were questionable. He had been the director of the Free German Youth organization and responsible for inculcating social values among the young. Krenz also was one of the most vocal supporters of the Chinese suppression of the democracy movement at Tiananmen Square.

Rapidly growing public protests increased the pressure on the government, and the continuing exodus to the West brought the economy to a near standstill. The Monday night protests outside the Nikolaikirche in Leipzig swelled in size. Protestors called for legalization of opposition groups, such as *Neues Forum*, and the actual guarantee of democratic rights stated in the GDR's constitution. In early November nearly a million people protested in East Berlin against the regime. The nation that was once known for its efficiency and order was plunged into political and economic chaos. The government did not govern, it barely existed. The government and the SED Politburo resigned in early November – the GDR was now a country without a government.

As a means of quelling the discontent and stemming the flow of refugees to the West, the government decided to allow East Germans the long desired right to free travel. At 6:57 pm on the evening of 9 November at a live press conference the spokesperson for the Central Committee, Günter Schabowski, announced that GDR citizens could now travel to the West.[2] East Berliners immediately began assembling at the Berlin wall to exercise their new right, and confused border guards let them through. In the former no-man's land of the Berlin Wall, Berliners from East and West joyously celebrated together. The unimaginable had become a reality.

"We are One People"

Once the euphoria of the opening of the Berlin Wall had passed, Germany had to address the question of "what next?" Helmut Kohl surprised most politicians, and most of the Federal Republic's allies, by announcing in November a 10-point plan to redefine relations between the two states. The most provocative part of the plan was Kohl's call for the development of confederative structures between the two Germanies. Kohl also offered the GDR financial support; both governments hoped that this aid would stem the tide of refugees flowing westward.

At the beginning of December Egon Krenz, the Politburo and the Central Committee all resigned, prompted by their inability

2. Egon Krenz claims that this announcement was actually a misstatement by the official, but once the border was forced open it could not be closed again (Krenz, 1991).

to control events and press reports of corruption and abuse of office. Hans Modrow, a little-known SED official, became the new prime minister of the GDR government. Gregor Gysi, who had been a government critic within the SED and represented dissidents at the expulsion hearings, was elected head of the SED at a special party meeting in December. The old communist leadership had simply left office voluntarily – East Germans had accomplished a "peaceful revolution."

Political power was now shared between the government, the SED, and opposition groups in meetings known as the "Round Table" (Glaeßner, 1991; Merkl, 1993). The Round Table included citizen groups formed during the democracy protests, such as Democratic Awakening (*Demokratischen Aufbruchs*), Democracy Now (*Demokratie Jetzt*), and New Forum (*Neues Forum*). The Round Table also included representatives of the political parties that formerly participated in the SED-led National Front (Eastern CDU, Liberal Democratic party [LDPD], National Democratic party [NDPD], and the Democratic Farmers' party [DBD]).

It was still unclear, however, where this new political leadership would lead East Germany. By mid-December, the continuing Monday night protests in Leipzig began to change their chant from their democratic slogan, "We are the people," to a new call for unification: "We are one people." Soon afterward, the reverberations of this chant were heard across Europe.

The prospect of unification was unsettling to many people who had become accustomed to the division of postwar Germany. Mauriac's satirical quote about Germany's division was still the opinion of many people: "I love Germany so dearly that I hope there will always be two of them." Among some of the Federal Republic's Western allies, the possibility of German unification created concerns that a new Germany would alter the international balance within Europe.[3] The Poles worried that unification might revive territorial conflicts between the two nations, and these concerns were heightened by Kohl's hesitancy in endorsing the Oder-Neisse agreement as a definite boundary for Eastern Germany. The Russians stated that any discussion of German

3. Margaret Thatcher was one of the most open skeptics of German union and created an international furor when her views (and those of her closest advisors) became public; Francois Mitterrand, in contrast, supported unification and visited Berlin before the end of 1989 (Livingston, 1991; Fritsch-Bournazel, 1991).

union was still premature, and that in any case a unified Germany would have to be a neutral Germany. Even the East Germans initially seemed hesitant about a full union with the West, and the first public opinion surveys in December 1989 found that most East Germans favored the continuation of a separate East German state, albeit of a different form than the old regime (Spiegel, 1989).

Critics of German union were also heard in the Federal Republic. The novelist Günter Grass was openly critical of the idea of German union, picturing it as the fruition of Nazi ideals and the destruction of socialist values. Other intellectuals called for a "third way" for the GDR, between the market economy of the West and the past socialism of the East. Many German leftists were obviously uncomfortable with the feelings of nationalism stimulated by the historic changes occurring in Germany, and openly expressed this concern.[4]

But in this case events, and not politicians, dictated the course of German history. The tide of emigrés to the West was not stemmed by the opening of the wall, and the continuing exodus further weakened the GDR economy. Amidst these problems a newly-freed press began providing exposés on the lavish lifestyles and abuses of power enjoyed by the past SED leadership. The offices of the secret security police were surrounded by masses of citizens calling for the end of the police state, and former SED leaders were placed under house arrest. The loss of legitimacy for the state and the declining vitality of the economy signaled the eventual demise of the GDR.

The Federal Republic, at least implicitly, encouraged this collapse. Kohl conditioned additional aid to the East on the implementation of democratic reforms, a byproduct of which was a further worsening of the economic situation in the East. The special social benefits available to immigrants from the GDR encouraged more people to immigrate to the West. Moreover, the image of a prosperous and pluralist Federal Republic was hard to resist as the situation deteriorated in the East.

Faced by mounting economic and political problems, the Round Table moved up the date of scheduled *Volkskammer* elec-

---

4. It should also be noted that other leftist politicians, such as Willy Brandt, openly embraced closer ties and even unification with the East and celebrated with Easterners their new-won freedoms.

14

tions to March 6. The public saw unification as the solution to the increasing political and economic chaos in the East. And perhaps most surprisingly, the Soviet Union seemed to accept the concept of a single united Germany. In January 1990, Modrow, and then Chancellor Kohl and Foreign Minister Genscher, visited Gorbachev in Moscow and apparently received his endorsement for the principle of a unified Germany. This was a stunning reversal of past Soviet policy.[5] The race to German union was on.

The Last Election

The March 1990 *Volkskammer* election would be the first (and conceivably last) free election of the German Democratic Republic (Wallach and Francisco, 1992). Because there was very little time to campaign before the election, the political parties were forced to develop new democratic identities very quickly (Niedemeyer and Stöss, 1993; Volkens and Klingemann, 1992).

The SED had been losing members by droves, and in some places whole local party groupings had disbanded (see Krisch's Chapter in this volume). In an attempt to save the party from complete dissolution and remain competitive in the new democratic environment in the East, the party changed its name in February 1990 to the Party of Democratic Socialism (PDS). Gregor Gysi remained the leader of the new party. Although the PDS suffered from the negative image of its previous identity as the SED, it would have advantages during the election campaign, namely its already well-organized party structure.

Many of the new opposition groups tried to develop into parties – such as Democracy Now, New Forum, and Alliance '90 – in order to compete in the first democratic elections. Other new political parties represented interests ranging from the serious (a women's party) to the sublime (the Beer Drinkers Union). As the campaign went on, however, it became evident that the parties allied to the established West German parties were usurping the electoral process, taking over the financing, tactics, organization and substance of the campaign. This occurred not only because the election was seen as a potential precursor to the December

---

5. As recently as 1988 Gorbachev had told Kohl that the Soviet Union would oppose unification. Following this meeting, Kohl was quoted as saying that he would probably not live to see German united.

1990 Bundestag election but also because the Eastern German parties felt that help from the West German parties allowed them to counter the organizational advantage of the PDS.

The first party to take the initiative was an Eastern Social Democratic party (SDP).[6] A new SPD-GDR founded itself two days before the Berlin Wall was opened, with the statement: "We have informed the state of our founding. We are not asking for legalization. We are legitimized by the citizens." The new party was free of past ties to the SED, and reflected a mix of traditional working-class interests with a concern for environmental and other New Politics issues. It campaigned on a platform emphasizing a federalist type of unification of the two German states within the context of European integration. It also promised to rewrite the Federal Republic's Basic Law if unification proceeded and to prevent the outright annexation of the East German state. The Western SPD assisted their comrades in the East by providing financial and political support. Willy Brandt and Helmut Schmidt were popular figures in the East, and both used their popularity to the benefit of the new party.

Conservative politicians in the East responded more slowly to the new partisan environment. In early 1990 a conservative "Alliance for Germany" combined the East German CDU with the newly formed Democratic Awakening and the German Social Union (DSU). The Alliance was an attempt to distance the Eastern CDU from its former identity as a bloc party and thereby gain the support of its Western sister party. The "Alliance for Germany" campaigned for a fast unification of the two German states and a quick introduction of the D-Mark in the East and a market economy. Helmut Kohl made whistle-stop tours for the conservative parties of the Alliance, and the Alliance soon became an extension of the Western CDU's electoral machine.

This pattern of East-West party alliances soon extended to the other parties. The Western FDP developed an electoral alliance with a coalition of liberal parties in the East and campaigned on the theme of unification at a measured pace. Hans-Dietrich Genscher, the West German foreign minister who was originally from

6. To highlight its separate identity, the Eastern SDP consciously chose different initials than the SPD in the West. Eventually, however, the Eastern party adopted the initials of the Western party and formally merged with the SPD in September 1990.

16

Table 1.2. East German Volkskammer Election Results, March 1990

	Percent	Seats
Alliance for Germany		
CDU	40.9	164
DSU	6.3	25
DA	0.9	4
SPD	21.8	87
PDS	16.3	65
Liberals	5.3	21
Alliance '90	2.9	12
DBD	2.2	9
Greens	2.0	8
NDPD	0.4	2
Women's League	0.3	1
United Left	0.2	1
Alternative Youth List	0.1	1
Other	0.4	—
Total	**100%**	**400**

East Germany, was the star attraction at FDP rallies in the East. The West German Greens assisted the Eastern Greens and the Independent Women's Association.

The elections provided an historic political opportunity, and the CDU and Helmut Kohl took the greatest possible advantage of this. While others looked upon the events with wonder or uncertainty, Kohl quickly embraced the idea of closer ties between the two Germanies that would lead to eventual confederation or unification. Thus when the election became a referendum in support of German unification, the Christian Democrats were assured of victory because of the party's early commitment to German union. The CDU/CSU was seen as the party representing the new Germany, and Kohl promised Eastern voters that they would be better off if they endorsed his unification proposals. This campaign led to a surprisingly strong showing for the Alliance in the March 1990 elections (Table 1.2). The Alliance stunned most political observers by winning over 48 percent of the popular vote, and Lothar de Maiziere (CDU) became the first freely-elected prime minister of East Germany.

Perhaps no one, except maybe the Communists, were more surprised than the SPD by the course of events in the GDR and the election results. The SPD expected the East to be a bastion of socialist support because of Weimar voting patterns, and yet the Christian Democrats captured the votes of this new constituency. The vote results reflect the inability of the SPD to respond to the new challenges of German unification. The Social Democrats stood by quietly as Kohl spoke of a single German *Vaterland* to crowds of applauding East Germans. The party's poor performance in the March poll thus reflects the SPD's inability to either lead or follow the course of German union.

The PDS campaigned as the representative of those who felt threatened by the potential economic and social costs of German unity. The party gained a significant share of the vote in the March election (16 percent), which was heavily concentrated in areas where the SED had a large membership, such as East Berlin.

Ironically, the citizen groups and political movements that produced the East German revolution gathered few votes in the elections. They were simply overwhelmed by the political machines of the parties with Western ties. One of their leaders observed philosophically after the election that they had moved from opposition to the GDR state to opposition to the new CDU-led government with barely a taste of political power.

In the end, the results of the *Volkskammer* election largely represented an extension of the Federal Republic's party system to the East. The rough balance of power was the same between the government and opposition parties as in the West, though the Left in the East was split between the social-democratic SPD and the communist PDS. The focus of the election had narrowed to the issue of German unification – it became a referendum on union. Morover, the election was a forerunner of things to come. The East German opposition groups that brought about the revolution were swamped by the better organized, better financed, and better known West German parties. This became a West German election on Eastern soil.

The Race toward German Union

Although the Alliance won the *Volkskammer* election, it did not win an outright majority of the vote, so it went into a Grand Coalition with the SPD and the Liberal party (BFD). The new government sought to solve the considerable economic and political problems facing the GDR, which included the high expectations of the electorate. Under Lothar deMaziere the government tackled the problems of the incorporation of a free market economy, the introduction of the D-Mark in the East, and the unification of the two German states.

One of the first steps was currency union. Kohl had promised voters during the *Volkskammer* campaign that their Ostmarks would be exchanged for Deutsche Marks (DM) at a 1:1 ratio. As soon as the election was over, the FRG's Bundesbank the Central Bank of West Germany recommended that the DM be brought into East Germany at a 2:1 exchange rate.[7] The East Germans balked at this rate; it would halve their savings and keep them from meeting cost of living expenses in a non-subsidized economy. De Maziere held firm against this rate and reminded Kohl of his campaign promises. When the day of Currency Union came, 2 July 1990, the 1:1 rate was the official rate for personal savings. Even so, most East Germans were disappointed. Although they finally had the coveted DM, shelves were still empty in the stores, which in turn charged vastly inflated prices on the products they did have.

At the same time that inter-German treaties were being worked out, so too were treaties between the two Germanies and the former World War II Allied governments. An official peace treaty had never been signed among Germany and the Allied governments because after the war there had not been a single Germany to sign one. With unification becoming more and more of a reality, questions concerning security and military alliances arose. Gorbachev, while agreeing in principle to German unification, would not agree to the new Germany's membership in the North Atlantic Treaty Organization (NATO). By the time of West German chancellor Kohl's trip to the Soviet Union in July 1990 the Soviet Union agreed to the membership of the unified Germany

7. In actuality, the Bundesbank initially had suggested a much higher exchange rate to reflect the different real values of the two currencies. Blackmarket rates, for example, were in excess of 10:1. But under pressure from the government the bank developed a plan closer to Kohl's preferences.

in NATO, which was seen as transforming itself from a military alliance into a political one. The Soviet Union's agreement came at a price. At a cost of over DM 15 billion, Germany promised to help cover the costs of a Soviet Red Army pullout from East Germany and to help support the failing Soviet economy.

At the "Two Plus Four" talks between the two German states and the four World War II Allied governments – France, England, the Soviet Union, and the United States – Germany finally received full sovereignty. The Germans promised no claims on territories lost during the war (such as Silesia), forfeited the right to have atomic, biological and chemical weapons, and promised to reduce its army to 370,000 soldiers in four years.

German unification proceeded under the terms of Article 23 of the Basic Law; that is, directly incorporating East Germany into the existing legal structure of the Federal Republic. This greatly simplified the unification process by using the West German system as a standard, but the union was also accompanied by extensive negotiations on the terms of union and exceptions to the provisions of the Basic Law. In September both German parliaments agreed to the provisions of a treaty on German union. On 3 October 1990, after a generation of separation, the two German paths again converged.

The All-German Election Campaign

As a prelude to the Bundestag election, the five Eastern Länder held elections for their new governments on October 14. Since the *Volkskammer* election in March, the CDU had ran substantially ahead of the SPD in the public opinion polls (see Figure 1.2). The elections confirmed these findings (Table 1.3). Although the CDU vote totals generally dipped slightly compared to the March election results, the CDU emerged from these elections as the largest party in every parliament except Brandenberg. In two states the CDU ruled as a majority party (Saxony and Thuringia) and in two states it ruled in coalition with the FDP (Mecklenberg-West Pommerania and Saxony-Anhalt). Only in Brandenberg did the SPD lead a coalition government.

After the *Länder* results in October, the Bundestag elections in December were somewhat anti-climatic. Kohl campaigned as the creator of German unity. The SPD chancellor candidate, Oskar

20

Table 1.3. Landtag Election Results, October 1990

	SAXONY	BRANDENBERG	MECKLENBURG	SAXONY-ANHALT	THURINGIA
CDU/CSU	53.8	29.4	38.3	39.0	45.4
SPD	19.1	38.4	27.0	26.0	22.8
FDP	5.3	6.6	5.5	13.5	9.3
Greens-Alliance `90	5.6	9.2	6.4	5.3	6.5
PDS	10.2	13.4	15.7	12.0	9.7
Republicans	—	1.2	0.9	0.6	0.8
Other Parties	6.0	1.9	6.2	3.6	5.6
Total	**100.0%**	**100.0%**	**100.0%**	**100.0%**	**100.0%**

Lafontaine, grumbled about the problems posed by unity but offered no clear alternative. Extensive discussions of what would be (and could be) done in the East were generally lacking. In large part, the election acted to legitimize the actions of the past year, rather than to discuss Germany's future.

The setting of the election was also affected by the decision of the Constitutional Court. The Court decided that this first all-German election must still use separate electoral lists in the East and West, and a party could win parliamentary seats by exceeding the 5 percent hurdle in either half of the country. The intent was to protect the small parties in the East which had not had time to organize nation-wide. In the future the system would revert to a single national system. This electoral provision encouraged mergers between East and West parties. The two branches of the SPD formed a single party in September, and the CDU and FDP soon followed suit. In fact, the Greens were the only significant Western party that avoided such an alliance with their comrades in the East as a protest against the absorption of the GDR into the Federal Republic. The Western and Eastern Greens agreed to merge the day *after* the Bundestag election.

In 1989, the SPD had looked forward to competing in the Bundestag elections. Public opinion polls showed the SPD running ahead of the CDU/CSU in voter support throughout most of 1989. In addition to its success in the Europarliament election, the

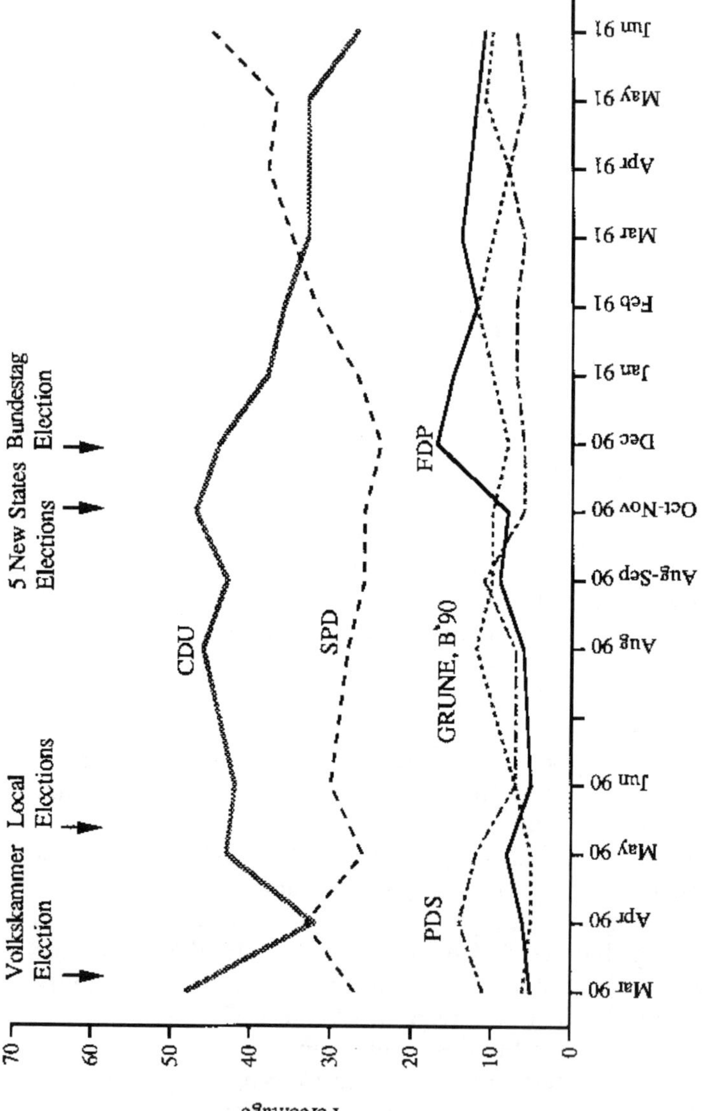

Figure 1.2. Party Support in the Eastern German Public, March 1990–June 1991.

SOURCE: Forschungsgruppe Wahlen Monthly Surveys.

party also won a decisive victory in the January 1990 Saarland *Land* election, where it controlled the state government with an absolute majority. Buoyed by this victory, Lafontaine, the Minister President of the Saarland, was chosen to be the SPD's chancellor candidate for the December election. On the face of things Lafontaine was a good choice. The SPD ruled the state with an absolute majority, and Lafontaine himself had won five straight elections. The SPD also hoped that Lafontaine would appeal to younger voters as a representative of the new generation of politicians rising to prominence in West Germany.

For Helmut Kohl and the CDU, the goal of the Bundestag campaign was to recover from their poor showing in the 1989 European parliament elections. By the end of 1989 the CDU/CSU had drawn even with the SPD in the poll standings in the West (Figure 1.1), but the party's ability to retain this support through the difficult process of unification was uncertain. Kohl also knew that all-German elections must take place quickly before the costs of unification made themselves felt. He wanted to bask in the success of being the chancellor of unification before Westerners realized they would have to pay for unification and Easterners realized the suffering that would have to endure. Because of the speed of unification and the election, Kohl got his wish. Portraying himself as the "Chancellor of Unification," Kohl and the CDU controlled the campaign agenda.

The smaller parties ran campaigns that were variants on the themes of the larger parties. The FDP campaigned on a theme of sensibility in politics, and promised that if it were to remain in government, Germany would stay governable. To stress their opposition to the fusion of both Germanies, the Western Greens refused to develop a formal electoral alliance with any Eastern party until after the 1990 elections. The Western Greens thus ran a separate slate from the Greens/Alliance '90 coalition in the East. The PDS, still under the leadership of Gregor Gysi, sought to expand its electoral base into the West through a coalition with a new Leftist List (*Linke Liste*). In addition to frustrated communists and social democrats, the PDS also wanted to draw support away from the Greens. Gysi pronounced his campaign an alliance of the left in both East and West.

Helmut Kohl emerged from the 1990 elections victorious, but with surprisingly little to show for his historic accomplishments during the preceding year. Kohl received almost the same vote share in 1990 as he had in the previous Bundestag election (Table 1.4). The big victor in the election was the FDP; it saw its vote share expand to 11 percent. The FDP had benefited from the international changes occurring in Europe. The FRG's foreign minister, Hans-Dietrich Genscher of the FDP, played a leading role in negotiating the international agreements that allowed the two Germanies to unite, and the party's stature gained from his accomplishments.

The SPD struggled through the election. Lafontaine might have been the right candidate for the party, but he had been fated to run at the wrong time. Lafontaine was a candidate of the New Left but the issues of the 1990 campaign focused on questions of national pride and economic reconstruction – something with which Lafontaine had trouble dealing. Lafontaine could not sense Germans' feelings about unification. He advocated slowing down the pace of unification because he felt that the costs were too great and potentially disastrous for both states. Lafontaine also argued

Table 1.4. Bundestag Election Results, 1987 and 1990

		1990 VOTES			1990
	1987	WEST	EAST	TOTAL	SEATS
Christian Democrats (CDU/CSU)	44.3	44.1	43.4	43.8	319
Social Democrats (SPD)	37.0	35.9	23.6	33.5	239
Free Democrats (FDP)	9.1	10.6	13.4	11.0	79
Greens	8.3	4.7	0.1	3.9	0
Greens/Alliance '90	—	—	5.9	1.2	8
Party for Democratic Socialism (PDS)	—	0.3	9.9	2.4	17
Republicans	—	2.3	1.3	2.1	0
Other parties	1.3	2.1	2.5	2.1	0
Total	**100%**	**100%**	**100%**	**100%**	**662**

NOTE: The 1990 West statistics are for the 10 *Länder* of the former FRG (excluding West Berlin) and the 1990 East statistics are for the 5 new *Länder* (excluding East Berlin). The CDU won 6 extra seats through their district victories, and the size of the Bundestag was therefore expanded to include these extra mandates.

that unification should take place through a series of well thought-out steps, enabling the two states to come together on a more equal basis. In the end, for nearly every vote that the SPD gained from young, middle-class voters, they lost another vote from their traditional working-class constituency. Lafontaine's doubts about unification also cost the party support in Eastern Germany. In the end, the party's Western vote share was just slightly lower than in 1987, and the party had a disastrous showing in the East.

The biggest losers in the elections were the Greens. The Greens had initially been ambivalent in responding to the German revolution in the East because they opposed the simple eastward extension of West German economic and political systems. Even worse, some Green party leaders had advocated an alliance with the recently dethroned communists in the East. On matters of German union, the party leadership was out of step with the public and its own electorate. Furthermore, by refusing to develop a formal electoral alliance with any Eastern party in the 1990 Bundestag elections, the Western Greens ironically suffered at their own hands. The Eastern alliance of the Greens/Alliance '90 won enough votes to gain 8 seats in the new Bundestag, but the West German Greens fell just under the 5 percent threshold and failed to win any parliamentary seats on its own. The Greens unconventional politics had finally caught up with them, at least temporarily.

Only the change in the electoral laws enabled the PDS to win representation in the 1990 Bundestag elections. The PDS captured barely 2 percent of the national vote, but it won 9.9 percent in the former territory of the GDR. The PDS should turn out to be an advocate for communist values and a vocal critic of the Bonn government, but without a broader base of popular support it is uncertain whether the party can establish itself as a permanent feature of the German party system.

Studying the New German Party System

Although this study primarily focuses on the elections, our larger concern is to track the evolution of a new party system in the East and to understand how this process is affecting the established parties in the West. Chapters 3–7 will explore the actions and reactions of the parties to the events of 1990, but also examine the political goals and calculations that explain party actions. Other chapters will explore how citizens have responded to events and the political cues provided by the parties and other actors.

The book is therefore divided into four sections. This chapter has described the flow of political events over the time of our study in order to provide a historical context for the volume. The following chapter by Manfred Kuechler discusses popular reaction to the collapse of the German Democratic Republic and the consequent process of German union. Kuechler had access to a series of public opinion surveys, from both East and West, beginning in December 1989, which enabled him to track the ebb and flow of public sentiments up to the present.

The second section of this book consists of five party analysis chapters by David Conradt (CDU), Donald Hancock (SPD), Christian Søe (FDP), Donald Schoonmaker and Gene Frankland (Greens), and Henry Krisch (SED/PDS). Each chapter considers how one political party responded to the unification process, and how this process affected the party. These chapters describe the motivations behind party actions, as well as the anticipated and unanticipated consequences of these actions. The authors also discuss how unification has affected the parties internally, creating contrasting electoral constituencies and different types of party activists East and West that affected the political divisions within the parties, and shifting the distribution of power. Each chapter closes with a discussion of the future prospects for the party.

The third set of chapters trace the flow of the campaign from the standpoint of the media and the electorate. Holli Semetko and Klaus Schoenbach's chapter draws upon a large scale study of the media's role in the Bundestag elections, analyzing how the campaign was presented to the voters. The chapter by Helmut Norpoth and Dieter Roth utilizes the rich storehouse of public opinion data collected by the *Forschungsgruppe Wahlen* for the Second German Television Network (ZDF). This chapter describes how voters made their decisions in the 1990 Bundestag election and discusses the likely implications of the election for future voting behavior.

The concluding chapter by Russell Dalton and Wilhelm Bürklin looks toward the future by drawing together the evidence of the volume and mapping out the future problems and prospects for the German party system, as well as for the German political system more generally.

As witnesses to a revolution, one can still be awed by the tremendous changes that have transformed Germany – and Europe – over this period. The pride of Easterners in their peaceful revolution is easy to understand, and admire. Yet the task of creating a single nation from the different experiences of East and West is still considerable. Much more remains to be done. The political parties and their leadership undoubtedly will play central roles in determining the success of this democratic transition. Thus the analyses we begin here are important both for understanding how unification occurred, and for looking forward to Germany's political future.

References

Cerny, Karl, ed. 1978. *Germany at the Polls: The Bundestag Election of 1976.* Washington, D.C.: American Enterprise Institute.
———. ed. 1990. *Germany at the Polls: The Bundestag Elections of the 1980s.* Durham: Duke University Press.
Dalton, Russell. 1992. "Two German Electorates?" in Gordon Smith et al., *Developments in German Politics.* London: Macmillans.
———. 1993. *Politics in Germany.* New York: Harper Collins Publishers.
Darnton, Robert. 1991. *Berlin Journal 1989–1990.* New York: W.W. Norton.
Dyson, Kenneth. 1982. "Party Government and the Party State," in Herbert Döring and Gordon Smith, ed. *Party Government and Political Culture in Western Germany.* New York: St. Martin's Press.
Fritsch-Bournazel, Renata. 1991. "German Unification: Views from Germany's Neighbours," in Wolfgang Heisenberg, ed. *German Unification in European Perspective.* New York: Brassey's.
Glaeßner, Gert-Joachim. 1992. *Der Schwierige Weg zur Demokratie.* Opladen: Westdeutscher Verlag.
Gleye, Paul. 1991. *Behind the Wall: An American in East Germany, 1988–1989.* Carbondale: Southern Illinois University Press.
Krenz, Egon. 1990. *Wenn Mauern Fallen: Die friedliche Revolution.* Vienna: Neff Verlag.
Livingston, R. Gerald. 1991. "Relinquishment of East Germany," in

Richard Staar, ed. *East-Central Europe and the USSR*. New York: St. Martin's Press.

Merkl, Peter. 1993. *German Unification in the European Context*. University Park, PA: Pennsylvania State University Press.

Niedemeyer, Oskar and Richard Stöss, ed. 1993. *DDR Parteien im Umbruch*. Opladen: Westdeutscher Verlag.

Roth, Dieter. 1990. "Sind die Republikaner die fünfte Partei," from *Politik und Zeitgeschichte* 6 October: pp. 10–20.

Spiegel. 1989. "Spiegel Umfragen: VEB in Privateigenntum?" *Der Spiegel* 52/1989: pp. 72–75.

Volkens, Andrea and Hans-Dieter Klingemann. 1992. "Die Entwicklung des deutschen Parteiensystems im Vereinigungsprozess," in Eckhard Jesse and Armin Mitter, eds. *Deutschland im Vereinigungsprozess*. Bonn: Bundeszentrale für politische Bildung.

Wallach, H. G. Peter, and Ronald Francisco. 1992. *United Germany: The Past, Politics, Prospects*. Westport, CT: Praeger.

Wildenmann, Rudolf. 1987. "Germany," in Richard Katz, ed. *The Future of Party Government*. Berlin: de Gruyter.

2

Framing Unification: Issue Salience and Mass Sentiment 1989–1991

*Manfred Kuechler**

OBVIOUSLY, THE PROCESS OF UNIFICATION – the debate about its advantages and disadvantages, merits and faults, and how unification could best be achieved – dominated the political agenda in the year before the 1990 elections. For East Germany, unification meant an almost complete restructuring of its political, economic, and social fabric. Unification affected every domain of public life: from schooling to retirement benefits, from health care to housing. Issues normally quite distinct became interrelated in the process of adapting to the standards and norms of the West. For West Germany, the impact was less dramatic. According to the unification treaty the West German laws, rules, and regulations would remain unchanged with the sole exception of abortion rights. Here, the far more liberal East German law was to stay in effect for the East; the newly elected parliament would reconcile the two laws within a two-year period. The incorporation of some 18 million East Germans was bound to have an impact on the economy, on the distribution of wealth and burdens, and on the social and political fabric in practical terms. To say that unification dominated the 1990 German elections is a truism, then.

This chapter examines the various facets of unification from the perspective of the public, both East and West. What exactly did unification mean to the Germans before the fact? How do they look at it now that unification has been formally established?

*I am indebted to the Forschungsgruppe Wahlen (Manfred Berger, Wolfgang Gibowski, Matthias Jung, and Dieter Roth) for continuously providing me with reports on their monthly Politbarometer surveys. A large portion of the data used in this chapter is extracted from these sources.

29

What were (and still are) their expectations, hopes, and fears? What costs were the Germans willing to bear? What role for Germany did they see in the new European order? Was Chancellor Kohl pushed by public opinion, or did he have to overcome reluctance at home in addition to the obstacles in the international arena? In short, I will try to shed some light on how the issue of unification was framed in the mind of the masses. Yes, unification dominated the campaign, but in exactly what way? Was unification an altogether "new" issue which transcended established cleavages and divisions, making the elections basically an *ex post* referendum? Or was unification framed and evaluated in standard categories like economic well-being, national power, and international prestige? What is the impact of the unification issue beyond the December 1990 elections? More precisely, I will address the following questions:

What was the salience of economic considerations compared to a sense of national and/or cultural identity at the onset of the process? Was unification a marriage of convenience or the consummation of genuine love and affection? To what extent were Eastern attitudes towards unification driven by expectations of quickly reaching economic affluence? To what extent were Westerners willing to share their prosperity? To what extent was the quest for unity related to a desire for political and/or economic hegemony? How have Germans reacted to the realities of unification? To what extent were the expectations of the public met, and what is the potential for lasting disenchantment? A year after the fact, have the views of Easterners and Westerners converged at all – that is, do they understand each other better, do they feel any closer?

These questions can be answered by analysis of available survey data. However, they constitute only part of a larger, more fundamental theme that at this point in time can only be addressed by way of informed speculation: Will the Germans live together happily and peacefully, continuing to be a good neighbor in a changing Europe? Will Easterners fully adapt to the new political and social order? What is the danger of internal strife and social conflict as an unintended consequence of unification? And what are the prospects for continued political stability in the now larger Federal Republic of Germany?

Longitudinal Trends in Support of Unification[1]

As a starting point, it is informative to look at the long term trend in support for unification. Drawing on data from various public opinion institutes, Jansen (1989: 1139) compiled several time series covering the period from the 1950s to 1987. Surveys until 1960, notwithstanding some variation in question wording, all show about 90 percent of the respondents to have been in favor of unification.[2] This figure dropped slightly to about 80 percent in the 1970s and 1980s, when the policy of peaceful coexistence, the strategy of "normal" relations between the two German states, replaced the cold war agenda.

In spite of high approval rates, the salience of unification as an issue declined. Unification became a hypothetical question. Up to the mid-1960s, the majority of the West Germans thought that unification was probable (Jansen, 1989: 1133), but concurrent with the emergence of a new "Ostpolitik," the percentage of respondents expecting unification dropped to below 20 points in the late 1960s and to less than 10 percent in the 1970s, finally reaching a low of 3 percent in 1987. Similarly, data from the Allensbach Institut für Demoskopie show that in 1955, in 1960, and in 1965 more than one third of the respondents named reunification as the most important issue facing the Federal Republic. This percentage dropped to a little over 10 points in 1970 and to just about 2 points in 1981 (Szumni, Lichtleitner and Bauske, 1990: 63). In the East, recently released youth studies from the Leipzig Central Institute for Youth Research (ZIJ) indicate that identification with the GDR as an entity in its own right rose continuously through the 1970s, well until at least the mid-1980s (Friedrich, 1990: 30–31).

In both parts of Germany the public had accepted the existence of two German states as a fact. The very idea of unification continued to be appealing, though on a more pragmatic level some degree of liberalization in the East (e.g., fairly unrestricted travel privileges for retirees, easier access for West Germans) seemed to satisfy the vast majority of all Germans. Family ties across the border were still maintained, but there was no grassroots move-

1. Several segments of this chapter are based on Kuechler (1992).

2. Up to early 1990 the term *reunification* (*Wiedervereiningung*) was used, implying – or at least not excluding – the restoration of a Germany with pre-1937 borders, containing territories now part of Poland and the former Soviet Union (Silesia, East Prussia, Pomerania).

ment actively pushing for unification. Moreover, the once powerful interest groups of expellees (*Vertriebenenverbände*) – Germans from what had become Polish and Russian territories – had lost their momentum due to generational replacement. Similarly, among the political elites the unification issue had become moot. Good for occasional partisan rhetoric, but no longer the subject of major debates. Even West German conservatives, including their prime spokesman Franz-Josef Strauss, sought to make deals with the other German state (Conradt, 1986: 236). Pragmatic economic interests had prevailed over pan-German ideology. On the international level most countries seemed to be quite content with the status quo. By the late-1980s, then, German unification was no longer on the political agenda.

Turning to the recent past, strong support for unification as a hypothetical question had continued. In March 1989 – well before the onset of the dramatic chain of events – 78 percent of West Germans were in favor of unification. The Politbarometer surveys of the Forschungsgruppe Wahlen allow us to very clearly track public sentiment on unification from this point on (see Figure 2.1). There is practically no change until early fall 1989, when a shocking reversal occurred. After the ousting of SED chief Honecker on October 18, making more sweeping changes conceivable, the West German public displayed more reluctance than jubilation. The slight decrease in the percentage of West Germans favoring unification in October 1989 could have been no more than a statistical random variation in a survey sample. But the November reading – with its interviews collected in the week immediately following the fall of the wall – showing public approval about 10 percentage points below the previous month's represented a statistically significant drop. The responses to a follow-up question are even more revealing. When asked if they were "still in favor (of unification) if a reunited Germany becomes neutral," only 53 percent of all respondents said they favored unification. Results from the December survey point in the same direction: faced with a balanced choice between one "common state" and "two independent German states," only a slight majority (56 percent) continued to opt for unification, with many seeing it as only a long term goal. Asked to look 10 years ahead, only 34 percent of all respondents envisioned a unified state, while 42 percent foresaw a confederation, and another 21 percent pictured maintaining the status quo of two independent states. After the 10 February 1990 meeting between Kohl and Gorbachev in Moscow, the previous level of about 80 percent approval for unification was reestablished (Figure 2.1).

The trends for the West German public at large are mirrored in the group most skeptical of the unification process: adherents of the Greens.[3] The support rate among these – on average much younger – respondents was 56 percent in March 1989, dropping to below 50 percent in late 1989 and early 1990, but climbing back to well over 60 percent later on (see Figure 2.1).

The data for East Germany show a dramatic increase in favor of unification from about 50 percent (including 32 percent who were "rather more in favor of than opposed") in November 1989 to around 80 percent in February and March 1990 (see Figure 2.1); there was also a rise from 16 to over 40 points in the percentage of those "very much in favor of" unification. However, these data (especially for November 1989) may be less than reliable. First, a still considerable reluctance to fully exercise the newly won right to freedom of speech may have biased the responses. Second, a substantial sampling bias may overrepresent adherents of the Communist party (SED/PDS), who were obviously less inclined to favor unification.[4] However, it seems safe to conclude that even in February and March there was no solid majority unequivocally in favor of unification, but that qualified support was very high. High support continued through the later part of 1990, reaching more than 90 percent – although it was based on responses to a differently worded question (see Figure 2.1).

Public reluctance about speedy unification showed in other ways. In both East and West Germany, the majority preferred a more measured and deliberate approach to unification even at a time when the political leaders had made their move and quick unification was agreed upon (see Chapter 1). In February 1990, two-thirds of the West German respondents judged the pace of unification to be "too fast," and only a quarter found it "just

---

3. Adherents of the Greens are those respondents intending to vote for this party: between 50 and 100 respondents for each time point leaves a fairly large statistical margin for error. For this reason, rather dramatic shifts from one point in time to the next are likely, but should not be overinterpreted. Rather, the trend over time should be considered.

4. A bias of this sort is suspected in most of the surveys conducted in the very early phase of liberation; see, e.g., Roth (1990: 391– 392). Given the data collection problems, it is difficult to separate response uncertainty from true change.

Figure 2.1. Support for Unification

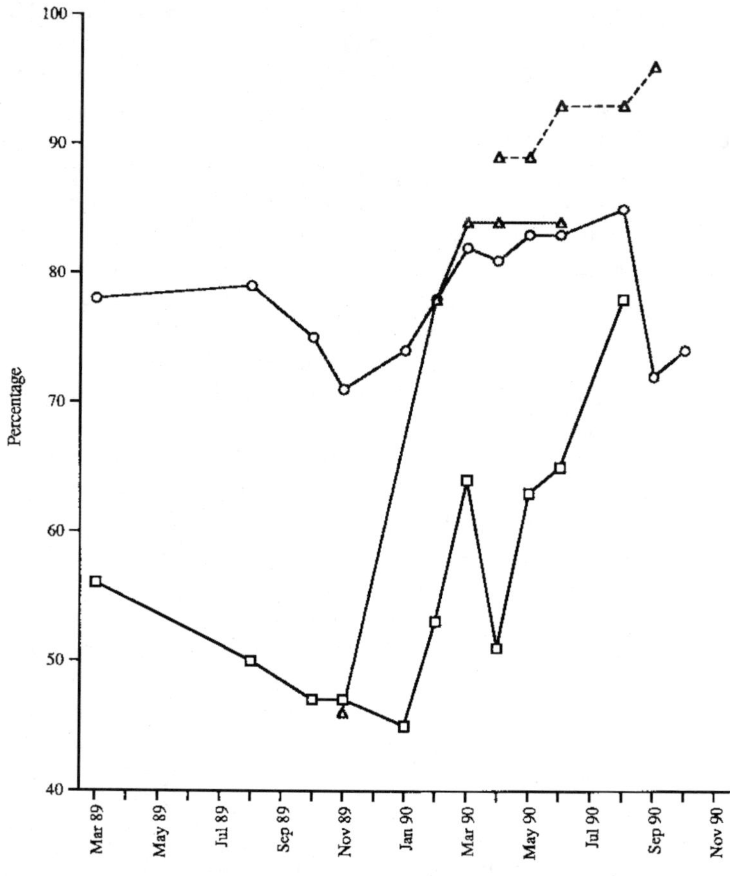

NOTE:

a) West German data up to August 1990 and East German data (April to September 1990) from Politbarometer surveys. Figures give percentage in favor of unification based on all respondents: "Are you personally in favor of unification of the two German states, do you oppose unification, or are you indifferent (gleichgültig)?" For September and October 1990, data excerpted from *Der Spiegel* (38/1990 and 47/1990). The "personal attitude towards unification of the two German states" was assessed on a scale from 1 ("very much opposed") to 10 ("very much in favor.") Table gives percentages for catagories 6 through 10.

b) Other East German data from general population surveys (M1–M5) of the Central Institute for Youth Research (ZIJ), Leipzig, East Germany. Question: "How do you feel about a unification of GDR and FRG?" Figures give percentages of those "very much in favor" combined with those "rather in favor that opposed" on a balanced 4-point scale.

34

right." In March, April, and May, two-thirds of the respondents preferred "to take time;" less than 20 percent favored "very fast" unification. The figures for East Germany are similar: in March and May 1990 more than half of the respondents found the pace of unification "too fast."

To summarize: West Germans have consistently exhibited strong support for reunification (in the abstract), but the issue began to lose salience in the late 1960s and eventually came to be seen as a hypothetical academic question rather than a concrete and immediate political goal. As unification became a tangible reality in the fall of 1989 support dropped fairly precipitously. Nevertheless, Chancellor Kohl embarked on a course of quick unification and the West German public responded with renewed support mitigated by concern over the pace of the unification process. By fall 1990, the support in the West started to slip again (see Figure 2.1), although due to the differently worded question the data are not fully comparable. The data for East Germany indicate a similar pattern: a continued high level of overall support, with underlying reservations and uneasiness about the pace.

In more general terms, the masses followed the leader. It appears that Kohl's stunning success in winning support for unification from the Soviet Union and his gaining full approval from the Western allies reversed the downward trend in West German public opinion – support that crossed partisan lines. In addition, the CDU's clear cut victory in the March 1990 *Volkskammer* elections all but eliminated the feasibility of any other option. A second German state simply did not appear as viable. Unification as such had become inevitable, an issue in which support – however grudging or reluctant – was the only rational choice. The question was how to go about it, how to implement it, how to best guard against unintended negative consequences.

Expectations, Hopes, and Fears

As is often the case, it is hard to find survey data that allow us to assess *why* the Germans favored unification, or *why* they were indifferent or even opposed to it. However, in some indirect way it is still possible to investigate the expectations, hopes, and fears associated with German unification. The Wildenmann surveys of April 1990 established both an overall effective response to unification, as well as the reactions to a series of possible consequences of unification on a four point scale.[5] Positive responses clearly outnumber the negative and indifferent ones among both German publics (see Table 2.1). Still, the feelings of one in four West German respondents fall far short of delight.[6]

Quick unification by way of extending the Federal Republic following the course prescribed in Article 23 of the Basic Law had been a highly partisan issue ever since Kohl's declaration in November (see Chapter 1). The high level of bipartisan support for unification noted above, then, may simply be due to the lack of viable alternatives. The partisan character of Kohl's specific agenda, however, should be detectable in the affective responses. Also, it is plausible to assume that 40 years of separation had left their mark, and that remaining family ties across the border would be more important for the older generation. As a matter of fact, the data in Table 2.1 show relationships of this kind. As to partisanship, among adherents of the SPD, Greens, and Republicans in the West and among the PDS followers in the East the proportion of respondents not pleased with unification was considerably higher. The age effect, however, differs between West and East. In the West, people under 35 were noticeably less enthusiastic about unification than their elders. A third of these younger respondents, moreover, were not pleased, compared to less than a quarter of their elders (see Table 2.1). This age effect, however, is contingent upon partisanship. There is no significant age difference among CDU adherents, and – in a reversal of the overall pattern – young Republicans are the most enthusiastic: 50 percent are "very pleased" in contrast to 11 percent among older Republicans and 20 percent among older CDU followers, the second most pleased

5. These surveys were conducted by the Research Unit for Societal Developments (RSD) at the University of Mannheim under the direction of Rudolf Wildemann. Largely identical questionnaires were used with representative samples in both East and West Germany. Field work was done by MARPLAN; N=808 (East) and N=1700 (West) face-to-face interviews were collected in March/April 1990.

6. The characterization of this question as measuring an affective response is bases on the original German question wording. The English translation given in Table 2.1 may not fully capture the semantics of the original. The crucial second sentence reads: "... *Was fühlen Sie dabei?*"

7. We need to be aware, though, that the absolute number of Republicans in the sample is rather small (N=28). Still, the partial association coefficient comes close to meeting conventional significance marks (.070). Allowing for partisanship, the full set of partial Cramer coefficients for the association of age group and feeling toward unification is: .058 (CDU), .130 (SPD), .110 (FDP), .150 (Greens), .435

Table 2.1. Feelings about German Unification, Spring 1990

WEST GERMANY	ALL RESPONDENTS	AGE		PARTY PREFERENCE				
		-34	35+	CDU	FDP	SPD	GRN	REP
very pleased	19%	14	21	24	19	16	10	25
pleased	55	52	57	57	62	56	41	36
not pleased/ indifferent	26	34	22	19	19	28	49	39
	100	100	100	100	100	100	100	100
(N of cases)	(1687)	(490)	(1197)	(669)	(89)	(747)	(98)	(28)
Cramer's V (significance)	.131 (.000)			.137 (.000)				

EAST GERMANY	ALL RESPONDENTS	AGE		PARTY PREFERENCE			
		-34	35+	CDU	FDP	SPD	PDS
very pleased	41%	35	44	49	50	36	13
pleased	50	55	48	46	42	57	44
not pleased/ indifferent	9	10	8	5	8	7	43
	100	100	100	100	100	100	100
(N of cases)	(806)	(271)	(535)	(397)	(24)	(316)	(61)
Cramer's V (significance)	.086 (.050)			.263 (.000)			

QUESTION: "Leaving aside detailed plans and procedures, German unification is more or less agreed upon. How do you feel about this? Are you very pleased (erfreut), pleased, not pleased, or are you indifferent (*gleichgültig*)?"

NOTE:: Data from surveys conducted by the Research Unit for Societal Developments (RSD) at the University of Mannheim under the direction of Rudolf Wildenmann. Largely identical questionnaires were used with representative samples in both East and West Germany. Field work was done by MARPLAN : N=808 (East) and N=1700 (West) face-to-face interviews were collected in March/April 1990. CDU+ for East Germany represents the "Alliance for Germany," i.e., it includes DSU and DA.

group.[7] In the East, the difference between young and old respondents was statistically significant, though not as impressive. Here, younger respondents were less exuberant but no more likely to be negative or indifferent. Other socio-demographic factors like sex, education, or income display no major differences.[8] Still, in the East and in the West, low income respondents were somewhat less enthusiastic than more affluent ones.

Beyond general affect, what consequences of unification did Germans expect as the unification process picked up steam in early 1990? Respondents in both Germanies were presented with a set of 12 statements to be rated on a four-point scale.[9] Unfortunately, these 12 statements only partially cover the range of questions pursued here (see Table 2.2). Most importantly, the prospect of political dominance in Europe by a unified Germany and the possibility of renewed military aggressiveness – at the heart of the concerns and reluctance abroad – are not covered. The reference to increased German self-confidence (statement F) is a distant proxy at best. Similarly, the possibility of internal strife due a deeply segmented labor market, unemployment, "dispossessed" segments of the population (e.g., East German military and secret police forces), and similar factors is not explicitly addressed. Finally, most of these items are worded from a Western point of view where the old FRG is taken as standard of comparison (most obviously, statements I, M, and L). The responses, then, may not fully capture the sentiments of East Germans.

Comparing the opinions of East and West Germans, in April 1990 the East Germans display a much more optimistic outlook. They consistently are more likely to agree with positive consequences and less likely to have negative or skeptical expectations. Almost half the East Germans "fully expect" a united Germany to be even stronger economically and for an upswing to occur in every conceivable aspect of public life, such as sports, cultural affairs, and even social interaction (*im Umgang miteinander*): an idyllic image of affluence in a kind and gentle society (see Table 2.2). In contrast, among West Germans two skeptical statements (A and B) draw the most agreement: 45 percent fully agree it would be difficult to reconcile the two social systems, and 36 percent foresee Germany as being preoccupied with its own prob-

8. For education, the Cramer coefficient is .075 (significance=.079) in the West and .121 (.091) in the East, but there is no clear linear trend across the 10 categories. Finally, for sex V=.051 (.106) in the West and V=.063 (.201) in the East.

9. In German, the scale was labeled as *"trifft voll und ganz zu," "trifft eher zu,"* and *"trifft überhaupt nicht zu."* It is difficult to find a full equivalent in English. The first category may best be translated as "absolutely true."

lems for years to come. On both counts the corresponding percentage in East Germany is about 10 points lower.

Returning to the overall feelings discussed above (see Table 2.1), we can now dig a little deeper: Are these feelings grounded in some calculus of rational choice? Do they reflect the outcome of a businesslike weighing of advantages and disadvantages or do they present a truly emotional response unfettered by practical concerns? If that is the case, feelings should be largely independent from expected gains and anticipated difficulties. In the West, however, feelings about unification with one exception are strongly associated with anticipated consequences (see third column in Table 2.2). Positive feelings tend to go along with positive expectations about the consequences, most prominently with expectations of quick and painless economic gains (statements C, I, and D) – and vice versa. In the East, the associations between overall feelings and the anticipated consequences are almost uniformly fewer, if not downright insignificant. By and large, the East Germans seemed to feel that they had no real choice and that unification was the only way to go – no matter what.[10]

Additional insight into the expectations associated with unification is provided by the Politbarometer surveys throughout 1990. The Western public was asked if they thought "that a reunification of the two German states will have mostly advantages or mostly disadvantages for the West German population in the short run, or if the advantages and disadvantages will even out," and how they felt "about the long run." Notwithstanding some minor fluctuations, only some 10 percent of the Westerners saw mostly advantages in the short run, while 35 percent felt that advantages and disadvantages would balance, and about half of the respondents perceived mostly disadvantages for West Germans in the immediate future. Most frequently named among the disadvantages were tax increases (up to 40 percent of all respondents), followed by a perceived burden on the economy, negative effects on the job market and on housing. In East Germany, a similar assessment produced distinctly more positive responses; about 20 percent saw mostly advantages, and an additional 40 percent felt that the advantages and disadvantages would bal-

10. In part, the low correlations for Easterners may be an artifact of the method used, due to a heavily skewed marginal distribution and the infelicitous wording of the statement battery.

Table 2.2. Anticipated Consequences of German Unification, Spring 1990

		AFFIRMATIVE RESPONSES		ASSOCIATION W/FEELINGS	
		WEST	EAST	WEST	EAST
C	The unified Germany will be even stronger economically than before	27.7	47.6	.264	.066
G	There will be a turn for the better in every aspect of public life, e.g., sports, culture	33.1	43.6	.250	.045
I	New investment opportunities in the GDR create new jobs and further stimulate the economy	30.8	39.0	.273	.029
F	German self-confidence will increase	21.6	37.7	.219	.174
A	Great difficulties in reconciling the social systems	45.5	36.8	-.170	-.182
B	Germany will be preoccupied with its own problems for years to come	36.5	26.5	-.187	-.091
H	There will be many more parties	20.1	20.9	-.076	-.054
E	The West Germans will get a little poorer, the East Germans will get a little richer	22.5	12.0	-.093	.018
K	A unified Germany will be neutral	9.2	9.4	.282	.147
D	Transition problems will be resolved quickly	9.2	9.4	.282	.147
M	A unified Germany will be less cosmopolitan than the FRG	10.9	4.5	-.204	-.252
L	The current "social market economy" as practiced in the FRG will be diluted	8.7	3.2	-.219	-.031

QUESTION: "On this list you will find a number of statements about what consequences the unification of the two German states into one single state might have. Please tell me for each one whether this is absolutely true, largely true, largely not true, or not true at all."

NOTE: Source as table 2.1. German wording: ". . . , ob sie Ihrer Ansicht nach voll und ganz zutrifft, eher zutrifft, eher nicht zutrifft oder überhaupt nicht zutrifft." In the first two columns the percentage of those finding a statement "absolutely true" are given – based on all respondents (N=1700 in the West and N=808 in the East). The differences in these percentages between the East German and West German samples are all statistically significant (on the .0001 level) except for items H, D, and K. Association is measured by the Somer coefficient d (symmetric) based on 4 x 3 tables. For West Germany, all coefficients are significant on the .05 level (except item K); for East Germany, coefficients are statistically significant for items F, A, B, D, and M only.

ance (Roth, 1990: 386, Table 8). The response pattern changes drastically, though, when the long term effect is assessed. When speaking of the long term, close to 50 percent of the West German respondents and about 60 percent of the East Germans see mostly advantages, and the percentage of those seeing mostly disadvantages drops to fewer than 10 points.

Unfortunately, only once in May 1990 (and in East Germany only), were respondents prompted in the additional open-ended probe to specify both the advantages and disadvantages they perceived. The responses are telling (see Table 2.3). A better standard of living tops the list of advantages named by 40 percent of all respondents; in contrast, freedom of speech or democracy trail far behind with only 13 and 4 percent respectively. At least one of the following five immediate economic advantages (standard of living, upswing, income, pensions, currency) is named by 75 percent of the respondents, and 49 percent name a few of these. Family reunion is conspicuously absent from the list of advantages, although freedom to travel ranks rather high with 18 percent. On the negative side, unemployment tops the list with 41 percent, followed by the loss of *sozialistische Errungenschaften* (by objective criteria, most prominently the easy availability of child care, low rents, and low cost health care) with 28 percent. However, a full 21 percent of the respondents did not see any disadvantage at all. Unification, then, was largely framed as an economic issue.

Solidarity and Sacrifice

Overwhelmingly, East Germans expected quick improvements in their standard of living. And most West Germans felt that the burden would fall on them – at least in the short run. But were they ready to make sacrifices for their "brothers and sisters in the other part of Germany" – as the East Germans were commonly referred to in pre-"Ostpolitik" rhetoric? Throughout 1990, the Kohl government tried to sell unification as a non-zero sum game with winners only. However, the West German public took a more realistic stance. Their willingness to bear the burden, then, is crucial for the process of truly reconciling the two social systems.

The solidarity theme was addressed in separate surveys commissioned by the two weeklies, *Der Spiegel* and *Die Zeit*, in February/March 1990. Using differently worded questions, the results

Table 2.3. Expected Advantages and Disadvantages of Unification in East Germany, May 1990

Overall	Short Term	Long Term
More advantages	16.5	54.6
More disadvantages	41.1	4.7
Balanced	38.0	39.6
No response	4.4	1.1
Total	**100.0%**	**100.0%**

Advantages		Disadvantages	
Better standard of living	40	Unemployment	41
Economic upswing	24	Loss of GDR specific gains	28
Freedom to travel	18	Sellout of GDR	8
Freedom of speech	13	Rising costs	8
Higher income	11	Higher rents	8
Stable currency	11	Crime	7
Social security	9	Drugs, AIDS	5
Occupational choice	8	Child care	5
Higher pension	8	Exploitation	4
Environment	7	Human relations	3
Democracy	3	Pensions	2
European unity	3	Discrimination against women	2
Better housing	2	Energy costs	2
Urban renewal	2	Xenophobia	2
Other	2	Housing shortage	2
Prestige	2	Other	1
Culture	1		
No advantages named	9	No disadvantages named	21

Source: FGW-Politbarometer (Ost) May 1990. Table entries are percentages based on all N=723 respondents. Closed question with non-filtered open-ended followup, allowing multiple responses.

were strikingly different. Forced to choose between two categorical statements, the Emnid/Spiegel survey found 61 percent of the respondents ready "to make personal financial sacrifices" and 36 percent unwilling to do so (*Der Spiegel* no. 14/1990). Over time, the percentage of those willing to sacrifice dropped to 45 percent in August and to 39 percent in October 1990 (*Der Spiegel* no. 38/1990). Using wording less prone to a social desirability bias, the Allensbach/Zeit survey found less than 25 percent of West Germans who said their willingness to make sacrifices was "great," 51 percent who said it was "not that great," and 25 percent who found the question impossible to answer (*Die Zeit* no.11/1990). As with general support for unification (see again Table 2.1), distinct age and partisan patterns emerged. For instance, only 16 percent of Westerners under age 30 were "greatly willing to make sacrifices" compared to 36 percent of those over 60. Similarly, 33 percent of CDU adherents, and only 17 percent of SPD followers, were fully prepared to make sacrifices.

Over time, Allensbach had measured the readiness to make sacrifices using a rather elaborate vignette question describing a possible political scenario and a 10 year surtax plan affecting all incomes beyond a moderate threshold (DM 1.90 on about $1200 per month in 1990). Unequivocal approval of such a plan dropped from 17 percent in 1959, to 16 in 1967, 12 percent in 1969, and to just 5 percent in 1990; staunch opposition, meanwhile, rose from 59 percent in 1959 to 77 percent in 1990. In 1959, 1967, 1969 the political scenario provided in the vignette was truly hypothetical; by February 1990, however, unification was a realistic policy option. No concrete tax plans had yet been introduced at the time of the survey, but 75 percent of the respondents anticipated "significant tax increases" and only 27 percent found this acceptable (see Table 2.4). More generally, major portions if not the majority of the respondents anticipated negative consequences: higher social security taxes, ever increasing budget deficits, higher interests on loans and mortgages, loss of currency stability, social security cuts, and more (see again Table 2.4). At best only 25 percent felt that these consequences were acceptable (*Das kann man in Kauf nehmen*).

In the same Allensbach survey of February 1990, 69 percent of the respondents were in favor of unification. The West German public seemed torn, at once seeming to voice massive support for unification, a realistic view of the considerable costs and difficulties, and a rather limited willingness to bear the burden. The *Zeit* headline said it all: "Unity? Yes, but cheap please!"

In contrast, Politbarometer data from the fall of 1990 show a somewhat more altruistic picture. In spite of Chancellor Kohl's

Table 2.4. Expectations and Tolerance of Effects of Unification in West Germany, February 1990

	EXPECTING	TOLERATING
Significant tax increases	75%	27%
Social security tax increase	61	26
Increasing federal budget deficit	61	26
Credit shortage, higher interest rates	47	24
DM loses stability	44	15
Cuts in social benefits	38	8
Pensions payment problems	35	3
No wage increases for some time	34	21
DM devaluation	29	8
Inflation	14	2

NOTE: Data as reported in *Die Zeit* No. 11 of 9 March 1990: p. 3, based on a survey conducted by Institut für Demoskopie, Allensbach.

frequent assurances that tax increases would not be necessary to finance German unity, the public read his lips differently: between 70 and 80 percent of the West German respondents expected a tax increase in the period between September and December 1990. At the same time, close to 50 percent agreed with this hypothetical increase.

Finally, the extent of German-German solidarity can also be assessed by Western attitudes towards East German refugees – later on: emigrants. Early support and sympathy quickly vanished after Honecker was ousted and the border between East and West was at last open. In December 1989 barely one quarter of the West Germans expressed full understanding for people still emigrating and their support dwindled to just 11 percent in April 1990 (see Kuechler, 1992 for more detail).

Unification on the Eve of the First Elections

Summarizing the situation in late 1990 and drawing on the data presented here as well as on qualitative evidence gathered from news reports, personal observation, and informal interviews, the following *gestalt* emerges. Above all, East Germans wanted their share of the "good life," not just material affluence, but also adventure, excitement, and personal freedom. The Leipzig studies provide ample evidence of this strong trend towards personal fulfillment among large segments of young adults in the late 1980s. Walter Friedrich (1990: 36) argues that this trend will continue, expressing mixed feelings about the social consequences. On the one hand, he sees people as ready and eager to take charge of their lives and to make the most out of their gifts and talents. On the other hand, he fears that people may become more self-centered, politically indifferent and/or opportunistic, and even that they may become more susceptible to extremism.

The East Germans seem to be thoroughly wary of ideology, any ideology restricting the individual pursuit of wealth and happiness. Consequently, the grassroots organizations pivotal in organizing opposition and in finally bringing down the old regime – most notably the *Neues Forum* and *Demokratie Jetzt* – were quickly abandoned by the masses. Their electoral alliance (*Bündnis '90*) received less than 3 percent of the popular vote in the March elections, with another 2 percent going to an alliance of green and feminist groups. As it turned out, the formal alliance between the Greens and *Bündnis 90* received 5.9 percent of the vote in the December elections, indicating a stable, if rather small voter clientele. The idealistic call for evolutionary renewal, for some sort of socialism with a humane face went largely unheard in the midst of a roaring desire for the quick affluence that unification on Western terms seemed to promise. In addition, the Eastern civil rights movement lacked a charismatic leader, a German Vaclav Havel, who could symbolize the hope for a more equitable and humane society, not just a more affluent one.

The East Germans wanted affluence and freedom, but with freedom suddenly and so easily won and secured, economic gains became the predominant concern. Quite a bit of help was expected from the West. The "poor relatives" were knocking on the door, not obsequiously, but with a sense of collecting an overdue debt. The West Germans, for their part, were not overly accommodating. They certainly welcomed the downfall of the Communist regime in East Germany, but for the most part felt reluctant to share and make sacrifices.

Unification had become an economic issue and as such it dominated the elections.[11] The delivery of promised affluence and reaching the Western standard of living were most prominent in the minds of the Eastern public; cost containment and minimizing the economic burden was the major concern of the Western electorate. Kohl's victory was less an unconditional mandate to lead the united Germany for years to come than the result of a qualified assessment that his government had the best chances for successfully coping with a tremendous array of economic problems. True unification was still to be achieved, and the public was withholding a final verdict.

Unification: A Perennial Issue?

Unification had dominated the public agenda since the fall of 1989, eclipsing previously salient issues like unemployment and the environment. Throughout 1990, consistently well over 50 percent of West Germans (and often up to almost 90 percent) named issues directly related to unification in response to an open probe about the two most important problems facing the nation (see Figure 2.2). The exact nature of these issues shifted over time with the changing political scenery: from concern about GDR emigrants, to the currency union, on to dealing with the cost of unity (though the majority of the responses was less specific). In absolute terms, the salience of unification started to decline by September 1990 – with a transitory resurgence in early 1991 – to a more constant level of some 30 percent in late 1991.[12] In the three-year period from 1989 to 1991 the salience of the unification issue stunningly complements the importance of another issue, how to deal with *Aussiedler*, asylum seekers, and foreigners. By early 1989, this issue topped the political agenda (see Figure 2.1), but quickly faded as the unification issue gained prominence. The trend is quite obvious: as the unification issue gains in salience, the "foreigners" issue declines and vice versa. Is this pure coinci-

11. For a detailed discussion of unification as a factor explaining the vote choice in the December 1990 election, see Kuechler (1991a); also see chapter by Norpoth and Roth in this volume.

12. The steep decline in January 1991 is due to the outbreak of the Gulf War. An open-ended question with just two possible responses like the one here is very sensitive to such a "period effect." The drop does not truly signify a salient decline of unification.

Figure 2.2. Most Important Problems in West Germany

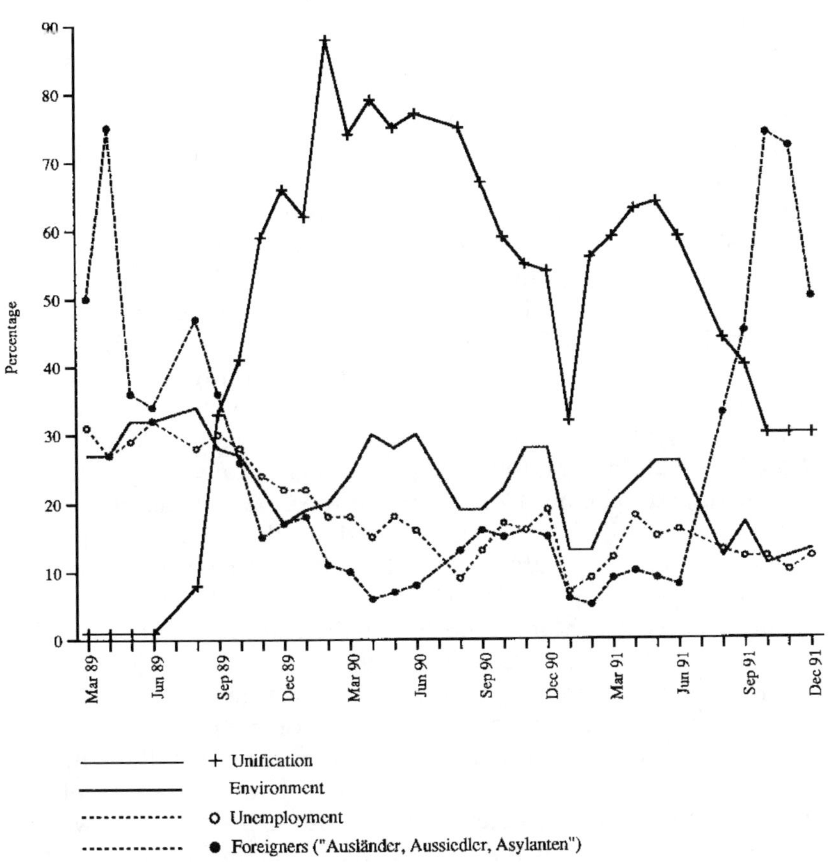

Source: FGW Politbarometer surveys. Percentages based on all respondents, each of whom could mention two problems in response to an open-ended probe.

47

dence? One may speculate that the issues of unification and "foreigners" are just two manifestations of the same underlying concern, for West Germans, who feel they must closely guard their affluence, are extremely wary of any demand that they share this wealth with others. Xenophobia may be too strong a word, but this seeming obsession with affluence and the status quo may turn out to be a profound liability if the Federal Republic's economy ever takes a serious downturn.

In the period considered here the Western economy, nonetheless, continued to prosper. As a matter of fact, it improved rather than declined during the process of unification. The inflation rate for 1990 was 2.7 percent (slightly down from 2.8 percent in 1989); the annual average number of unemployed was below two million for the first time since 1982; and the GNP increased by 4.5 percent (compared to 3.9 percent in 1989), the strongest growth in 14 years. However, new debt in the federal budget increased markedly compared to 1989, from some DM 25 billion to about DM 60 billion for both 1990 and 1991 (with a projected DM 50 billion for 1992). In 1991, the average number of unemployed further dropped to below 1.7 million and the GNP rose another 3.2 percent; only inflation increased to a still rather modest 3.5 percent. The objective state of the economy is mirrored in public opinion. The salience of unemployment steadily declined from some 30 percent in March 1989 to less than 20 percent at election time and to about 15 percent by the end of 1991 (see Figure 2.1). Concern about inflation and the economy at large never exceeded 10 percent of West Germans during the whole period.

For East Germany, the unification issue was framed differently and is more succinctly dissected into several concrete facets. Unemployment quickly became the overriding problem, followed by concerns over how to improve or even maintain the standard of living in the face of quickly rising prices and wages improving only slowly at best (see Figure 2.3). The approaching currency union in particular seemed to cause great anxiety. In May and June 1990 – the months immediately preceding the monetary union – 38 and 27 percent respectively saw this as one of the two most important problems facing the GDR. Starting in the fall of 1990 and continuing throughout all of 1991, concern about unemployment rose steadily to over 60 percent before leveling off, though it continued to outnumber all other economic concerns combined.

48

Figure 2.3. Most Important Problems in East Germany

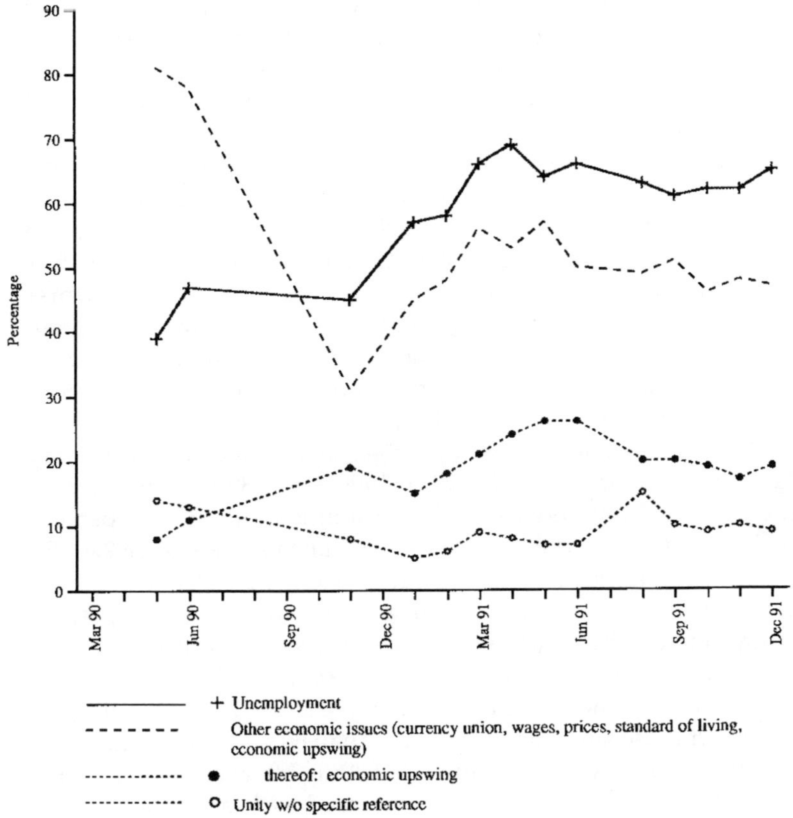

SOURCE: FGW-Politbarometer surveys. Percentages based on all respondents, each of whom could mention two problems in response to an open-ended probe. The December 1990 survey was omitted, since it used a different format (three problems instead of two).

The Eastern concerns reflected objective conditions. Labor statistics showed a steady increase in unemployment after formal unification. The official unemployment rate reached 9.2 percent in March 1991 and 11.8 percent in December 1991. These figures camouflage the true extent of the job shortage, however. About another 20 percent were "working reduced hours," often not doing any real work at all, yet receiving a government subsidized salary rather than unemployment benefits. Until 1 July 1991, temporary protection measures guarded against layoffs in many formerly state-owned and now defunct companies. After that, "employment associations" (*Beschäftigungs-gesellschaften*) were formed as a functional equivalent to alleviate growing dissatisfaction. At the time the government maintained that the worst would be over by the end of 1991, that an upswing was imminent. In early 1992, however, even the government had to concede it expected a further rise in the official unemployment rate to about 17 percent over the course of the year.

Dissatisfaction in the East with the general state of the economy had been high in the early fall of 1990. Over 80 percent felt that the present situation was "bad," with little more than 50 percent feeling that it would be "better" a year ahead (see Figure 2.4). By the time of the elections, however, the trend had shifted dramatically. In December 1990, only 60 percent still felt that the present situation was bad and a positive outlook on the future was spreading. But the reversal was short lived. In the first few months of 1991 negative assessments reached the previous high levels. Of those still employed, more than 60 percent felt that their jobs were not secure (see Figure 2.4). Only after the Bonn government decided on a program of increased assistance for the East did this trend change once again. Still, by December 1991 about 55 percent of Easterners saw the economic situation as bad, while the number with an optimistic outlook on the future had increased only temporarily, and more than 50 percent of those employed still felt that their job was not secure (Figure 2.4).

The disenchantment of the people in the East shows in many other ways as well. Throughout 1991, some 70 percent were "rather dissatisfied" with their progress in reaching the Western standard of living, and more than 75 percent felt that the Bonn government was not providing enough help to reach this goal (see Figure 2.5). By the end of 1991, more than 40 percent still felt

Figure 2.4. Economic Outlook of East Germans

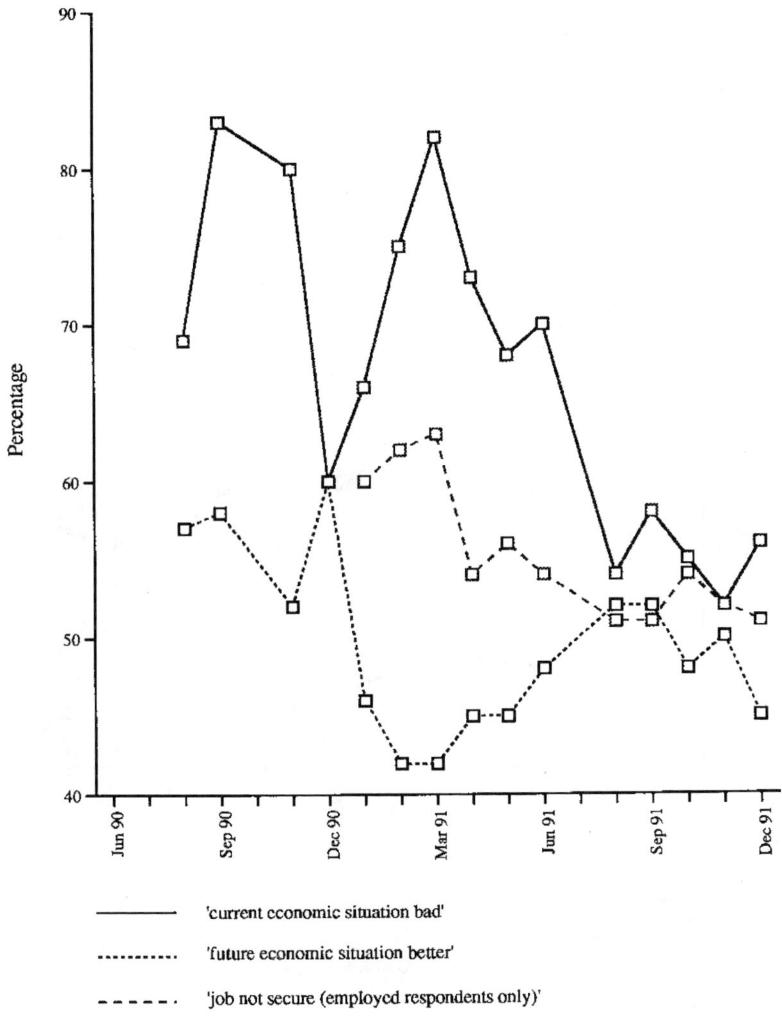

Source: See Figure 2.2.

Figure 2.5. Selected Assessments of Unification after the Fact

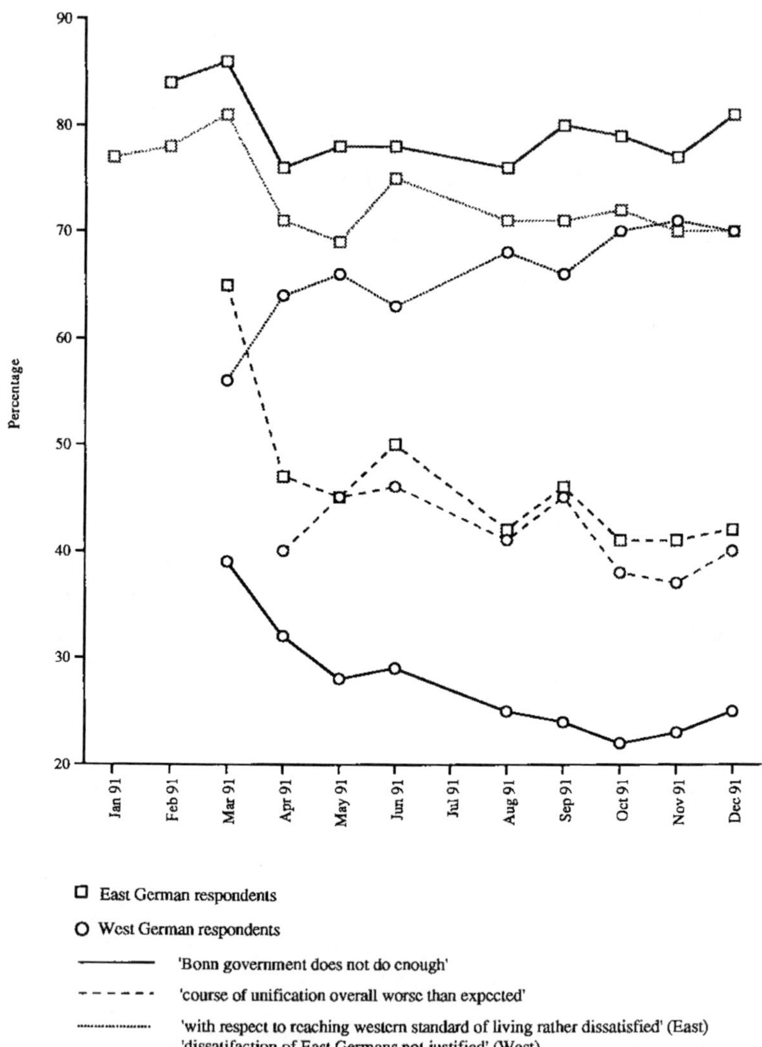

SOURCE: See Figure 2.2

that unification had gone "worse than expected," and less than 15 percent were positively surprised. After the peak of dissatisfaction in March 1991 the share of disenchanted Easterners declined, though this downward trend was very gentle.

As to unmet expectations with the course of unification, the Westerners show a similar pattern. Throughout 1991 some 40 percent felt it had gone worse than expected, and about 15 percent felt it had gone better. The similarities end here, however. By the end of 1991, only a little more than 20 percent in the West felt that the Bonn government did not do enough to help the East and, increasingly, a clear majority of Westerners felt that the dissatisfaction of Easterners was "not justified" (Figure 2.5). By December 1991, some 70 percent felt that way.

Conclusion

As an abstract idea, a vast majority of Westerners – and it seems safe to assume Easterners as well – had always been in favor of (re-)unification. However, by the late 1980s unification had become a hypothetical question, and the reality of two German states had been widely accepted. The fall of the Communist regime in the GDR, then, took everybody by surprise. While all Germans were united in celebration of the newly-won freedom for the East, the public was not prepared for a quick unification of the two states. Chancellor Kohl took the lead, and the masses eventually followed – somewhat reluctantly and wary of negative consequences.

The data show that economic expectations strongly shaped mass sentiment toward unification in both East and West. Easterners expected rapid and significant improvements in their standard of living, while Westerners were not eager to share and showed little inclination to make sacrifices. Initially, Easterners were more enthusiastic about unification than Westerners. After the fact, by spring 1991, the situation was reversed: a vast majority of people in the East showed marked signs of disappointment with the unification process and its economic benefits. Westerners, however, seemed reasonably assured that the cost of unification – while not negligible – could be tolerated and thus a mild optimism prevailed. The economic disappointment Easterners felt marred their view of the Federal Republic's political system in general – a phenomenon observable in other countries as well (see Kuechler, 1991b). Consistently fewer than 50 percent of Easterners are "rather satisfied" with democracy and the political system at large whereas about two-thirds of Westerners continue to be "rather satisfied" throughout 1991. It remains to be seen whether the East will successfully adapt to the new political and social order – particularly if economic improvements continue to come slowly if at all.

There are some early warning signs that internal strife may emerge. The surge of manifest xenophobia in late 1991 and throughout 1992 in both parts of Germany, the reemergence of the "foreigner" issue on top of the political problem list (see again Figure 2.2), may both be seen as foreboding indicators of a still latent conflict. Asylum seekers and immigrants may be surrogates for the "other" Germans; for now, open conflict is avoided by zeroing in on a common enemy. Easterners and Westerners have not grown any closer during the process of unification. The majority of Westerners feel that Easterners want too much too quickly, while most people in the East still feel like second class citizens, failing to get the respect of the *Besserwessies*.[13]

The on-going process of unification will no doubt continue to dominate the political agenda. The issue may take on different shapes and forms, but it seems safe to predict that the fate of the governing coalition in the next elections will be determined by its handling of the unification process. Among the various aspects of unification, preservation of Western affluence during the attempt to improve economic blight in the East will be the top criterion the public will use to evaluate the work of the current government. In March 1991, about two-thirds of Westerners considered Kohl's promise not to raise taxes a fraud and a lie (*Wahlbetrug* and *Steuerlüge*), and the popularity of both the government and Kohl declined. The CDU/CSU was the "party liked best" by 47 percent of the electorate in December 1990. By late 1991, the slide had stopped at approximately 37 percent. In addition to low standings in the polls, the Christian Democrats lost the state elections in Rhineland-Palatinate – Kohl's home state where the CDU had

---

13. "*Besserwessie*" has been chosen as the most characteristic word of 1991 by the Society for German Language from more than ten thousand entries. It combines the slightly derogatory term *Wessie* (for West German) with "*Besserwisser*" – wise guy (*This Week in Germany*, 20 December 1991: 7).

ruled since the end of World War II – in April 1991. Yet, as long as the Federal Republic's economy continues to prosper, as it did in 1990 and 1991, the unification issue may turn out to be an asset for the coalition in the 1994 elections. More importantly, continued prosperity will keep the latent conflicts between East and West Germans in check. It will also prevent radical parties from capitalizing on disappointment and dissatisfaction. There will be no serious threat to the basic political order – as long as affluence prevails.

References

Conradt, David P. 1986. *The German Polity*, 3rd ed. New York: Longman.

Friedrich, Walter. 1990. "Mentalitätswandlungen der Jugend in der DDR." *Aus Politik und Zeitgeschichte. Beilage zur Wochenzeitung Das Parlament* No. 16/17: pp. 25–37.

Jansen, Silke. 1989. "Zwei deutsche Staaten – zwei deutsche Nationen? Meinungsbilder zur deutschen Frage im Zeitablauf." *Deutschland Archiv* 22: pp. 1132–1143.

Kuechler, Manfred. 1991a. "Anschluss über alles? What did the Voter decide in the 1990 German Elections?" Paper presented at the Annual Meetings of the Midwest Political Science Association, April 18–20, Chicago, IL.

————. 1991b. "The Dynamics of Mass Political Support in Western Europe," in Karlheinz Reif and Ronald Inglehart (eds.), *Eurobarometer: The Dynamcis of European Public Opinion*, London: Macmillan.

————. 1992. "The Road to German Unity: Mass Sentiment in East and West Germany." *Public Opinion Quarterly* 56: pp. 53–76.

Roth, Dieter. 1990. "Die Wahlen zur Volkskammer in der DDR." *Politische Vierteljahresschrift* 31: pp. 369–393.

Szumni, Birgit, Isabell Lichtleitner and Franz Bauske. 1990. "Datenreport: Die Vereinigung der beiden deutschen Staaten." *ZA-Informationen* 26: pp. 62–71.

II. THE POLITICAL PARTIES

3

The Christian Democrats in 1990: Saved by Unification?

David Conradt

T HE CHRISTIAN DEMOCRATIC UNION has been the dominant political force for most of the Federal Republic's history. Like the Republic itself, the party is a postwar creation. The CDU also pioneered a new style of German politics because unlike parties during the Weimar Republic, the CDU after 1949 avoided any narrow ideological direction. It demanded little of its supporters besides a general commitment to the "social market economy" and a pro-Western, anti-Communist foreign policy. These were the party's only "essentials." It offered a political home for Catholics and Protestants, blue-collar and white-collar workers, urban and rural interests. The stunning electoral successes of the Union's first leader and chancellor of the Federal Republic, Konrad Adenauer, held this coalition together. In the first three national elections held between 1949 and 1957, the CDU/CSU's proportion of the vote increased from 31 percent to over 50 percent – a total no German political party has ever achieved before or since. The Union delivered on its promises of security and mass prosperity. Its successes transformed the FRG party system as the numerous small, special interest parties disappeared and the Social Democrats eventually moved into the center of the political spectrum.

The Christian Democrats soon became a prototype for the "catchall parties" that emerged in postwar Europe: parties that sought through their pragmatic, non-ideological images to attract as broad an electoral base as possible. The CDU has always wanted voters, if not necessarily believers. This openly pragmatic approach was criticized by more traditionally-minded politicians and most intellectuals as being opportunist. But to many voters

59

the Union represented a welcome relief from the ideological rigidity that had characterized past German parties.

The 1990 elections, first in the former GDR and then the December national election, showed that this 1949-style of Western party politics was equally successful in the East. The Union, led by Chancellor Kohl, responded to what most East Germans wanted as quickly as possible: the freedom, security and prosperity of the West. The party did not hesitate or agonize over the questions of East German identity, or over what "achievements" of the communist system should be preserved. Neither did it agonize over the costs and possible resistance of West Germans to the process. As in 1949 under its first leader, Konrad Adenauer, the Christian Democrats had the right message at the right time to attract the greatest amount of electoral support. The path to victory in 1990, however, was far from smooth.

The Union in Disarray, 1987–1989

Until the opening of the Wall in November 1989 the prospects for the Union's return to power after the 1990 election were anything but bright. In the 1987 election the Christian Democrats, with their 44.3 percent of the vote, dropped to their lowest level since 1949. Losses to the Free Democrats (intra-camp desertions), low turnout (especially in rural areas), and overconfidence among the party's activists were the major factors cited by the party's leadership in explaining the outcome (Conradt and Dalton, 1988: 23; Schultze, 1991). Moreover, the Union lost votes to the SPD largely because of the still high unemployment level among manual workers.

The election postmortem in 1987 included mutual recriminations between the CDU and CSU. Kohl's supporters in the CDU blamed Strauss and the Bavarians for their attacks on the Free Democrats, which caused some moderate government supporters to vote for the liberals. Strauss, in turn, attributed the decline to Kohl's relatively low popularity. In 1987, the CSU wanted the Union to make an all-out effort for an absolute majority, thus making a coalition with the FDP unnecessary.

But as 1987 progressed the political fortunes of Chancellor Kohl's party did not improve. At four state elections in May and October 1987 the CDU lost support due to the slow economy, internal party conflicts, and scandals. The party was further shaken in September 1987 when the young premier of the northern state of Schleswig-Holstein, Uwe Barschel, was accused of using governmental agencies and funds for a Watergate-style dirty tricks campaign against his Socialist challenger. Shortly before he was to testify about the charges before a parliamentary investigating committee, Barschel, who had been in ill health because of an airplane accident, was found dead in a Zurich hotel room – an apparent suicide. A few months later in 1988 the Union lost its forty-year old majority in Schleswig-Holstein, as the Social Democrats, led by Björn Engholm, won an absolute majority.

In the 1989 city elections in Berlin and Frankfurt, and in the June 1989 European parliamentary election, the CDU lost heavily to the Social Democrats and in some cases to the radical-right Republican party. The Union lost support in all but one of the seven state polls held between the 1987 general election and the opening of the Berlin Wall. At the four West German state elections in 1990, which preceded the national vote, the party was able to reduce its losses, mainly due to state-level factors and not to any national trend against the government.

These losses in state elections were mirrored in the declining support it garnered in the monthly polls of the national electorate (see Chapter 1). By the end of 1987, the Christian Democrats had lost their advantage over the SPD and soon entered the mid-term decline common for all governing parties. In early 1989, the Social Democrats moved ahead of the CDU and held this lead until July. The nadir of the Union's fortunes was reached in April 1989 when only 36 percent of the electorate supported the party. Kohl's popularity level dropped to 34 percent and one poll found that 73 percent of the voters preferred Lothar Späth, then minister president of Baden-Württemberg, over Kohl as chancellor (*Der Spiegel*, No. 17, 1989: 24).

Adding to the party's problems in 1989 was the appearance of new competition on the right, the Republicans (*Republikaner* [REP]). Spreading out from their Bavarian base, the REPs entered the city parliament in Berlin in January 1989 and scored similar victories in local elections in Frankfurt. In the June 1989 European election the party received 7.1 percent of the vote. Surveys found that over 40 percent of REP voters had supported the CDU/CSU in 1987, while only 20 percent came from the SPD camp (Roth, 1990; Stoess, 1991).

There were numerous reasons for voter discontent with the CDU and Chancellor Kohl. The 1988 tax law changes, especially the provision for a withholding tax on interest and dividend payments, were very unpopular with his party's middle-class clientele. Cuts in the health insurance system upset broader sectors of the population. The extension of the length of compulsory military service from 15 to 18 months did not help the party's status among younger voters, and shortage of affordable housing in many large cities cost the government support in urban areas. This housing problem, coupled with the generous support of ethnic German resettlers from the Soviet Union and Eastern Europe, provided the right-wing Republicans with an effective anti-foreigners campaign theme.

In April 1989, Chancellor Kohl attempted to appease his critics and stem the loss of voters. The unpopular withholding tax on dividends and interest was repealed and the government announced new restrictions on foreigners seeking asylum as well as cuts in benefits for ethnic-German settlers. Some social programs, such as family allowances, were expanded and a new five-year public housing program was passed, the first since 1986. Kohl also dismissed or transferred unpopular cabinet ministers for Defense, Finance, the Interior, and Housing.

These changes were not enough, however, to satisfy some of the chancellor's critics in the Union. By the summer of 1989 reports of intra-party opposition to Kohl, as well as a possible "coup" at the party's September Parteitag in Bremen, were widespread in the media. The leaders of the opposition were the Union's General Secretary, Heiner Geissler, Späth, Bundestag President Rita Süssmuth, former General Secretary of the Union Kurt Biedenkopf, and Labor and Social Welfare Minister Norbert Blüm. Geissler and his supporters wanted to make the party more independent of the CDU government, that is, of the Chancellor's office and parliament. They believed the party organization and its staff should be more involved in policy development, more concerned with putting together the "majorities of tomorrow." In actual terms this meant that the Union's thinkers would develop positions on "new politics" issues such as the environment, womens' rights, foreign residents, and at least discuss such "unthinkable" topics as the Union's future relationship with the Greens. For the party in government and especially Chancellor Kohl –

such concern about "tomorrow's majorities" ran the risk of disturbing the majority of the here and now. And in fact, when party dissidents such as Biedenkopf and Süssmuth made public statements about the Greens or gay rights, they provoked sharp criticism from the Union's traditionalist wing and the Bavarian CSU.[1]

As the date for the 1989 party conference approached, however, Kohl was able to marshal support within the party. Späth, who would have replaced Kohl, was interested in the job only if he were drafted. When Kohl announced that Geissler would not be reappointed for a second term as general secretary, the mini-revolt collapsed. Yet several months later a member of the party's executive could still remark that "without the unification process there would have been another uprising within the party after the election in Lower Saxony [May 1990] at the latest" (Sommer, 1990). Having won reelection as national chairman of the party with over three-fourths of the vote, Kohl purged Späth from the National Executive.

In spite of these problems, the party's position before the collapse of East Germany was far from hopeless. The political business cycle was alive and well in the Federal Republic even before the dramatic developments in the GDR. West Germany in 1989 was in its seventh consecutive year of economic expansion, with real economic growth in the fourth quarter of 1989 exceeding 4 percent, the highest level in 10 years.

Unification sparked a major economic boom in West Germany that reached a peak by the fourth quarter of 1990. The real growth figure of 4.5 percent in 1990 was the highest since 1976 (see Table 3.1). While unemployment remained high by German standards, the trend going into the election was downward and hence favorable to the government. Inflation was generally modest, although an upward trend was noticeable by the end of the year. It would become a problem in 1991 and 1992. The sharp increase in federal deficits was due to the costs of unification. The positive foreign trade figures attested to the vitality of the German export machine. In 1991, however, both Germany's current account and

---

1. In 1988 Kohl supported Geissler's proposal to remove references to reunification in the party's program and to make any future restructuring of Germany dependent on the consent of all European nations. Kohl, however, withdrew his support for the change in the face of opposition from the party's right wing.

trade balance would show small deficits, mainly due to a sharp increase in unification-related imports.

Table 3.1. The Kohl Ecomomic Record, 1982–1990.

	1982	1986	1990*
Real Economic Growth (in%)	-1.0	+2.3	+4.5
Unemployment (Annual average in millions)	1.8	2.2	1.9
Inflation (in %)	+5.2	-0.1	+3.0
Federal Deficit (billions)**	23.1	14.4	41.8
Balance of Payments (billions)	6.2	43.8	69.4
Balance of Trade (billions)	32.1	70.4	65.6

SOURCE: Sachverständigenrat figures cited in *Die Zeit*, no. 49 (30 November 1990): 24. *1990 figures are for West Germany only. **$1.00 = 1.60DM.

Unification, Helmut Kohl and the Christian Democrats

While Kohl did not create the conditions that led to the collapse of the Soviet empire in Eastern Europe, he did seize the opportunity to end Germany's division. Less than three weeks after the breaching of the wall, he took the initiative on unification with his ten-point program for eventual unification. Kohl's plan envisaged, first, a package of treaties between the two states, leading in four or five years to "confederal structures," and eventually to a confederation (*Staatenbund*) and, finally, to a federation (*Bundesstaat*) between them. The whole process would take about ten years and the two states would remain equal partners throughout this period. The proposal drew widespread support, including that of the political opposition in Bonn, although some of Germany's allies thought that the chancellor was moving too fast and had failed to consult them before announcing the plan. His proposal in early 1990 for a currency union between the two states intensified the movement towards a speedy unification process.

The surprise victory of the Union at the GDR's first (and last) free parliamentary election in March 1990 also yielded sharp gains for the CDU in West German polls. Until about mid-February, polls in the East pointed to a solid SPD victory with only about 20 percent supporting the CDU and other center-right parties. But a fundamental shift took place in voter preferences during the last month of the campaign. This shift can be traced to several important developments in the strategies and programs of the major parties. First, Chancellor Kohl personally intervened to create the "Alliance for Germany," an electoral alliance composed of East German Christian Democrats, the CSU-backed German Social Union, and a former dissident movement turned conservative party, the Democratic Awakening (DA). Kohl was initially wary of any close association with the East German CDU because of its satellite status in the GDR's National Front. Kohl was also concerned about the apparent support by several of its leaders, particularly Lothar de Maiziere, for some of the former GDR's socialist "achievements," such as full employment and public housing. Kohl was determined, however, to present the East German electorate with a center-right alternative to the surging Social Democrats (this would also create a forum for his own campaign appearances in the GDR). But perhaps more important, Kohl and the West German CDU were fearful that an unchallenged SPD victory would have a negative impact on their own chances in the December 1990 national election.

Second, the East German SPD changed its position on the question of the pace of unification mid-way through the campaign. With West Germans such as Willy Brandt setting the tone, the Social Democrats initially proposed a speedy unification process and an end to any Four-Power residual rights in the two states and Berlin. The indigenous Social Democrats began to emphasize a more gradual approach to unity, however, and this shift produced a drop in the party's potential share of votes.

Finally, the rejection by the Kohl government of the GDR's request for DM 15 million in emergency aid in mid-February 1990 sent a clear message that West Germany was not willing to finance any major economic reconstruction in the GDR until there was a legitimate government in East Berlin. For many East Germans, Kohl's action was also interpreted to mean "no money until there is a government to Bonn's liking." This decision was followed by an increase in support for the Kohl-inspired Alliance for Germany. After the elections the Social Democrats accused the Alliance of using Kohl's decision to withhold aid to, in effect, buy the election, contending that a vote for the SPD would mean a further delay in aid from Bonn.

The victory in the East in March also affected the Union's level of support in the West. Until March, the SPD and CDU were deadlocked in the West German polls. The GDR election also revealed the surprising weakness of the Social Democrats in an area of Germany where they had historically been one of the strongest parties. The SPD's increasingly indeterminate position on the crucial question of the timing of unification had eroded its support during the campaign, especially among manual workers. It received only 22 percent of the working-class vote, as compared to over 55 percent for the center-right Alliance (Forschungsgruppe Wahlen, 1990: 14). Since the SPD was in the opposition in Bonn, it was also seen by many voters as being less able to deliver on its promises of prosperity than the ruling Christian Democrats.

A New Relationship with the Bavarians

Unification also produced a fundamental change in the Union's relationship to its sister party, the Bavarian Christian Social Union (CSU). The CSU has dominated politics in Germany's most distinctive *Land*, Bavaria, for most of the postwar period. Its unique position of strength in Bavarian politics also has enabled it to play a major role at the national level. Bavaria is the largest German state in area and by far the most particular in its relationship to the rest of the country. After 1945 it was the only large state to reemerge with its historical borders and identity relatively intact.

While the CSU at the national level has always been aligned, if sometimes uneasily, with the Christian Democrats, it has been far from a mere appendage to this larger partner. First, the party is more homogenous and programmatically consistent than the Christian Democrats. It draws its strongest support from Bavaria's large Catholic, small-town, middle-class population. At the same time the party has also played a key role in Bavaria's postwar transformation into a modern industrial society with numerous high-tech growth industries. The CSU's programs have been more conservative and nationalist than those of the Christian Democrats. The party, for example, has been the staunchest opponent of any liberalization of Germany's abortion law. During the early 1970s it rejected the *Ostpolitik* (Eastern Policy) of the SPD-FDP governments as a sell out of Germany's interests.

Second, the CSU became a modern, well-organized mass membership party long before the Christian Democrats changed from a loosely-organized election association into a modern party. Third, the CSU has outperformed the CDU in national elections and hence made a proportionally greater contribution to the Union's combined national share of votes. Since 1972, the CSU, campaigning only in Bavaria, has averaged about 57 percent of the vote in Bundestag elections there, as compared to 43 percent for the CDU running in the rest of the country. This large Bavarian contribution to the CDU's national vote total of the conservative parties has given the CSU substantial influence in Bonn, enabling the party to be both the dominant political force in Bavaria and a major player on the national scene – where it is careful to protect and promote Bavarian interests.

Finally, the CSU has had far more continuity in leadership for most of its history than the Christian Democrats. Until his sudden death in 1988, the CSU was led by Franz-Josef Strauss. Strauss had been the unchallenged chief of the party since the 1950s as well as the major architect of its transformation from a regional party into a national political force. He was also the dominant figure on the center-right of Germany's political spectrum. Since his death the party has been led by a triumvirate consisting of Theodor Waigel, finance minister in the Kohl government, Max Streibl, Strauss' successor as minister-president of Bavaria, and Edmund Stoiber, the party's chief ideologist. Neither individually nor collectively, however, have these leaders been able to compensate for the loss of Strauss.

Unification represented a new challenge to the CSU's national position and its relative weight within the governing coalition. From 1987 to 1990 the party had 49 seats in the West German parliament. This was about 10 percent of the total, and 18 percent of the coalition's 269 seats. With the addition of the East German *Länder*, the Bundestag would be expanded by about 150 seats and the CSU's proportion of the total consequently be reduced to less than 8 percent. Within the government the CSU share would thus decline to 13 percent and for the first time in the history of the Federal Republic the CDU would not need the CSU to maintain its parliamentary majority.

Mindful of these new realities and desiring to preserve Bavaria's special position, the CSU went looking for a new partner in East Germany. In the neighboring *Land* of Saxony, the CSU helped to establish an Eastern affiliate, the German Social Union (DSU), from conservative and church groups in early 1990. The DSU, led by a Lutheran pastor from Leipzig, took policy positions roughly equivalent to those of the CSU. Its relationship to the East German CDU also paralleled the CSU's position vis-a-vis the CDU in the Federal Republic. During the campaign for the March 1990 *Volkskammer* election the DSU received massive financial and organization assistance from the Bavarian party, managing to secure about 6 percent of the vote in the territory of the former GDR and about 13 percent in its home state of Saxony. But following the March election, the party was plagued by a variety of personnel and programmatic conflicts. Many of its early leaders switched to the Christian Democrats and DSU's ability to surmount the 5 percent hurdle within the former East Germany was in doubt.

After the 1990 Bundestag election the CSU went from having 6 to having 4 ministers in the Kohl government, and the CSU currently finds itself with its weakest position in national politics since the early 1950s. In other words, the current coalition could stay in power without the Bavarians. It can no longer maintain a two-track approach to the national CDU, a practice characteristic of the Strauss era: that is, participating in the national government in Bonn while firing shots at the chancellor from Munich. Neither Waigel in Bonn nor Streibel in Munich are willing or able to continue this type of relationship with the Union.

The National Campaign

The CDU's Bundestag campaign in 1990 began and ended with Helmut Kohl. For the first time in his four campaigns as the chancellor candidate, Kohl was more popular than his party. Between April and November in 1989, his popularity level doubled from 34 percent to a record 68 percent. While polls showed that the Union would receive about 44 percent of the vote, Kohl was favored over Lafontaine in final surveys by a 54:45 ratio (*Der Spiegel*, No. 46, 1990: 24). The party's planners believed that Kohl personified the unity issue in 1990, just as Willy Brandt had personified *Ostpolitik* in 1972, or Ludwig Erhard the market economy in the 1950s (Reicherzer, 1990: 28). Only three slogans were used under the numerous Kohl portraits: *Kanzler für Deutschland* (Chancellor for [all of] Germany); *Ja zu Deutschland, Ja zur Zukunft* (Yes to Germany, Yes to the Future); and *Gemeinsam schaffen wir's* (Together we can do it). At the end of the campaign a fourth slogan, *Zweitstimme ist Kanzlerstimme* (The second ballot is the Chancellor's ballot), reminded voters not to split their ballot (Pursch, 1990: 3). Kohl's 28 campaign appearances drew record crowds, especially in the former East Germany.

Yet the party's program broke no new ground, emphasizing its record of modest but steady economic growth, low inflation, and the stability of the DM. The problems arising from the need for economic reconstruction in the East were all attributed to the former communist regime. The CDU promised to amend the constitution to make environmental protection a formal goal of the state. In the area of *Rechtspolitik* both the CDU and CSU took a hard-line position on law and order, with the CDU's program emphasizing the threat posed to the country by internationally-organized crime and calling for the creation of a European-wide police agency modeled on the American FBI (a favorite project of Chancellor Kohl's). The CSU echoed this position, but added a strong endorsement for local police officials. Both parties affirmed their opposition to any liberalization of the 1975 abortion law. On the critical question as to how the economic reconstruction of the former East Germany should be financed, the party program declared that this could be accomplished through new borrowing, the privatization of state-owned enterprises, and private investment. There was no mention of tax increases.

The unification process dominated the list of voter concerns, benefiting both the governing parties and the chancellor (see Chapter by Norpoth and Roth). Domestic issues, which had plagued the CDU since the 1987 election – unemployment, cuts in health care, the instability of the pension system – became less relevant to the electorate. The unification process, especially Kohl's summit meetings with Gorbachev in February and July 1990, increased his popularity to record levels. Unification changed Kohl's image even among his opponents. Absent from media coverage in 1990 were references to his lack of vision, his lack of interest in complex theoretical topics, and his tendency to commit clumsy mistakes (*Pannen*). He had come to be seen as an innovative policymaker rather than just a mediator between conflicting interests.

Kohl's image during the 1990 Bundestag campaign was also enhanced by comparisons to his opponent, Oskar Lafontaine. Lafontaine's ambivalence about unification and his pessimism about the costs of blending the two economies and societies were major handicaps that he never managed to overcome. By the end of the campaign Lafontaine had also alienated the SPD Right, particularly those in the trade unions and those who had been followers of former Chancellor Schmidt. In an interview with a Dutch newspaper in the last weeks of the campaign, Schmidt predicted that Lafontaine would lose, and moreover, deserved to lose. Lafontaine, unlike all previous SPD candidates since 1972, refused to display the national colors in his campaign material and would not allow the national anthem to be sung at the end of his rallies. In contrast to the meetings of the CDU, Lafontaine also rejected the term Fatherland as being "a form of the past." But Kohl led crowds in singing the anthem and rejoiced in calling unification the fulfillment of the national longing for "Germany, One Fatherland."

The Results

In spite of the chancellor's record-high popularity, the booming West German economy, and the still-high level of optimism in former East Germany, the Christian Democrats' share of the vote actually dropped from 44.3 percent in 1987 to 43.8 percent in the all-German election in 1990. (see Table 1.4). The Kohl-led coalition, however, increased its combined percentage of the vote slightly from 53.4 percent to 54.8 percent. This increase, coupled with the vagaries of the electoral system and the addition of about 150 parliamentary seats from the former GDR, gave the coalition a majority of 134 seats in the new all-German Bundestag. Nonetheless, the question remains why the Union did not increase its vote. First, viewed from the perspective of early 1989 when the Union dropped to around 30 percent in some polls, the December 1990 result of 43.8 percent of the vote represented a substantial improvement. Second, some analysts argued that the 11 percent of the vote racked up by the FDP partially contained a "tribute" the CDU had to pay to its junior coalition partner for its contribution to the successful unification process. From this perspective, the Kohl-led government received a clear mandate. The Union was also hurt by the traditional FDP tactic of appealing to the electorate's traditional aversion to one-party government. In the final weeks of the campaign some polls showed the Union at or near the 50 percent mark. This was the signal for the FDP to remind voters of the alleged dangers of one-party government in the German context. In fact most voters, regardless of party, are opposed to a single-party government.

Third, in 1990 as had been the case in the elections of the 1980s, tendencies toward dealignment were noticeable in spite of the singularity of the unification issue and the addition of 12 million new voters from the former GDR. The turnout of 77.8 percent was the lowest level in the history of the Federal Republic. Both major parties continued to lose support. Since 1976 the combined two-party proportion of the Western vote has declined from 91.2 percent to 80 percent, with ticket-splitting over this same period showing an increase from 7 percent to 16 percent. Finally, the CDU had difficulty mobilizing its potential vote during the final stages of the campaign because of the almost universal (90 percent) expectation that the government would win the election. Never before in recorded German electoral history had so many voters been so sure of the outcome.

While the Union received about the same amount of support in both the "old" Federal Republic and the former GDR in 1990, wide social-structural disparities existed between Eastern and Western Germany in the party's vote (Kaase and Gibowski, 1991). The CDU electorate in the Eastern states is younger, more Protestant or secular, and far more concentrated among manual workers than in the West. From the perspective of these variables, the CDUs in the East and West would seem to have little in common. While one of every three Christian Democrats in the West is over 60, only about one in five in the East is in this age group. There are almost three times as many manual workers in the Eastern electorate than in the West. Almost 90 percent of Eastern Christian Democrats are either Protestant or have no religious affiliation, as compared to 49 percent in the old Federal Republic. How much longer will these topsy-turvy electoral demographics continue?

Epilogue: Germany Continues to Vote

After having benefited from the upside of unification in 1990, the Christian Democrats experienced unification's downside in 1991. In February Chancellor Kohl announced a variety of tax increases, including a 7.5 percent "Solidarity" surtax on income and a hefty rise in oil and gasoline taxes. Kohl cited the unexpectedly high costs of unification and the German financial contribution to the Gulf war as the reasons for these actions. The opposition Social Democrats reminded voters of the chancellor's no new taxes pledge and quickly denounced the increases as "the biggest fraud" in German political history. Voter reaction, as measured in state elections and public opinion polls, was swift and negative. In April 1991 the Union lost heavily in Kohl's home state, the Rhineland-Palatinate, and was thrust into opposition for the first time in the state's history. In January it fell further behind in the state of Hesse, and later in the year the party fared poorly in elections in Hamburg and Bremen. In the East the Union's level of support in public opinion polls dropped from 42 percent in December 1990 to only 29 percent by July 1991 (*Der Spiegel*, No. 30, 1991: 29). In the West the Union went from 44.4 percent to 34 percent during the same period. Over 60 percent of the electorate considered the increases a "tax lie," and over 70 percent did not believe that the surtax would last for only one year as Kohl announced (*Der Spiegel*, No. 11, 1991: 32).[2]

The party's string of losses at state elections in 1991 had four common characteristics: 1) lackluster leadership in the states; 2) voter backlash over the tax increases; 3) diminished competence in all issues except the economy; and 4) low turnout among traditional CDU voters. The more post-materialist West German electorate in these state elections also gave the Union low marks for its policies on the environment, housing, and transportation. In the Rhineland-Palatinate, for example, the four most salient issues in April 1991 were: 1) the environment; (2) the economy; (3) transportation; and (4) kindergarten space. Thus the CDU has lost support in the West in spite of a booming economy, and in the East because of a depressed economy. These defeats at the state level also meant the loss of the party's majority in the Bundesrat.

Facing the Future: The Union in the New Eastern States

The decision to build on the bloc-CDU in the East gave the Union a short term advantage, although it is now turning into a long

2. In surveys conducted during the campaign, the great majority (over 80 percent in one study) of voters expected tax increases to finance unification (Konrad Adenauer Foundation Survey No. 9002).

term disadvantage. After the *Wende*, the West German CDU decided with some hesitation that while the leadership of the East-CDU was corrupt, most of the party's rank and file membership was "basically healthy" ("people like us," in the words of the then Interior Minister Wolfgang Schäuble). Following the election, a division emerged within the East-CDU between Blockers – members of the old bloc party – and Reformers who had joined since the *Wende*. The party became identified less with Kohl and his promises of Western-style prosperity and more with the former loyal and subservient *Anhängsel* of the communists. Throughout 1991 the party in the East lost members and support in the polls because of this issue. The conflict has been especially severe in Saxony, Saxony-Anhalt and Thuringia. In the latter two states the Blocker minister-presidents have been forced to resign since the 1990 elections. Their replacements came from the West.

The Eastern CDU is not only characterized by a high proportion of *"Block-Flöten,"* it is also a very secular party in comparison to the West. About three-quarters of the population in the former GDR has no religious affiliation at all, the rest being 24 percent Protestant and only 3 percent Catholic, though about half of these people with a religious affiliation are over 60 years of age (Perger, 1992: 1–9; Haungs, 1989). Unification has thus added to the internal divisions in the party.

Leadership Questions: The Union after Kohl

Unlike the Social Democrats, the Union has no strong leadership tier at the state and cabinet level. Like the SPD under Helmut Schmidt in the 1970s, the CDU under Kohl in the 1990s has become a *Wasserkopf* party, possessing a strong head but lacking support throughout the rest of the organization. Potential national-level leaders and possible successors to Kohl are few in number. Since the failed uprising in June 1989, once prominent Union leaders such as Heiner Geißler, Lothar Späth, and Rita Süssmuth have been isolated within the party organization. Späth, the long-time chief executive of Baden-Württemberg, had to step down in early 1991 following revelations that he had accepted free vacation trips from business interests in the state. Gerhard Stoltenberg, once considered the strongest member of the government, has been damaged by his performance first as finance minister and then as defense minister. His age also works against his having any chance for the chancellorship.

The one remaining figure in the party who is generally considered to possess both the ability to become chancellor and, perhaps more important, Kohl's support is Wolfgang Schäuble, the former chief-of-staff in the chancellor's office who is currently Interior Minister and the chairman of the Union's parliamentary party (*Fraktion*). Schäuble, however, has serious health problems. In October he was shot by a deranged man following a campaign rally, and the attack has left him paralyzed and confined to a wheelchair. Schäuble was able to resume his duties as interior minister in 1991, but he faces a larger challenge as leader of the Union in the Bundestag. If his health permits, he would be the strongest candidate to succeed Kohl.

The Union's grassroots organizations in the West, which Kohl (and Biedenkopf) built up in the early 1970s, have declined from years of neglect coupled with the general trend away from the established parties. Following rapid growth from 1970 to 1983, the party's membership has stagnated at about 700,000 (Wiesendahl, 1990: 4). Membership in the party's youth organization has dropped from 260,000 in 1983 to 196,000 in 1991. Most of these young Christian Democrats are over 25. In the party's 9,000 local organizations (*Ortsvereine*), older males are heavily overrepresented. Two-thirds of all local party officials are over 50 and about 2,000 of the *Ortsvereine* have no female members (*Frankfurter Allgemeine Zeitung*, November 7, 1991: 5).

Unification and its victory in 1990 gave the Union an excuse for not dealing with these problems. The party is divided and has no clear cut policy for major issues such as the foreigner question, abortion, immigration, the environment, poverty, the aversion young people have to the party, and the general phenomenon of voter dealignment.

References

Conradt, David P. and Russell J. Dalton. 1988. "The West German Electorate and the Party System: Continuity and Change in the 1980s," *Review of Politics* 50: pp. 3–29.

Der Spiegel (1989), No. 17; (1990), No. 46; (1991), Nos. 11, 30.

Forschungsgruppe Wahlen (1990). "Wahl in der DDR," Report No. 56.

Haungs, Peter. 1989. "Die CDU: Krise einer modernisierten Volkspartei," *Der Bürger im Staat* 39: pp. 237–241.

Perger, Werner A. 1992. "Die CDU," *Aus Politik und Zeitgeschichte*, No. 5.

Pursch, Günter. 1990. "Kanzler-Stimme mit leiseren Tönen," *Das Parlament*, No. 48.

Reicherzer, Judith. 1990. "Der Kanzler und die Gartenzwerge," *Die Zeit*, No. 48.

Roth, Dieter. 1989. "Sind die Republikaner die fünfte Partei? *Aus Politik und Zeitgeschichte* (6 October): pp. 10–20.

Schultze, Rainer-Olaf. 1991. "Bekannte Konturen im Westen – ungewisse Zukunft im Osten," in Hans-Georg Wehling (ed.), *Wahlverhalten*. Stuttgart.

Sommer, Theo. 1990. "Gerettet von der deutschen Einheit," *Die Zeit*, No. 48.

Stöss, Richard. 1991. *Politics Against Democracy: The Extreme Right in West Germany*. Providence / Oxford: Berg Publishers.

Wiesendahl, Elmar. 1990. "Der Marsch aus den Institutionen," *Aus Politik und Zeitgeschichte*, No. 21.

4

The SPD Seeks a New Identity: Party Modernization and Prospects in the 1990s

M. Donald Hancock

"THE WRONG CANDIDATE with the wrong ideas at the wrong time." This uncharitable judgment succinctly expresses the view of many critical commentators concerning both Oskar Lafontaine's campaign strategy and the disastrous performance of Germany's Social Democratic party (SPD) in the all-German election of 2 December 1990. Chosen as his party's candidate in large measure because he represented more youthful "postmaterialist" views on ecological and economic issues, Lafontaine then emerged as a negativist who failed to resonate to the historical moment of unification. His emphasis on the projected costs of unification cast him in the role of spoiler, reminding voters of unpleasant economic and social realities at a time when Helmut Kohl and Hans-Dietrich Genscher, the "stars" of the Christian Democratic-Free Democratic unification team, exuded a far more hopeful vision of united Germany's future.

The result was the most devastating outcome for the SPD since 1957 (when the party received 31.8 percent of the vote). From their electoral zenith of 45.8 percent in 1972, the Social Democrats began a downward slide commencing in 1976 that led to their receiving only 33.5 percent of the vote in the all-German 1990 election. While the SPD's decline in the "old" states of the Federal Republic was only 1.1 percent when compared to the 1987 Bundestag election results, its performance in the former German Democratic Republic (GDR) was a dismal 23.6 percent. Confronting an ebullient Kohl, fresh from being reelected federal chancellor by the Bundestag in January 1991, and a Christian Democratic majority in the upper house of parliament (*Bun-*

desrat), the SPD seemed consigned to a hapless minority status at a time when German politics was entering a significant new phase of economic and political development.

Events during 1991 swiftly altered this prognosis. Hans-Jochen Vogel announced his decision to relinquish the party chairmanship in the immediate aftermath of the December election, opening the way for the election of fifty-one-year-old Björn Engholm as his successor. Engholm, the minister-president of Schleswig-Holstein who represents a vision of Social Democratic pragmatism reminiscent of the nearby Scandinavian countries, promised to breathe new life into the upper echelons of the party. Eastern Germany's worsening economic plight throughout the winter and spring of 1991 – coupled with the government's unpopular decision to raise consumer taxes to help pay the staggering costs of unification – belied Christian Democratic and Free Democratic campaign promises that unification could be achieved relatively painlessly, without a tax increase.

Capitalizing on the growing popular dissatisfaction with Kohl's leadership and the government's economic performance, the SPD outpolled its CDU rivals in three Landtag elections during the first half of 1991. The SPD's resumption of power in Hesse in January, its stunning victory over the CDU in Rhineland-Palatinate in April, and its retention of power in Hamburg in June enabled the Social Democrats to gain a majority of seats in the Bundesrat and thereby a bigger voice in national policy making. The largely unanticipated swing in public opinion in favor of the SPD (especially in the ex-GDR) by the early spring of 1991, constituted – in the words of the weekly newsmagazine *Der Spiegel* – nothing less than "a political avalanche" (*Der Spiegel*, 13 May 1991: 65). By August 1991, fully 44 percent of German voters preferred the Social Democrats, compared to the 38 percent favoring the Christian Democrats (*Der Spiegel*, 16 September 1991: 45).

Beginning in the fall of 1991 and continuing into 1992, electoral disenchantment with both of Germany's principal political parties caused the SPD's post-unification resurgence to abate. The SPD lost support in *Land* elections in Bremen in September 1991, and in Schleswig-Holstein and Baden-Württemberg in April 1992 (see Table 10.1). Nonetheless, the Social Democrats remained in office as the largest party in the first two states and joined the Christian Democrats in a "grand coalition" government in the latter. As the governing party in nine western states, Brandenburg in the former GDR, and in Berlin, the Social Democrats thus appeared *regierungsfähig* (capable of governing on the national level) less than two years after their overwhelming defeat in the all-German election of 1990.

These rapid fluctuations in Social Democratic electoral and political fortunes are conditioned by both contextual (external) factors and internal party dynamics. Externally, the breathtaking pace of German unification caught the party (as it did virtually all Germans) by surprise. Relegated since October 1982 to opposition status in the Bundestag, the SPD was unable to lead or capitalize on the unification process. On the contrary, Lafontaine seemed to begrudge Kohl the historic achievement of national unity. His choice of issues and campaign tactics during the fall of 1990 would have been more appropriate for an election to the Bundestag of the 10 Western *Länder* than to an all-German parliament. Conversely, other external factors, in the form of a dawning economic sobriety among citizens on both sides of the former East-West German boundary, contributed to the resurgence in popular support for the SPD in various Landtag elections during the first half of 1991.

At the same time, the ebb-and-flow of SPD electoral fortunes in the early 1990s is not due to the changing context of national German politics alone. Instead, programmatic innovation during the 1980s, Engholm's election as party chair, and the party's self-proclaimed goal of "modernization" have all contributed to the SPD's emerging image as a realistic alternative to the dominant CDU.

This chapter explores efforts by Social Democratic leaders to establish a new party identity based on organizational reform and continuing programmatic change, and discusses the prospects for their political success or failure during the present decade. My thesis argument is that the SPD's response to the institutional and policy challenges of the 1990s reflects a broader process of adaptation to changing domestic and international conditions on the part of European social democracy as a whole.

Postwar Electoral Trends and Programmatic Adaptation

As Germany's oldest mass political party, claiming a continuous existence since 1875, the SPD reemerged after 1945 as an important actor in the democratic, social, and economic reconstruction of Western Germany and West Berlin. The party disappeared as a distinct entity in the Soviet zone of occupation in April 1946, when its Eastern branch was forcibly merged with the smaller Communist Party of Germany to form the Socialist Unity Party (SED) (although the SPD's West German organization and leadership remained intact). During the formative phases of postwar occupation and the institutionalization of the Federal Republic, Social Democrats exercised power in a number of *Land* (state) governments and local councils, and played a constructive role as the dominant opposition faction in the Bundestag. The SPD assumed national power in 1966 as a junior partner in a grand coalition cabinet with the Christian Democrats. Under Chancellors Willy Brandt and Helmut Schmidt, the Social Democrats served as the senior government party in coalition with the Free Democrats from 1969 until October 1982.

Consigned once again to opposition status following the FDP's switch of coalition partners in favor of the CDU/CSU, the SPD suffered successive electoral declines during the remainder of the decade. Popular support fell from 42.9 percent in 1980, to 38.2 percent in the 1983 Bundestag election, to 37.0 percent by 1987. Accounting for most of the party's losses was the rise of the Greens, whose pro-environmentalist stance appealed to many socially-conscious and younger voters who might otherwise be expected to vote for the SPD. Another contributing factor was the absence of charismatic leaders comparable to either Brandt or Schmidt. When former Chancellor Schmidt announced that he would not lead the SPD's challenge to CDU Chancellor Helmut Kohl in the special March 1983 election, the Social Democrats hastily nominated Hans-Jochen Vogel, the party's parliamentary leader, as their chancellor-candidate. Vogel's largely lackluster campaign proved disappointing, prompting the Social Democrats to choose Johannes Rau (minister-president of North Rhine-Westphalia) as their candidate four years later – to no avail.

The SPD's electoral slide during the 1980s coincided with a protracted ideological debate among opposing factions concerning programmatic principles and the party's response to the electoral challenge of the Greens. Historically, the SPD has been characterized (similar to socialist parties elsewhere in Europe) by recurrent ideological conflicts between radical Social Democrats who advocated the attainment of democratic socialism – abstractly defined in terms of collective ownership and control of the principal means of production – and more pragmatic party leaders who espoused political democracy and piecemeal social and economic reform. Throughout the Second Empire and the ill-fated Weimar Republic the SPD formally espoused Marxist-inspired principles of economic and social reform, though in practice it pursued a "revisionist" strategy affirming parliamentary democracy and the extension of workers' rights (e.g., in the form of works councils).

Contradictions between its radical programmatic principles and moderate behavior persisted following the end of World War II. Ideologically, the SPD reaffirmed its traditional demands for nationalization and economic planning as the key features of a transition to democratic socialism. In their day-to-day political behavior, however, party leaders cooperated closely with Allied officials and their Christian Democratic and Free Democratic rivals in the parallel restoration of a market economy and representative democracy in Western Germany. Their most prominent partisan priorities included the extension of social benefits, the affirmation of a viable trade union movement, and the introduction of parity codetermination (*Mitbestimmung*) in the iron, coal, and steel industries as a further step (alongside the works councils) toward industrial democracy.

The SPD's string of losses to the Christian Democrats in Bundestag elections from 1949 through 1957 compelled the Social Democrats to confront the need for programmatic revision. Prominent revisionists, among them Willy Brandt (who had returned from Scandinavian exile in 1945 to assume a leadership role in West Berlin politics), seized the initiative from party traditionalists in order to press for a wholesale revision of its formal ideological principles. Efforts by the revisionists to transform the SPD from a working-class party that claimed the continued allegiance of the majority of industrial workers (who by the mid-1950s were already dwindling in number in the wake of post-industrializing economic and social change in West Germany) into a more broadly-based *Volkspartei* (people's party) with a more promising electoral future culminated in the adoption of the Bad Godesberg program in 1959.

With this step, the SPD abandoned its traditional Marxist ballast in favor of what Gordon Smith describes as "a quite eclectic view of 'democratic socialism'," (Smith, 1986: 101) characterized by demands for "freedom, justice, and solidarity." Affirming Judeo-Christian principles of a just and humane society, the SPD advocated measures to promote international peace and solidarity, a full cultural life, and the enhancement of individual "social consciousness" through citizenship training "in the broadest sense." The only explicitly socialist demand in the party's catalogue of basic ideological objectives was its call for a "new economic and social order" in which the "collective interest" would prevail over "special interests" (SPD Bundesvorstand, 1959).

Under Brandt's chairmanship during the 1960s and 1970s, the SPD capitalized on its more moderate image to reverse its earlier electoral decline by mobilizing increased support among members of the middle class (including salaried employees and professionals), as well as women and younger voters. The party steadily expanded its share of votes in Bundestag elections from 36.2 percent in 1961, to 42.7 percent in 1972, to a peak of 45.9 percent in 1976. This unbroken advance, coupled with a corresponding decline in CDU/CSU strength, enabled the Social Democrats to join the West German government in 1966 and form the first of a series of social-liberal coalitions with the Free Democrats in 1969.

The years of Social Democratic governance (1969–82) unleashed renewed internal ideological controversy (Braunthal, 1983). Young Socialists (*Jusos*) attacked what they perceived to be an abandonment of socialist principles in favor of short term political expediency, as epitomized in particular by the economic and social policies implemented by Brandt's non-ideological successor as Federal chancellor, Helmut Schmidt. Their demands for the restoration of a long term perspective on democratic socialist transformation, which were endorsed by sympathetic traditionalists within the SPD's leadership ranks, culminated in the adoption in 1975 of a more radical statement of party objectives in the Economic and Political Orientation Framework for the Years (*1975–85*) *Ökonomisch-politischer Orientierungsrahmen*) (SPD Bundesvorstand, 1975). The "OR '85," as the document became popularly known, reaffirmed the principles of Bad Godesberg but simultaneously advocated the extension of worker codetermination and the implementation of state investment controls as essential measures to "subordinate economic power to democratic control." While worsening economic conditions in the aftermath of destabilizing increases in the international price of oil during the latter part of the decade prevented any attempt by the Social Democrats to radicalize their domestic economic policies, the very language of "OR '85" provoked widespread consternation both within and outside the party. One prominent critic interpreted the document as a "militant" return to the political vocabulary of conflict, as well as a symbol of both the SPD's retreat from a Volkspartei and the end of Germany's postwar process of ideological "deprogrammization" (Hennis, 1977).

The SPD's fall from power in October 1982, its subsequent loss of electoral support, and the emergence of the Greens as a non-Marxist yet radical alternative to the Social Democrats confronted the party with a changed agenda for programmatic adaptation. Recognizing the need to update the Godesberg principles of 1959 in the face of the sweeping domestic and international changes since then, SPD leaders appointed a program commission at the party's 1984 convention to recommend appropriate revisions. Its members, representing diverse ideological factions within the party, deliberated five years in their effort to devise a suitable and acceptable document. The outcome was the Berlin program of December 1989 (SPD Bundesvorstand, 1989).

Far from embodying the ideological militancy of the *Jusos* and other traditionalists, the Berlin program constitutes a modification of Godesberg in the spirit of adaptive moderation. It reaffirms the core SPD values of "freedom, justice, and solidarity," as well as the party's self-identity as a "Volkspartei of the Left." Similarly, the program reaffirms the SPD's historical commitment to democratic socialism, defining it as the attainment of a "solidaristic society of free and equal [citizens] without class privileges in which all people can decide their life and their work on the basis of equality" (ibid.: 22). At the same time, the SPD pledged its continuing support for both a strong labor movement and extended rights of worker codetermination. Significant departures from Godesberg include lengthy sections on environmentalism, the value of labor and leisure, equal economic and social rights for women, and the need for greater North-South cooperation on behalf of economic development in the Third World. The Berlin program also emphasizes the necessity of protecting and extending fundamental principles of political democracy, and warns against uncritical efforts to reify the state:

> The state should promote democracy and social justice in society and the economy, guaranteeing the public the necessary decision-making means for achieving [them]. At the same time the state cannot solve all social problems. Whoever makes excessive demands of the state encourages the growth of bureaucracy, which loses thereby its effectiveness and can be neither controlled nor [adequately] financed. We are opposed to subordinating society to the state. (ibid.: 46)

The SPD's renewed commitment to economic and social reform seemed to augur well for the future. Under Vogel's leadership, (Vogel had been elected Brandt's successor as party chair in June 1987), the Social Democrats sought to enhance voter confidence in their economic policies by endorsing proposals to promote "entrepreneurial activity and performance" through a corporate tax reform, the development of new environmental technologies, and a reform of local government finances. Members of a party commission (*Fortschritt 90*, or Progress 90) chaired by Lafontaine, the minister-president of the Saarland, explicitly eschewed "socialist experiments" in redistribution. The Social Democrats simultaneously acted to broaden their appeal among female voters by pledging to increase the number of women members in top party positions to 40 percent by 1994.

The "greening" of the SPD was accompanied by the formation of admittedly fragile local coalitions with the Greens in West Berlin in March 1989 and in Frankfurt the following month that pointed toward the possibility of a national coalition of the two parties. Encouraging such a prospect was the erosion of the CDU's electoral strength in tandem with increased support in regional elections during the late-1980s for both the FDP and the rightist Republican party (REP). Party strategists calculated that increased support for the Republicans at the expense of the Christian Democrats would enhance the SPD's image as a solidly centrist party – much to the political consternation of the Christian Democrats (Süddeutsche Zeitung, 1989: 1). Lafontaine led the SPD to a resounding Landtag victory in the Saarland, which won 54.4 percent of the popular vote in January 1990. In May, Social Democrats won an absolute majority of 50 percent in the Landtag election in North Rhine-Westphalia, scoring a noteworthy advance from the 42.1 percent they had captured in 1986 by winning 44.2 percent in Lower Saxony. Throughout much of 1988 and 1989 the SPD outpolled the Christian Democrats in opinion surveys (see Figure 1.1), with 49 percent of voters favoring Lafontaine in December 1989 compared to 45 percent who preferred Helmut Kohl. Programmatic and generational changes within the SPD thus seemed to set the stage for a change-of-government following the next scheduled Bundestag election in 1990.

Germany's Rush to Unification: A Campaign Gone Awry

Externalities dramatically intervened to alter the SPD's electoral prospects. The precipitous implosion of the authoritarian regime in the GDR – which began with the onset of massive emigration to the Federal Republic during the summer of 1989 and accelerated with Erich Honecker's resignation as SED and government leader on 18 October and the opening of the Berlin wall on 9 November – prompted the incipient democratization of the East German political system. A crucial consequence was the revival of a competitive multi-party system. First to emerge was *Neues Forum* (New Forum), an umbrella organization representing a variety of citizen-level protest groups. On 7 October 1989 a clandestine group of democratic socialists proclaimed the establishment of the Social Democratic Party (SDP), a movement allied with but organizationally distinct from the West German SPD. Other opposition movements and parties rapidly followed, including *Demokratischer Aufbruch* (Democratic Awakening), *Demokratie Jetzt* (Democracy Now), the *Initiative für Menschenrechte und Frieden* (the Initiative for Human Rights and Peace), the *Unabhängiger Frauenverband* (the Independent Women's Association), and the Greens. Simultaneously, the former bloc parties that had been nominal coalition partners with the SED – notably the East German CDU and the Liberals – initiated internal democratization and leadership renewal. The SED itself sought to distance itself from its Stalinist past by electing reformist members to a new Politburo, endorsing an action program in November promising free elections and the formation of a democratic coalition government, and changing its name to the Party of Democratic Socialism (PDS).

Democratization in the GDR swiftly yielded to Westernization (Richter, forthcoming). Deeply concerned about the financial and social costs of a swelling tide of East German immigrants (*Übersiedler*), whose numbers had jumped from 39,832 in 1988 to

343,854 a year later (Statistisches Jahrbuch, 1991: 94), Chancellor Kohl hastily proposed a ten-point program on 28 November 1989 calling for German unification on the basis of "confederative structures" contingent on "the election of a democratic government in the GDR". By December, public protesters began unfurling banners in Leipzig and other East German cities proclaiming "One fatherland, one state." In response to both Kohl's initiative and citizen demands, opposition spokesmen began increasingly to advocate the transformation of the GDR into a constitutional democracy with a social market economic system as a prelude to the creation of a united German state. On 6 December the PDS concurred with representatives of the democratic opposition groups in the first of a series of informal Roundtable negotiations on scheduling free elections in the GDR in early 1990.

Leaders of both the Western SPD and the newly formed Eastern SDP initially qualified their support for German unification. While West German Social Democrats promptly claimed credit for Kohl's ten-point plan as an extension of their own earlier efforts to promote closer ties with East Germany, Lafontaine declared on 19 December that "the attainment of greater social justice in the Federal Republic and the GDR has priority over efforts to force the Germans into a national state" (quoted in *Deutschland-Nachrichten*, 20 December 1989: 4). At the Berlin conference devoted to the adoption of the party's new program of 1989, delegates overwhelmingly affirmed German unity – albeit on the basis of a confederation that could eventually "lead to a unified state" (ibid.: 3). East Germany's Social Democrats similarly endorsed the concept of a united and confederal Germany at a conference on 13 January 1990. That same month, Lafontaine, exultant over the SPD's victory in the Saarland state election that confirmed his nomination as his party's chancellor candidate in the 1990 Bundestag election, warned against a rush to unification in the absence of prior economic reforms in the GDR (*Der Spiegel*, 26 February 1990: 16). In addition, the Social Democrats declared an explicit legal recognition of Poland's western border along the Oder-Neisse rivers to be a necessary condition for German unification and asserted that unification should be accompanied by a dissolution of the existing Western and Eastern military alliances within the framework of a European-wide security system.

The rapidity of events culminating in Germany's unification in

1990 as a member of NATO negated the need for a confederation and an East-West agreement on a new security arrangement. The pace of unification also ultimately undermined the SPD's electoral credibility in both the 18 March election to the East German *Volkskammer* and the national election to the Bundestag on 2 December. While many reformers had hoped that democratization would ensure the survival of the German Democratic Republic as an independent state, East-West agreement in February on a "two plus four" formula for negotiations on German unification and the accelerating pace of Westernization of the East German parties had clearly pointed toward the creation of an all-German economic and political system. East German Social Democrats tacitly acknowledged that prospect in mid-January 1990 when they adopted the traditional designation of SPD, endorsed the Berlin program as their own, and elected Willy Brandt as the party's honorary chair. As the campaign progressed, they willingly accepted financial and material support from the West German SPD. Lafontaine, Brandt, and other prominent Social Democrats crisscrossed the GDR to speak at public rallies on behalf of their fledgling sister party.

Public opinion surveys initially indicated that the Ost-SPD would win a majority in the *Volkskammer* election. In mid-February 1990, the Youth Research Institute in Leipzig reported that fully 53 percent of East German voters preferred the SPD compared to 13 percent who supported the CDU and 12 percent who favored the PDS (*New York Times*, 21 February 1990: A8). As the prestigious British weekly newsmagazine *The Economist* opined in March: "Most pundits reckon the Social Democrats will be easy winners. East Germany has a strong Social Democratic tradition, especially in the industrial south, and unlike the (eastern) Christian Democrats the party has not been tainted by decades of kowtowing to the communists" (*The Economist*, 10 March 1990: 53).

The "pundits" proved devastatingly wrong. Chancellor Kohl's and Foreign Minister Hans-Dietrich Genscher's own intervention in the campaign on behalf of the CDU and the FDP, respectively, mobilized vast public support in favor of a federal government proposal in February to achieve rapid economic and monetary union. The SPD's own campaign efforts were hampered by its weak organizational structure as a new party and its ideological emphasis on the attainment of an "ecologically-oriented social democracy" that seemed to pale in comparison with conservative promises of prosperity under a social market economy. The result was a disappointing 21.8 percent for the SPD in the March election compared with 40.9 percent for the CDU (see Table 1.2). Social Democratic leaders joined the non-communist government that had displaced the former SED regime, although they played a distinctively subordinate policy role in subsequent negotiations between the Christian Democratic-led majority in East Berlin and the federal government in Bonn on treaties to achieve German economic and monetary union on 1 July and political union on 3 October.

Despite the Ost-SPD's loss in the March election, West Germany's Social Democrats remained confident that they could defeat the CDU/CSU in the all-German election set for December. Party strategists were banking heavily on Lafontaine being successfully promoted as a representative of a new generation of German leaders – youthful, unencumbered by personal involvement in the Third Reich, and possessing the managerial skills for governing the Federal Republic's advanced industrial economy. The SPD's chancellor candidate had a proven record of electoral success in his home state of the Saarland, and both party stalwarts and members of the general public appreciated his political competence, wit, and energy. Public sympathy surged for Lafontaine, at least it did temporarily, following an attack on his life by a knife-wielding woman at a campaign appearance on 25 April.

Fatefully, Lafontaine chose a campaign strategy in the months following his recovery that proved largely discordant within the changed context of all-German politics. He repeatedly charged that Chancellor Kohl had blatantly lied to voters by making campaign promises that he could not deliver (notably Kohl's pledge of "no new taxes" to finance German unity). Lafontaine declared at a meeting of the SPD executive committee in late-March: "The election in the Federal Republic will not be decided on the basis of German nationalism but instead on the idea of social justice" (*Der Spiegel*, 26 March 1990: 22). He emphasized the principal themes of his campaign, the postmaterialist ecological and social components of the Berlin program – thereby failing to address the historical significance of Germany's impending unification. Underlying Lafontaine's campaign rhetoric was his continued ambivalence toward the rapid resolution of the German question.

His views were not shared by Brandt, Vogel, and other Social Democratic notables, who as early as January had all affirmed unification on West German economic, social, and political foundations. Even after the SPD endorsed the cabinet's plan in March to achieve economic and monetary union by mid-summer, Lafontaine remained personally convinced of the need for a transitional period of economic reform in the GDR prior to unification.

An Emnid survey conducted in May 1990 revealed that 50 percent of those surveyed declared they would vote for Lafontaine in a direct election of the federal chancellor, compared to the 44 percent who favored Kohl. Most voters believed that the SPD was more capable than the Christian Democrats in promoting social justice and improving Germany's housing situation. Significantly, however, a majority viewed the CDU/CSU as more capable than the SPD in virtually every other policy area – including the attainment of better environmental protection. Overwhelming public majorities considered the CDU/CSU more competent in helping the GDR achieve economic growth (63 percent), attaining German unification (62 percent), and maintaining a stable D-Mark (58 percent) (*Der Spiegel*, 28 May 1990: 44).

By June, continued momentum toward unification on terms mandated by the federal government had yielded a popular majority in both West and East Germany in favor of the CDU/CSU and FDP. The monthly Emnid survey revealed that 42 percent favored the CDU/CSU, 9 percent the FDP, 39 percent the SPD, and 8 percent the Greens. In contrast to earlier polls, Kohl was now the favored candidate with 47 percent, compared to Lafontaine's 44 percent (Der Spiegel, 25 June 1990: 45). When asked who of the two candidates was better qualified to solve the problems of German unity, 53 percent of GDR voters and 50 percent of West Germans said Chancellor Kohl – compared to 42 percent and 43 percent, respectively, who expressed greater confidence in Lafontaine's ability (ibid.: 41).

The SPD never recovered from the groundswell of popular support in both parts of Germany for the Christian Democrats and the Free Democrats as the principal architects of German unification. An institutional merger of the Eastern and Western branches of the party on 27 September provided little organizational strength to the party's campaign efforts, given a paucity of SPD members in the newly-reconstituted East German states and the party's continued organizational weakness there. The SPD-Ost had optimistically claimed 70,000 members at its founding in 1989 (Bauman, et al., 1990: 305). This membership figure was at best an estimate; interview sources in Western Germany assert that a more realistic total was 30,000. As the campaign mounted in intensity during the fall, Lafontaine failed to launch what party leaders had originally anticipated would be an offensive campaign against the Christian Democrats. A conspicuously missing symbol at many of Lafontaine's public appearances, as if emphasizing his distrust of the speed of German unification, were Germany's national colors of red, gold, and black on the speaker's platform. Lafontaine constantly reiterated his arguments about social justice, the ecology, and Kohl's misleading statements about the economic and social costs of German unification. In the process, the SPD candidate seemed constantly on the defensive.

The election results on 2 December confirmed the outcome of the East German election of March. Overwhelmingly, the German electorate affirmed the Christian Democratic-Free Democratic commitment to rapid union and their vision of a social market economy. From the heights of a prospective victory early in 1990 in what party leaders and the electorate had anticipated would be a "normal" West German election, the SPD had plummeted to its lowest national status in more than three decades.

SPD "Modernization": Propaganda or Substance?

In the aftermath of the party's massive defeat, the SPD confronted simultaneous organizational and programmatic challenges to redefine its role in unified Germany. A first priority was to fashion an effective party apparatus capable of mobilizing the partisan loyalties of an expanded membership. The SPD has consistently claimed a larger number of members than its principal rivals (thanks primarily to membership drawn from unions belonging to the German Confederation of Trade Unions (*Deutscher Gewerkschaftsbund*, or DGB). The party, however, had actually experienced a steady erosion of membership from a postwar peak of 1,022,191 in 1976 to 910,063 in 1987 (see Table 4.1). The SPD's loss of members during the mid-1980s was attributed to at least two causes. One was the SPD's fall from power in October 1982, which abruptly decreased the incentive among aspiring

Table 4.1. Membership of the Principal German Parties, 1946–1990

YEAR	SPD	FDP	CDU	CSU	GREENS
1946	711,448	45,000	n/a	69,370	
1950	683,896	82,890	n/a	n/a	
1955	589,051	n/a	245,000	35,000	
1960	649,578	n/a	255,000	52,501	
1965	710,448	n/a	n/a	70,302	
1970	820,202	56,531	329,293	76,655	
1975	998,471	74,032	590,482	132,593	
1976	1,022,191	79,162	652,010	144,000	
1977	1,006,316	79,539	664,214	159,475	
1978	997,444	80,928	675,286	165,710	
1979	981,805	82,546	682,781	169,247	
1980	986,322	84,865	693,320	172,419	n/a
1981	954,119	86,931	705,116	175,273	n/a
1982	926,070	78,763	718,889	178,523	n/a
1983	925,630	71,456	734,555	185,428	25,222
1984	916,485	71,183	730,395	184,626	31,078
1985	919,457	65,552	718,590	84,228	37,024
1986	912,854	64,622	714,089	182,369	38,170
1987	910,063	65,200	705,821	184,293	42,419
1988	911,916	64,417	676,747	182,738	40,829
1989	921,430	65,485	678,592	185,853	41,127
1990	960,000	n/a	658,584	183,853	n/a

SOURCES: Hübner and Rohlfs (1990: 312–13), and Scarrow (1991: 91).

civil servants and professionals to join what was no longer a government party. A second cause was the parallel growth in popular support for the Green party, which attracted the partisan loyalty of many otherwise potential SPD adherents. Once the political novelty of the Greens began to wane, however the party experienced an incipient growth of membership in the ten Western states by the end of the decade.

The attainment of German unification underscored the need to expand the party base in the new *Bundesländer*. Party stalwarts addressed this challenge in the months following the December 1990 election by pursuing multiple strategies of institutional innovation. The first involved the creation of branch organizations in the ex-GDR as a means of recruiting and socializing an expanding core of partisan supporters. Similar to the simultaneous efforts by trade union officials to extend their structures and democratic principles to the East, SPD functionaries from the Federal Republic served as party consultants who assisted in the establishment of local and regional organizations. Second, the Social Democrats elevated several prominent East Germans – including Manfred Stolpe (minister-president of Brandenburg) – to visible positions of authority within the party. This was a calculated effort to legitimize their all-German status and thereby broaden their electoral appeal.

Vogel's decision to relinquish the party's chairmanship, and Björn Engholm's election as the new party chair on 29 May 1991 at the SPD's congress in Bremen, signalled a simultaneous SPD initiative to refurbish its stature under the changed conditions of German unity. Apart from the symbolic importance of his relative youth and electoral successes in Schleswig-Holstein, Engholm embodied a strong personal commitment to Social Democratic "modernization," as revealed through both the themes he addressed in his keynote speech at the Bremen convention and his subsequent actions as party chair. The SPD has a *"modern* program," he proclaimed to the party delegates, and is committed to "achieving the foundations of *modern* organizational and personnel leadership" (Engholm, 14, 21; italics added for emphasis). With this characterization of the Berlin program of 1989, Engholm affirmed the SPD's incorporation of stronger ecological, internationalist, and democratic perspectives into its formal statement of ideological principles. At the same time, the new party chair added his own prescriptions for Germany's intermediate future.

Modernization is admittedly an ambiguous concept. Engholm's use of the term – which some domestic skeptics have derided as political "propaganda" – is rooted in pragmatic partisan politics rather than academic abstractions. He made no effort to define modernization as such in his Bremen address. Instead, he declared that "[Germany] stands at the beginning of a new era . . . [that] demands new answers." Refuting those who "speak of the end of the Social Democratic epoch" in light of the alleged "victory of capitalism over communism" in Eastern Europe, Engholm declared: "I am convinced that there is a lasting new opportunity for Social Democracy throughout Europe. We are not at the end of a Social Democratic century; [instead], we stand at the beginning of a new century of reform" (ibid.: 1–2).

Such reforms, Engholm went on to explain in his address, embrace Germany as a whole as well as the SPD itself. On the national level, Engholm called for the wholesale reconstruction of the ex-GDR and a comprehensive commitment to social and political change. For the SPD, as a political organization, modernization requires greater "openness" and extended dialogue among its adherents. "We live in an open society," he observed. "Open societies . . . do not tolerate closed parties. The SPD is therefore neither a closed-shop nor a party of dogmatic beliefs" (ibid.: 10). Engholm added:

> We will be more successful as a party the less we formulate our intentions behind closed doors. Only a party that engages in . . . open and broad discussion with people where difficulties actually exist and draws on the fantasy, the creativity, and enormous strength of the citizens themselves – only such a party will remain in the center of development (ibid.: 13).

To promote his goal of organizational modernity, Engholm promptly moved to revitalize the SPD's professional staff. A key figure in the new managerial team assembled by Engholm during the spring and summer of 1991 is Karl-Heinz Blessing, elected party manager at the Bremen meeting. Blessing, thirty-four years old at the time of his appointment, previously served as a personal assistant to Franz Steinkühler, chairman since 1986 of *IG Metall* (Germany's largest trade union). In this capacity Blessing not only demonstrated impressive qualities of professional competence and dependability, but also developed close working relations with strategically placed contacts throughout organized labor and corporate enterprise. Blessing has been joined at the party's headquarters in Bonn by other academically trained experts who share his penchant for pragmatic efficiency.

The expansion of the party's organizational base in the new *Bundesländer*, the recruitment of new leaders, Engholm's plea for greater openness, and staff reorganization will not suffice alone to restore the SPD to national executive office. Instead, the party's success or failure in public office will prove of equal or greater relevance. And therein lies the substantive challenge of social democratic modernization – in Germany as elsewhere in Europe.

Prospects in the 1990s

The most compelling domestic issues facing Germany today are associated with the aftermath of unification. Laggard economic performance and soaring unemployment in the ex-GDR, and public discontent over higher taxes in the Western states are key examples. Criticizing these patterns from an obviously partisan perspective, Engholm advocated in Bremen an aggressive program of economic and social reconstruction in the new *Bundesländer* that encompasses five specific proposals: 1) government measures to increase employment opportunities among qualified workers, salaried employees, technicians, and scientists; 2) the maintenance, where possible, of existing industrial structures; 3) financial support for employment services to facilitate the retraining and relocation of workers; 4) government support for the improvement of the East German infrastructure (including telecommunications, urban renewal, and environmental protection); and 5) the expansion and democratization of public administration (Engholm: 3–4). Failure to ameliorate deteriorating economic and social conditions in the Eastern part of the country, in the SPD's eyes, will seriously hamper progress toward the social integration of Germany as a whole and may well prove the precursor to future political instability.

In the months immediately following unification, public dissatisfaction over Germany's economic performance contributed decisively to the SPD's electoral gains in the Landtag elections during the first half of 1991 in Hessen, Rheinland-Pfalz, and Hamburg (see Table 10.1). Their advances in these states enabled the Social Democrats to recapture their previous majority in the Bundesrat and contributed to the surge of popular support for the SPD measured in opinion surveys during the spring and summer. Subsequently, however, the Social Democrats (as well as both members of the governing coalition) have lost support in the wake of persisting economic malaise and an increase in social tensions. A continuing influx of economic and political refugees from Eastern Europe and third world countries has generated a resurgence of racist and anti-foreigner sentiment among many Germans, especially the unemployed and younger "skinheads." Disaffected voters have expressed their mounting protests against prevailing economic conditions and the immigrant issue, either by abstaining altogether in Landtag elections midway through the 1990–94 national legislative period, or by supporting the Republicans and other rightist parties. As indicated in Table 10.1, rightist parties won 6.2 percent of the vote in the September 1991 election in Bremen, 6.0 percent in Schleswig-Holstein in April 1992, and fully 10.9 percent that same month in Baden-Württemberg. In all three elections the Social Democrats lost ground (as did the CDU in Baden-Württemberg).

Electoral volatility in the wake of German unification offers no reassuring prospects for either the SPD or the governing coalition. Landtag officials confront electoral displeasure with economic and social conditions over which they have little or no control. Nationally, the Social Democrats remain shackled by their opposition status in the Bundestag, where they are unable to enact national policies of their own with respect to tax reform or economic reconstruction in the former GDR. Moreover, the party's image as a credible alternative to the Christian Democrats has been tarnished by the personal rivalry between Engholm (whom some Social Democratic critics charge is too aloof from parliamentary politics in Bonn because of his day-to-day responsibilites as minister-president in distant Kiel), and Lafontaine, who despite his defeat in December 1990 views himself as a potential chancellor candidate in the next scheduled election in 1994.

At the same time, social democratic efforts at programmatic and organizational modernization, coupled with Engholm's performance as party chair, potentially bode well for forthcoming elections. Despite the party's loss of electoral support in recent Landtag elections, Emnid reported in May 1992 that 39 percent of West Germans and 29 percent of East Germans favored the SPD (*Der Spiegel*, 11 May 1992: 51). Both totals are somewhat lower than the levels of mass support the party registered during the spring, but they are nonetheless higher than the election result of

December 1990. Public confidence in Engholm personally is significantly stronger than support for the party generally: 49 percent of those polled would vote for the SPD chair in a direct election of the federal chancellor, as compared to the 41 percent who would favor Kohl (ibid.: 50).

The SPD thus faces an uncertain future. Some leading Social Democrats, including Engholm himself, have suggested that the party should share government responsibility through at least an informal grand coalition with the CDU, enacting a more activist program of structural reform and employment creation in the new *Bundesländer*. Others have argued that the SPD should press for a change of government – conceivably in coalition with the Greens – and thereby pursue a partisan approach to the economic and social problems caused by unification. Engholm's capacity to determine the course of the SPD's strategic choices will no doubt be enhanced by Lafontaine's fall from grace during the summer of 1992 as a result of revelations that he has received considerable remuneration in lieu of a pension for his services as a former mayor alongside his salary as minister-president of the Saarland. The resulting political scandal means, in the view of *The Economist*, that Lafontaine "can probably abandon his hopes of a national career" (*The Economist*, 13–19, June 1992: 56).

While the political choices and electoral prospects facing the SPD during the 1990s seem specific to Germany, they in fact epitomize a more general plight of social democratic parties elsewhere in Europe. Social Democrats have relinquished power and languished in opposition in recent years in a number of countries, notably the United Kingdom, France, Denmark, and Norway. In Sweden, the Social Democrats lost the September 1991 election to a coalition of centrist and conservative parties after serving for over five decades in executive office (except for the period 1976–82). A principal reason for this reversal of fortune on the part of European social democracy, which underlay the SPD's own electoral decline during the late 1970s and 1980s, was an erosion of the postwar Keynesian consensus that had previously favored interventionist policies and corporatist policy-making arrangements associated with social democracy as an international phenomenon (Hancock, Logue, and Schiller, 1991). The successive economic crises of 1973–74 and 1979–80 encouraged national electorates throughout North America and Western Europe to endorse alternative approaches to economic management, such as "Reaganomics," "Thatcherism," and a return to classical social market principles under CDU/CSU-FDP aegis in 1982 in the Federal Republic. By the early 1990s, in contrast, higher inflation rates, sluggish economic performance, and the neglect of pressing social issues in most of the industrial democracies have begun to pose a cyclical electoral challenge to the restoration of market-oriented strategies. Evidence of renewed support for Social Democracy can be seen in the return of the Labor party to power in Norway (albeit as a minority government), the Labour party's advance from 30.8 to 34.4 percent in the April 1992 election in the United Kingdom (even though it was insufficient to dislodge the Conservatives from power), and Engholm's popularity in Germany.[1]

The SPD's multiple strategies of programmatic and organizational modernization may therefore prove appropriate in today's rapidly changing times, especially in light of heightened public expectations concerning material progress and social security under the conditions of economic liberalization and political democratization in Eastern Europe and the ex-GDR. If so, Germany's Social Democrats could well displace the Scandinavian model of reform in a new era requiring a creative synthesis of public and private measures to maintain an acceptable mixture of stability and growth.

1. Editor's note: After this chapter was completed, investigators found evidence that Engholm and his lieutenants were involved in the CDU dirty-tricks scandal in Schleswig-Holstein. This investigation forced Engholm from his position at the head of the SPD. In June 1993 the SPD selected Rudolf Scharping, MInister President of Rhineland-Palatinate, as the new head of the SPD. Scharping has expressed his commitment to continue the modernization course for the SPD outlined in this chapter.

References

Baumann, Eleonore, et al., 1990. *Der Fischer Weltalmanach. Sonderband DDR*. Frankfurt am Main: Fischer Taschenbuch.

Braunthal, Gerhard. 1983. *The West German Social Democrats, 1969–1982. Profile of a Party in Power*. Boulder, Colorado: Westview Press.

Engholm, Björn. n.d. "Rede Engholm." Address by Björn Engholm at the SPD party congress on 29 May 1991. Bonn: SPD, xeroxed.

Hancock, M. Donald, John Logue, and Bernt Schiller, eds. 1991. *Managing Modern Capitalism: Industrial Renewal and Workplace Democracy in the United States and Western Europe.* New York: Greenwood Press.

Hennis, Wilhelm. 1977. *Organisierter Sozialismus. Vom strategischen Staats- und Politkverständnis der Sozialdemokratie.* Stuttgart: Ernst Klett Verlag.

Hübner, Emil and Horst-Hennek Rohlfs. 1990. *Jahrbuch der Bundesrepublik 1990/91.* Munich: Deutscher Taschenbuchverlag.

Richter, Michaela W. Forthcoming. "Exiting the GDR: Political Movements and Parties Between Democratization and Westernization," in M. Donald Hancock and Helga Welsh, eds., *German Unification: Process and Outcomes.* Boulder, Colorado: Westview Press.

Scarrow, Susan Edith. 1991. "Organizing for Victory: Political Party Members and Party Organizing Strategies in Great Britain and West Germany, 1945–1989." Unpublished dissertation presented to the Faculty of the Graduate School of Yale University. New Haven, CT.: Yale University.

Smith, Gordon. 1986. *Democracy in Western Germany: Parties and Policies in the Federal Republic,* 3d ed. New York: Homes & Meier Publishers.

SPD Bundesvorstand. 1959. *Grundsatzprogramm der Sozialdemokratischen Partei Deutschlands.* Bonn: Social Democratic Party.

SPD Bundesvorstand. 1975. *Ökonomisch-politischer Orientierungsrahmen für die Jahre 1975–1985.* Bonn: Social Democratic Party.

SPD Bundesvorstand. 1990. *Grundsatzprogramm der Sozialdemokratischen Partei Deutschlands beschlossen am 20. Dezember 1989 in Berlin.* Bonn: Social Democratic Party.

Süddeutsche Zeitung. 1989. "CDU: Anschlag auf politische Kultur. Die SPD nimmt bewusst Anwachsen rechter Parteien hin" 15/16 July.

5

Unity and Victory for the German Liberals: Little Party, What Now?

Christian Søe

AMONG THE INCUMBENT BUNDESTAG PARTIES in united Germany's first national election, the liberal FDP was the only one to feel wholly jubilant over its share of the poll. By winning 11 percent of the nationwide party-list vote, the Free Democratic party registered its best overall performance in almost three decades. The small party had done better in 1961 by winning 12.8 percent of the West German vote, but even that distant electoral record could be said to have been topped in 1990 – if only within the region covered by the five new Eastern states. Here, in the area that for four decades had comprised the German Democratic Republic (GDR), the FDP received 13.4 percent of the vote in 1990. Within the electoral region of the "old" Federal Republic, the FDP captured 10.6 percent of the vote, itself an outstanding result for a party that had received single-digit scores in all but one previous Bundestag election since 1961.

Shortly before entering its quadrennial struggle for survival and influence as both a member of parliament and government in Bonn, the Liberal coalition party had pulled off another political feat. In August 1990 it had been the first of the established West German parties to unite with its counterparts in Eastern Germany. As a result of what could be described as a friendly takeover, the FDP had suddenly seen its official membership triple – from close to 67,000 to over 200,000. It was a new situation for the FDP, whose West German membership had reached a

*My research and writing have been made possible by grants from California State University, Long Beach; Internationes; the German Academic Exchange Service; and the Marshall Fund of the United States. I am grateful to these institutions as well as to many persons in Germany who have been willing to inform me about the FDP and other parties.

99

plateau after declining from its previous peak of nearly 87,000 in the early 1980s. All but a very small fraction of the Eastern members had belonged to two of the old satellite or bloc parties, which had cooperated closely with the Communist rulers of the GDR until late 1989. The rest had belonged to two tiny dissident Liberal parties that had formed in East Germany at the beginning of 1990. Even though no one expected the high figures in the East to hold steady, the sudden growth in members and organizational resources made wits speak of a *liberale Massenpartei*. There could be no comparable growth when the West German *Volksparteien* – the CDU and SPD, with their much larger party organizations – joined up with their Eastern counterparts a few weeks later.

The Liberal electoral triumph also stood in marked contrast to the results of the other Bundestag parties. The Christian Democrats had recorded their worst tally since the first Bundestag election in 1949, while the Social Democrats turned in their poorest showing since 1957. Most unexpected of all, the electoral nightmare that has so often haunted the Liberals suddenly became reality for the West German Greens, when they failed to win the minimum five percent necessary for a return to the Bundestag.

In the year of unification, the small party of Foreign Minister Hans-Dietrich Genscher had been able to play some strong cards in Eastern Germany. The breakthrough in this electoral *terra nova* was nevertheless both impressive and ironic. The area's recent experience under Communist rule had been a far cry from the kind of political rhetoric and behavior normally associated with the FDP. Liberals could even be portrayed as an ideological antipode to the old regime in such matters as their celebration of market economies and promotion of entrepreneurial interests, their exhortations against state bureaucracy and incantations of individual achievement, their concern for civil rights and liberties, and, not least, their eloquent defense – by no means disinterested – of the principle of coalition government as a form of checks and balances.

The Liberals clearly had reasons for celebrating a great victory. But they left for the evitable "morning after" some stubborn structural and political problems that will preoccupy the small party in the years ahead. This chapter focuses on the background leading up to the superb electoral performance in 1990. It briefly examines the small party's ability to struggle through the electoral doldrums in West Germany during the late 1980s and adjust to the unexpected change in political parameters brought about by national unification in 1990. Special attention is given to the manner in which the FDP managed, after some initial setbacks, to forge an organizational unity among Germany's rival Liberal parties as a precondition for its later electoral breakthrough. The conclusion returns to some nagging questions about the FDP's future course that have been left unresolved by the triumph of 1990. Will the small party squander its electoral windfall, as it had on other occasions in the past, or will it be able to invest its new political capital in the construction of a stronger and more solid base for itself within an expanded and altered German system of politics?

An Uneven Electoral Recovery

In the summer of 1989, when the FDP began systematically preparing for the Bundestag election of December 1990, the planners had no reason to expect that the campaign would be dominated by the issue of national unification. They assumed like everyone else that the contest would be fought within the established framework of West German electoral and party politics. As in the past, the minimum goal of the FDP would be a return to both parliament and cabinet in Bonn.

For the FDP, a Bundestag election had come to be seen as the most important of a seemingly never-ending series of challenges to its continued role as small but vital majority-maker in the coalition politics of Bonn. In the first eleven Bundestag elections, voter support for the small party reached two-digit figures in only three cases (1949, 1961, and 1980). Still, its electoral performance at the federal level was generally better than in state politics. It had always passed the five percent hurdle in Bundestag elections, despite some fairly close calls, and polls gave no reason to think that 1990 would be any different. However, the FDP's electoral outlook was inevitably influenced by some traumatic experiences in Landtag contests. In the first four decades of the Federal Republic (mid-1949 to mid-1989), the FDP had failed to gain parliamentary representation in 18 of the 111 state elections – with 12 of these routs taking place in the 28 state elections of the 1980s alone (Ritter and Niehuss, 1991: 158–179). Even though the staggered contests at the state level are not accurate indicators of what will happen in a federal election, they have come to serve the small party as on-going reference points in gauging the political problems and opportunities it faces in the electorate.

When taking stock in mid-1989 of its electoral performance since the last Bundestag election, the FDP could look back upon a record underscoring the continuing weakness and volatility of its electoral support. Still, the uneven results did reflect an overall improvement in the party's position compared to the previous legislative period. In the Bundestag election of January 1987, the FDP had received 9.1 percent of the vote, an impressive improvement of 30 percent over its result of 7 percent four years earlier. There had been eight state contests since then, as well as an election to the European Parliament. The state contests had been a "mixed bag" for the FDP. Its position had improved somewhat in the first five, all held in 1987, thus continuing the party's modest recovery in state politics that had begun in the mid-1980s. As a result, the party was able to remain in one legislature and return to four others, from each of which it had been excluded in a preceding election. The upturn was desperately needed, for it followed the most severe loss of voter sympathies in the small party's history due to its controversial mid-term switch of coalition partners in Bonn in 1982 (Søe, 1985, 1990).

The electoral upturns in 1987 had also helped the FDP recover at least some of its lost territory on another important front, that of acting as a junior coalition partner at the state level of government. The FDP, once a major presence in state politics, had almost disappeared from view until it entered two new cabinets, one with the CDU in the Rhineland-Palatinate and one with the SPD in the city-state of Hamburg. The new partnership with the SPD aroused considerable attention, it being the first Social Democratic-Liberal coalition formed since the FDP had left Helmut Schmidt's cabinet in 1982. The Hamburg coalition inevitably led to speculation about the FDP possibly inviting a new national alliance with the SPD. Because the political Left had itself become fragmented since the SPD-FDP era of government (1969–1982), the discussion of alternative coalition scenarios now sometimes included the so-called "traffic-light" combination, in which the Greens would join the SPD ("red") and the FDP ("yellow"). In reality, there was no political basis for such a coalition in any of the states, nor was the matter given serious consideration at the federal level. The national party was led after 1988 by Count Otto von Lambsdorff, a figure identified with the center-right wing of the party that had broken with the Social Democrats in 1982. In Bonn, the FDP looked toward a continuation of the coalition with the CDU/CSU.

In the Landtag elections in 1988 the FDP suffered setbacks for reasons special to each case. In Schleswig-Holstein, where the recently elected state legislature was dissolved early as a result of a political scandal involving the former CDU premier (the Barschel Affair), the FDP failed by a fairly small margin (0.6 percent) to maintain the slim parliamentary foothold it had gained less than a year earlier. The 1988 election in Baden-Württemberg was another story, and in some ways an even more discouraging one. This was the only one of the eleven states in which the FDP had always scored above the five percent threshold, and it was returned to parliament as usual. However, the result of 5.9 percent was embarrassing in a state that had always been considered a Liberal stronghold.

The West Berlin election of 1989 was an outright disaster for the FDP, although once again for reasons that appeared mostly to be locally defined. The Liberals had won 8.5 percent of the vote in that city's previous election and had entered into government office with the CDU. In January of 1989, however, the two governing parties were the victims of an electoral revolt. After capturing only 3.9 percent of the vote, the Free Democrats were excluded from both legislature and city government. Two other "third" parties, which had attracted protest votes, had no such problems in Berlin. The leftist Alternatives rose to 11.8 percent and the new right-wing party, the *Republikaner*, made a surprising breakthrough with 7.5 percent.

After these three electoral disappointments the contest for the European Parliament in June 1989 took on even more symbolic importance. In the previous European election, held at the time of the party's political nadir in 1984, the FDP had for the first time ever failed to pass the five percent electoral threshold within West Germany as a whole. In the election of June 1989, however, the FDP was able to repair part of the damage and return to the European Parliament (see Table 1.1). The Liberal outcome was undeniably modest (5.6 percent), however, and resulted in a distant fifth place for a party that liked to present itself as the "third force" in West German politics. The Greens placed third (8.4 percent), while the Republicans came in fourth (7.1 percent) by again mobilizing protest votes from the Right.

The unexpected emergence of the Republicans aroused concern in the FDP for a couple of reasons. Ideologically, the new party represented an illiberal right-wing populism. That could conceivably be turned into an opportunity for the FDP to display its own liberal credentials. Politically, however, the new grouping seemed to have the potential for upsetting the delicate balance of party politics in Bonn, from which the FDP had benefited so much over the years. The Liberals acted by preparing special argumentation for its members concerning this danger from the ultra-right. Yet by the time the materials became available, in November 1989, the Republicans were in decline, at least for the time being. Instead, the issue of *Deutschlandpolitik* had moved to center stage.

The Early Campaign Planning

The FDP's early stages of preparation for the Bundestag election of December 1990 did not seem in any way extraordinary. As in the past, the FDP established a small campaign group (*Wahlkampfgruppe*) at the party headquarters in Bonn a year and a half in advance of the election. As usual, it was headed by the federal party manager and included the head staffers in the Thomas Dehler House. More general direction came from the FDP's general secretary, Cornelia Schmalz-Jacobsen. The party's presidium and executive committee (*Vorstand*) regularly received reports and reviewed campaign proposals, beginning with a five-hour executive committee meeting on 11 September 1989 that issued directives for the election platform.[1] As always, the party organization seemed to take pride in drafting early and lengthy platform proposals, drawing upon the party's policy work groups (*Fachausschüsse*) for ideas. The first complete draft was to be ready by January 1990, yet as it turned out this meant that the proposals would first be ventilated just when the national parameters of postwar German politics were about to be shaken apart.

In the weeks and months that followed, the initial campaign

1. Generalsekretär der FDP, *Informationsbrief* Nr. 8/89, September 1989, pp. 2–3.

plans would be altered repeatedly to take into account the political dislocations accompanying the rush toward German unification. In their responses to exigencies, the FDP leaders and staffers would sometimes play by ear and sometimes change the score of the campaign strategy. Throughout this period of confusion, improvisation, and change that was to come, however, the FDP's small and simple system of campaign planning appears to have functioned with relative flexibility and efficiency.

At its 11 September 1989 meeting the party executive had paid special attention to *Deutschlandpolitik*, prompted in large part by the swelling number of German refugees from the East. The intensive discussion, as later reported by the general secretary to leading party members, provides a useful summary of where the FDP stood on the German Question a few weeks before the GDR's rapid disintegration opened the door for national unification. The members of the executive had consciously avoided "illusionary visions," as Cornelia Schmalz-Jacobsen put it, and had emphasized the need for continuity rather than new directions. Her report referred in very general terms to "new opportunities to overcome the division of Germany" as a "logical result of our efforts to overcome the division of Europe." It also stressed the continuing need to work within existing structures and convince neighboring countries that the Federal Republic would avoid unilateral directions (*Sonderwege*).[2] The report appears to be a quintessential statement for the FDP as well as for Minister Genscher's foreign policy at this point – in its cautionary tone, its stress on the larger European arena, and its emphasis on working through established structures and contacts. Only a short reference to FDP support for "old and new opposition groups" in the GDR seemed to go a step beyond the usual, and it was immediately balanced by an emphasis on the need for continuing a critical dialogue with the *real* powerholders, who alone were in a position to carry out reforms. In the following weeks the party leadership repeated the same basic message.

The Liberal policy on the "German Question" had been strongly national in the early years of the Federal Republic before undergoing a major transformation in the 1960s. Although the

---

2. Ibid., pp. 2–5. The same message is carried in the monthly membership magazine during the fall and winter months. See *Die neue Bonner Depesche*, 1989.

FDP's change in policy is often seen as part of a more general reorientation and "modernization" of the party at that time, it was also an attempt to come to terms with what appeared to be a consolidation of the division of Germany after the building of the Berlin Wall in 1961. Like the SPD, the FDP came to view political recognition of the East German state as a practical means of improving East-West as well as intra-German relations. Still, although the FDP had come to base its *Deutschlandpolitik* on the formula "one nation, two states," and sometimes appeared studiously to avoid the term "reunification," its leaders continued to pay homage to this goal in more distant metaphors and indirect formulations. Normally, they referred to "self-determination" and "overcoming the German division" within a new and peaceful European order. Leading Free Democrats thus tended to shy away from traditional nation-state formulations that came more easily to some conservatives in the CDU and CSU. They also differed markedly from at least some Social Democrats and many Greens by clinging more tenaciously to the special status accorded to the East German state and its citizens, rather than seeking to redefine them as *Ausland* and *Ausländer* respectively.

In the weeks and months following the FDP executive's September meeting, the German Democratic Republic went through a dizzying transformation that soon would be recognized as a revolution. By December 1989 and January 1990 it had become increasingly clear that the quick succession of reforms undertaken by the regime – such as the sacking of Erich Honecker and other leading communist officials, the relaxation of political controls, the opening of the Berlin Wall, and the hesitant moves toward a form of power-sharing – would not be able to conserve a separate statehood for East Germany. Still, it was not immediately clear or certain that a rapid unification would follow.

The general uncertainty found a somewhat belated reflection in the FDP's draft election program, finished according to plan in January 1990. It continued to speak in measured terms of the small party's *Deutschlandpolitik* as aiming at a peaceful order in Europe that would make possible for Germans "in free self-determination to regain their unity." The draft document spoke very generally about improvements in this area, though it paid considerably more attention to new possibilities for promoting democratic and economic reforms within the German Democratic

Republic. Internationally, it envisaged a reformed GDR as being a full member of the European Community.[3]

By the time the document reached its Liberal readership in February this section of the platform draft was already history. A free election of the *Volkskammer* had been scheduled early, for 18 March 1990. Thereafter, it was generally assumed, German unification would be on the agenda of the first democratically legitimate government in the GDR. In other words, the question had shifted to the timing and manner of German unification, something bound to give additional publicity to Foreign Minister Genscher.

The almost strained verbal caution of the FDP's initial draft undoubtedly reflected the small party's close identification with the Foreign Ministry. On the German Question, Hans-Dietrich Genscher had been characteristically undramatic in public. This was in marked contrast to such leading politicians as Helmut Kohl (CDU) and Willy Brandt (SPD), who already before the New Year had spoken less hesitantly and more emotionally of an early unification. During the following months, however, the Foreign Minister would play a highly visible role in the international negotiations dealing with reunification as well as in making frequent visits to calm neighboring countries concerned about a powerful 'new Germany'.

It had long been clear that Genscher would be an enormous asset for the FDP among West German voters in the coming Bundestag election, as he already had been in 1987. Since then, he had continued to rank in Politbarometer and other polls as the most popular politician in West Germany, where he was widely perceived as being a prudent and knowledgeable promoter of East-West detente. His popularity reached into East Germany as well, where Genscher's willingness to play upon his links to the hometown of Halle easily made him appear to be 'one of ours.'

The West German FDP and the East German LDPD

The FDP differed from its Bundestag rivals in having a long record of maintaining contacts with one of the bloc parties in the GDR. By the time several West German parties united as the FDP in December 1948, they had already broken the organizational tie

3. See first draft of the election platform, Wahlprogramm '90, in *Die neue Bonner Depesche*, February 1990, p. 28.

to the East German Liberal Democratic Party (LDPD). Then and later, they condemned the LDPD's increasing subservience to the Communist rulers of Eastern Germany. Still, many personal contacts to Liberal Democrats appear to have been kept up throughout the Cold War. There were also intermittent formal contacts with the LDPD. By the 1980s, Liberal party members and officials in the two German states met with some frequency.[4]

The links to the LDPD fit in well with the FDP's concern for improving relations between the two German states by working within existing structures. Contacts were facilitated by the fact that a considerable number of Free Democrats had begun their political careers in the early postwar LDP, before relocating in West Germany. The two best known were Foreign Minister Genscher and Wolfgang Mischnick, the veteran Bundestag leader of the FDP. Such Free Democrats were well aware that the LDPD had long since been reduced to a useful satellite party for the communist rulers of the GDR, and they had no illusions about its serving as a place of liberal opposition to the existing order before 1989. At the same time, there were indications that in some cases the LDPD may have filled a latent function for rank-and-file members by serving as a convenient political niche or half-way house (Lapp, 1988: 36–38).

Contacts to members of the LDPD were thus nothing new for the FDP, though their numbers swelled between October 1989 and the end of the year. The visitors included Mischnick and other FDP members of the Bundestag, as well as the EC commissioner and former party leader, Martin Bangemann. On 26 November, Lambsdorff arrived with Mischnick for a talk with the LDPD leader, Professor Manfred Gerlach, a talk that both sides have described as critical. By this time Free Democrats were also networking at lower levels of the LDPD, and would soon be talking to dissidents wanting to organize as Liberals outside the LDPD. It appeared like a whipsaw approach, and Professor Gerlach would later complain in his memoirs about the FDP's "double-strategy" of putting pressure on his own party (Gerlach, 1991: 336). As the party leader since 1967, he had led the LDPD in giv-

---

4. The subject needs to be systematically researched. Manfred Gerlach mentions that he had discussions with Mischnick eight times between 1973 and 1987, and several times afterwards. He lists other discussion partners and concludes that "there was nothing similar to this in the other parties" (Gerlach, 1991: 308 ff., 435).

ing unqualified support to the goal of "building socialism" in the GDR. Yet he showed himself to have fine political antenna by developing a mildly reformist posture during the last full year of the state's existence. It was a reasonable conclusion for the FDP to see him as being a possible promoter of reform within the existing state structure. The report on the FDP executive meeting in September 1989 includes an approving comment on the "remarkably open" manner in which Gerlach now spoke about "conditions in his country."[5]

Ironically, Manfred Gerlach would turn out to be a political handicap, a common fate for early reformers in a revolutionary situation. On 6 December Gerlach had succeeded Egon Krenz (himself Honecker's successor) as head of the moribund East German state council, but by this time his mild latter-day reformism had been overtaken by far more determined demands for thorough political change in the GDR. In his emperor's new clothes, Gerlach now seemed to many to be the personification of the opportunistic turn-coat or *Wendehals*. Yet he had a strong following at the higher levels of the LDPD, and he managed to hold on to the leadership of the party during a time that in the view of many called for a thorough clearing out of the old power structure. There was now a real danger that the LDPD, which earlier had appeared to be such a useful channel for reform, would now instead become identified through its leader with the old regime in its last stage of decay. Even the old ruling party, the SED, had thoroughly revamped itself as early as December 1989, while the Christian Democratic bloc party carried through a major change of leadership and program in January 1990. By this time the Eastern CDU had also made a show of its new independence by pulling out of the party coalition that made up Hans Modrow's government in East Berlin, while the LDPD executive decided that the Liberal Democrats would remain in the coalition despite what Gerlach interpreted as pressure from the Western FDP to make a similar demonstrative exit (Gerlach, 1991: 415).

The LDPD had not been wholly inactive. In several successive steps throughout December its executive had issued a series of announcements from the top in which it simply scrapped the party's long support for a socialist society, embraced the goals of

5. *Informationsbrief* Nr. 8/89, p. 5.

a free society and a market economy, and even began to speak in favor of an "incremental" (*schrittweise*) unification of the two German states (Gerlach, 1991: 351–370) Yet despite urgings from within the LDPD as well as the West German FDP, it delayed major self-reform until a party conference on 9 and 10 February , just five weeks before the *Volkskammer* election. In a symbolic move to emphasize its transformation, the February conference decided to return to the old and shorter party name and abbreviation, LDP. In addition to this facelift, the Liberal Democrats underwent an ideological metamorphosis by inscribing a commitment to the market economy, the rule of law, and pluralist democracy in their program (Friedrich Naumann Foundation, 1990: 36 ff). They also replaced Gerlach and some of the other leading Liberal Democrats. Thus the old bloc party managed to strike a balance between political continuity and discontinuity. Gerlach attended, spoke, and was honored for his contributions to the party. The new leader was Rainer Ortleb (born 1944), a soft-spoken professor of mathematics who had been a member of the LDP in Rostock since 1968. Like so many others inside and outside the party, he had apparently found ritual ways of accommodating himself within the old socialist system. Compared to Gerlach, he seemed like a fresh voice without close and disqualifying ties to the old powerholders.

Old and New Liberal Parties in a Free East German Election

The LDP's relatively long delay of any self-reform had raised suspicions among the members of two new Liberal groupings, the FDP of the GDR, and the German Forum Party (DFP). The Eastern FDP had been founded on 4 February, after more than a month of networking among some individuals who included dissident former LDP members as well as some people who had kept away from political involvement until very recently. Dr. Bruno Menzel, who belonged to the latter category, became leader of the new party, which claimed to represent "real" Liberals as opposed to the collaborators and turncoats of the LDP. The West German FDP had early contacts to the founders and encouraged their venture.

The Forum Party was a very small and fragmented group. Its members had distanced themselves from the opposition group,

New Forum, when it decided against revamping itself as a political party. The DFP described itself as a party of the center, though in fact its members were divided and confused about both program and strategy. Both the CDU and FDP had courted the group, yet it decided in the end to go with the Liberals, a decision that appears to have been decisively influenced by the Forum Party's first leader, Jürgen Schmieder, a former member of the LDP who had a personal following among the DFP's membership in Chemnitz. He would eventually be replaced (in May) by a new acting leader, Lothar Ramin of East Berlin. But Schmieder, who had far more political experience than his replacement, was by that time abandoning a mutinous and wayward vessel. He later managed to end up as the only former member of the Forum Party to secure for himself a good list place for election to the Bundestag.

Both the new Liberal parties were at first reported to have several tens of thousands of members – vastly more than could be substantiated by later, more careful estimates. The West German FDP, clearly aware that there were gross discrepancies in the membership figures, remained politely discrete about such matters, at least in public. The membership of the new East German FDP reached about 1,500 by August 1990. The Forum Party at one point claimed to have a membership of 50,000, though it actually amounted to about five hundred, concentrated in a few cities (East Berlin, Leipzig, Dresden, and Chemnitz).[6] What the Forum Party lacked in membership numbers, it made up for in factional divisions. The DFP was a difficult partner for everyone, though it had some symbolic value to the West German FDP at this time. Like the small new East German FDP, the tiny Forum Party could be presented as a part of the liberal democratic opposition in the East. The reformed LDP, by contrast, could boast of a much larger membership (about 110,000), a network of 1,500 full-time party workers, and a valuable organizational infrastructure. But these riches carried political embarrassment with them, for they

6. The claim of 50,000 members was made by the Forum Party in its self-presentation that accompanied its party program in *Parteien und Wahlbundnisse in der DDR. Programme und Statuten*, p. 15. The deflated membership figures for the DFP are based on information from a former leading member of that party. They correspond to estimates given by other German Liberals who had worked with the small party. The membership figures for the FDP in the GDR are given as 1,500 for August 1990, by Veen et al. (1990: 20). The same source also lists 500 for the DFP.

derived from the LDP's comfortable former life as a privileged bloc party in communist East Germany.

The West German FDP clearly had an interest in maintaining contacts to both the old and new Liberal parties. Leading Free Democrats attended and spoke at the founding congress of the Eastern FDP on 4 February and at the reform congress of the LDPD a few days later. Already before the New Year, there had been some 200 regional "cooperation contacts" between Western Free Democrats and their counterparts in the LDPD and what later became the separate Eastern FDP.[7]

The West German FDP pushed for organizational unity among the East German Liberal parties in advance of the elections to the *Volkskammer*. That turned out to be difficult. By early–February, all three parties wanted to be tied in some way to their West German counterpart, though they had little if any affection for each other. It was only as a concession to political practicality, backed by considerable pressure from the West German FDP, that they finally agreed to campaign not so much together as under a shared label, League of Free Democrats (*Bund Freier Demokraten* or BFD). The three dissimilar parties were equally represented (three members each) on a coordination committee, headed by Wolfgang Mischnick. Its job was to promote cooperation, but five long meetings in the five weeks before the election did not bring harmony. The two new parties understandably distrusted the Liberal Democrats, whom they regarded as an opportunistic and privileged part of the old GDR establishment. The LDP reacted defensively to such charges, accusing the newcomers of political naivite and charging them with using highly inflated membership figures in order to gain a better share of representation in the electoral alliance. Not surprisingly, the most difficult task turned out to be the allocation of the list placements under the shared BFD label. Here the LDP was forced to make major concessions to its rivals.

The West German FDP played a major role in supporting and promoting the BFD in the *Volkskammer* election. The party headquarters in Bonn took credit for sending 47 campaign workers to

7. The account in this and the following paragraphs is based on interviews with FDP campaign planners, as well as with several East Germans who were involved in Liberal party work. The FDP made available a detailed internal report, dated 16 March 1990, written by Rolf Berndt, federal manager of the FDP, and Hans-Jürgen Beerfeltz, head of the political planning section (Berndt and Beerfeltz, 1990).

the GDR, but there appear to have been many others representing the lower levels of the party organization as well. They brought with them all kinds of technical help, such as photocopiers, computers, electrical typewriters and, not least, special telephone lines. To overcome the information problems caused by the technically backward communication structures in the GDR, the FDP also used five couriers who delivered messages between the fifteen campaign centers (one for each *Bezirk*) when all else failed. The printing of BFD campaign posters and other advertising lay mostly in West German hands, although each party also used some of its own advertising materials. To better promote the BFD, it had been decided in the coordination committee to use the blue-and-yellow colors and distinctive lettering that have become part of the corporate image of the West German FDP. The dominant role of the Western FDP took an even more striking form when the parties in the BFD agreed to use only prominent West German politicians to personalize the advertising, rather than their own, relatively unknown leaders. As a consequence, the countenances of Genscher and Lambsdorff were included with much of the BFD's advertising. It was inevitable that there would be a reaction against the West playing such a visible role, and the BFD responded somewhat tardily by presenting their own leaders in a final electoral pamphlet (*Wahlaufruf*).

Western experience and funding also lay behind a great deal of the other political advertising, such as one television and one radio commercial for the BFD as well as ads in most regional newspapers and some other publications. Two of the three most commonly used slogans, in addition to one that simply encouraged voters to vote for List 4, used Lambsdorff and Genscher to attract attention: "Trust the economy to those whom Count Otto Lambsdorff trusts; . . ." and "Trust your future to those whom Hans-Dietrich Genscher trusts." Somewhat more memorable, perhaps, was a slogan which ran, "You've had the Left, You don't want the Right. Good that there's the Strong Center Now." Another slogan, widely used on posters, had been borrowed directly from the West: "Freedom is Achievement." Some Easterners objected that the typically Liberal reference to achievement or performance (*Leistung*) could run into cultural difficulty in the GDR because the old regime had used a similar slogan in some its neo-stakhanovite appeals.

The Western campaign planners later reported that their partners in the GDR tended to take little initiative in shaping the course or contents of the campaign. They would "react, rather than act," partly from lack of experience, but also because the BFD lacked its own identity and cohesion. The Western visitors even prepared a recommended plan for the course of a campaign meeting, crafting a model speech on a topic that clearly had priority for people in the GDR, namely the social safety net in a market economy. There were 210 separate political meetings in which politicians from Bonn addressed East German voters. Lambsdorff, Genscher, and Mischnick were among the most frequent speakers, but others included Irmgard Adam-Schwaetzer, Gerhart Baum, and Jürgen Möllemann. Like West German politicians from other parties, the Free Democrats would report that they had frequently been met by a more interested audience than they were used to at home. There were a few mass meetings, with the biggest turnout – 80,000 – recorded for Genscher in Chemnitz on 24 February.

After all these efforts the outcome of the *Volkskammer* election on 18 March was a disappointment but not a surprise, since the polling reports had been consistently dismal. The League of Free Democrats attracted only 5.3 percent of the vote, giving it 21 of 400 seats. As in West Germany, the Liberals did best among middle-aged voters in middle-class professional or independent occupations. The list placements, based on a pre-election agreement that clearly had been very generous to the two small new parties, resulted in ten delegates elected from the LDP, seven from the DFP, and four from the FDP-East.

Since the Alliance for Germany had won a total of just over 48 percent of the vote, it would have been possible, arithmetically at least, to build a new non-Communist government in the GDR similar to the conservative-liberal coalition of Christian and Free Democrats in Bonn. Politically, however, a much wider base would be necessary for decisions that were to result in the dissolution of the GDR. Lothar de Maiziere, the leader of the East German CDU, therefore formed a broader government coalition that included the Social Democrats as well as the Liberals. The BFD was given three of the 21 ministries, considerably more than its relative share of the total vote for the parties making up the coalition. In the new government, the BFD was usually overshadowed

by its much larger partners, although it did receive some unwanted attention as a result of agreeing with de Maiziere to fill the
Ministry of Justice with an old and compromised LDPD politician, Kurt Wünsche. He had already served as Minister of Justice
between 1967 and 1972, and that associated him with the politically repressive use of the state's criminal code and judicial
machinery, even though his supporters argued that he had
attempted to ward off still worse abuses. Wünsche finally
resigned in July 1990, although he nonetheless continued to symbolize a major problem in the takeover of the old satellite parties.

As could be expected, there were mutual recriminations following the poor electoral performance on 18 March. And the LDP
did not make itself any more loveable when it decided to accept
an offer to merge with a remnant of the National Democratic
Party of Germany. The NDPD was by this time largely another
middle-class satellite party, though it had originally been created
by the communists in the late-1940s to attract "nationally" oriented East Germans – often politically cleared, former members of
the German officer corps. The election had been a total disaster
for the NDPD. As a bloc party, it (like the LDPD) had been used
to occupy a guaranteed share of 52 seats (or 10.4 percent) in the
old (and larger) Volkskammer. Now it was reduced to only 2
seats (or 0.5 percent of the seats), based on an even smaller share
(0.4 percent) of the vote. There had been only slightly more than
44,000 ballot supporters for this old block party that had recently
claimed a membership of over 110,000 and 1,600 full-time party
workers (Lapp, 1988: 81 and 143)![8] The NDPD's only conceivable
link to liberalism was sociological – its middle-class membership
– rather than ideological. It did, however, have some valuable
organizational resources in addition to a small remnant membership that now joined the LDP at the end of March. By this time the
Liberal Democrats had unilaterally appropriated for themselves
the campaign name, League of Free Democrats (BFD), after a first
post-election attempt to bring in the two new Liberal formations
had failed. The union of the two old bloc parties as BFD could

8. This section also draws on data from Rolf Berndt's internal party report,
"Wiedervereinigung als Organisationsproblem: Gesamtdeutsche Zusammen-
schlusse von Parteien und Verbanden." The author, who is the FDP federal manager, has described in detail the 'organizational problems and successes' of party
unification. He lists the number of full-time party workers of the LDP and NDPD
on page 5.

thus only add to the general confusion surrounding political identities in the dying East German state.

In the GDR's local elections on 6 May the three Liberal parties did not form an electoral alliance and competed separately. The two former bloc parties (the LDP and NDPD), now running as the League of Free Democrats, improved slightly upon the low Liberal results attained in the *Volkskammer* election of seven weeks earlier by winning 6.6 percent of the vote. Still, the electoral outcome reflected the organizational weaknesses and spotty geographical presence of the two new Liberal parties. The Eastern FDP won only 0.5 percent of the vote, while the German Forum Party registered a minuscule 0.03 percent of the total.

The Unification of Germany's Liberal Parties

All three Liberal groupings in the GDR wanted to achieve full corporate unity with the West German FDP, the latter having a strong interest in such a move as well. Only a united Liberal party would be likely to make a credible showing in the upcoming state and Bundestag elections in the Eastern part of a united Germany. The old LDPD (and the rump NDPD) were politically compromised in many ways, but they offered considerable organizational resources – including party members, functionaries, press organs, political bureaus, valuable real estate, and other assets. A July 1990 report by the party's treasurer held the BFD's total assets to be worth about DM 200 million, including about DM 13.5 million in cash (Veen et al., 1990: 20), a figure later reduced to DM 91 million by a Treuhand estimate (Süss, 1992). The new Liberal groupings had tiny memberships and their only organizational resources consisted of what they had received from the West German FDP in the frenzied political build-up of the first few months of 1990. Their real value was symbolic: they represented a liberal democratic legitimacy that the LDP could not seriously lay claim to, despite its name.

The groundwork for the merger was decided upon in the interparty commission during the summer of 1990, and a special FDP unification congress took place in Hannover, on 11 and 12 August 1990. The parties were represented on the basis of a combination of their official membership and their absolute vote in the last Bundestag or *Volkskammer* election. This meant that the East German Liberals, with a total of about 137,000 members at the time but only about 600,000 votes in the March election, received 260 delegates out of a total of 662. Of these, 160 were allocated to the BFD, 55 to the FDP-East, and 45 to the Forum Party. There were complaints from the Liberal and National Democrats in the BFD that their huge combined membership of about 135,000 (Veen et al., 1990: 20) had been grossly underrepresented in the numbers of delegates awarded them, not only in comparison to the minuscule East German rivals but also to the West German FDP, which had a party membership of close to 67,000 (see Table 5.1). Party leaders and staffers appeared to have done their work well in preparation for a harmonious ceremony at this political wedding of convenience. The only acrimonious notes heard were when some members of the two small East German parties once again used the opportunity to remind delegates from the former satellite parties of their past political sins.

It had been evident in advance that a delegate key that combined party membership and total vote received by the party in the previous election would give the lion's share of conference votes to the Free Democrats from the four times more populous Federal Republic. There was, however, a conscious attempt to include each of the Eastern parties in the allocation of top party offices. Lambsdorff was reelected as leader, two of his five deputies being from the GDR (Rainer Ortleb from the former LDP/BFD, and Dr. Bruno Menzel from the former Eastern FDP). Four of the thirteen members of the party presidium were from East Germany (including a little known representative from the DFP), and the party's executive committee was expanded to provide similar representation to the newcomers.[9] The FDP had suddenly tripled its official membership to over 200,000, of whom two-thirds were concentrated in a region that would constitute only one-fifth of Germany's population after unification. Nevertheless, it was obvious that the West German FDP had largely absorbed its East German counterparts in Hannover, and that this process would soon be repeated by the West German SPD and CDU when they held their unification conferences.

The FDP had scheduled a pre-election convention for 29 and 30 September 1990 in Nurnberg. Party delegates, as expected, decid

9. The unification congress is the major topic of the renamed membership journal, *Die liberale Depesche*, Nr. 9–10, September–October 1990.

Table 5.1. FDP Membership in the Old and New States of the Federal Republic, 1990–1992

	30 June 1992	1 Oct. 1991	31 Dec. 1990	31 July 1990
Baden-Württemberg	7,244	7,363	7,496	7,440
Bavaria	6,078	6,257	6,385	6,432
West Berlin*	2,607	(2,600)	(2,600)	(2,600)
Bremen	624	629	598	618
Hamburg	1,899	1,958	1,987	1,899
Hesse	7,512	7,638	7,759	7,361
Lower Saxony	8,256	8,315	7,948	7,989
North Rhine-Westphalia	20,188	20,367	20,652	20,519
Rhineland-Palatinate	5,217	5,306	5,375	5,390
The Saar	2,686	2,808	2,878	2,931
Schleswig-Holstein	3,192	3,208	3,278	3,296
Old States: Total	65,503	66,449	66,956	66,475
East Berlin*	2,352	(3,046)	(4,412)	(5,444)
Brandenburg	6,931	11,651	15,853	19,865
Mecklenburg-Pomerania	7,836	9,636	13,154	17,744
Saxony	12,918	21,280	25,363	35,832
Saxony-Anhalt	9,355	19,831	24,171	29,151
Thuringia	18,774	22,556	28,425	28,129
New States: Total	58,166	88,000	111,378	136,165
Total Membership** East and West	123,669	154,449	178,334	202,640

* No breakdowns for East and West Berlin were contained for the 1990 and 1991 data, but West Berlin's figures have changed very little during the two-year period. It has been estimated at a constant of 2,600, based on the June 1992 membership figure of 2,607. This has been subtracted from the total Berlin membership data to arrive at the East Berlin figures.

** The nearly 300 members who reside abraod and belong to the *Auslandgruppe Europa* have not been included.

SOURCES: F.D.P. Die Liberalen, *Geschäftsbericht 1990–1991*, p. 36, for the 1990 and 1991 membership figures. The 1992 figures were provided by the FDP party headquarters in Bonn.

ed overwhelmingly and without formal debate to continue the coalition with the Christian Democrats. Genscher was chosen as the FDP's top candidate for a cabinet position, as foreign minister and deputy chancellor. Otherwise it was a busy meeting, much of the time being devoted to combining, discussing, and voting on what had been 1097 motions for a change of the platform – something of a record even for the FDP. Lack of time finally made it necessary to leave the final formulation of a few policy areas to a later meeting of the party executive.[10] In certain civil libertarian matters the party included as always what it likes to call "sharp edges" (*Ecken und Kanten*), a few demands that the conservative coalition partner would never support. But the main emphasis was on foreign and economic policy. In the former area, the party congratulated Genscher and itself on great accomplishments for Germany and Europe, while emphasizing the need for continuity in leadership and policy. On economic policy, the party stressed market-oriented solutions, advocated a reduction of bureaucracy, and emphasized that the FDP could never agree to new taxes to finance German unification. Such taxes, the FDP argued, would reduce the productivity of the German economy. Instead, there should be savings in the state budget, along with a reduction in subsidies.

The FDP's Bundestag Campaign

The Bundestag campaign was unusually long in 1990, in part because it overlapped six state elections in October. Earlier in this busy political year there had been three additional state contests, and their coinciding with unification efforts had strained the small party's energies to the limit. Following the disappointing results in both 1988 and 1989, the first state election in 1990 was hardly auspicious. In late-January the FDP managed to squeeze into the state parliament of the Saar with 5.6 percent of the vote, though this result constituted a sharp setback from the previous tally of 10.0 percent. It was yet another unnecessary reminder of the volatility of the FDP's electoral support. In May 1990 the Liberals finally managed to hold back the electoral tide in two more state elections. The FDP hung on to its previous share of 6.0 per-

10. For a good overview of the conference, see *Die liberale Depesche*, Nr. 11–12, November-December 1990, pp. 1–12. The daily press also covered the event.

cent in Lower Saxony, although it had to leave the state government in Hannover when its CDU coalition partner suffered a major electoral setback. In the populous state of North Rhine-Westphalia, the Liberals suffered only a slight erosion of their small previous share of the vote (5.8 percent, down from 6.0).

Despite the SPD's three victories in Western state elections between January and May 1990, the FDP decided in May and June to base its Bundestag campaign strategy on the expectation of a relatively weak SPD and a relatively strong CDU/CSU. Until late spring the planners had basically planned a West German campaign, assuming that the SPD, with Oskar Lafontaine as chancellor candidate, would make a very strong showing. The results of the state elections seemed to support such a view. Yet when it became clear that the rapid progress in negotiating, adopting, and implementing the unification arrangements would make it possible to have an all-German Bundestag elections at the end of the year, Lambsdorff convinced a somewhat skeptical party presidium to adopt the strategy of running against the Christian Democrats. The FDP assumed that the SPD and Oskar Lafontaine would be overshadowed by the CDU/CSU in the first all-German Bundestag contest. As a consequence, the FDP planned to fight a campaign directed at winning coalition supporters away from the CDU/CSU, arguing that a single-party conservative government must be prevented (Beerfeltz, 1991: 22–25).[11]

The new campaign budget also reflected the changed geographical and political framework of the Bundestag election. Originally, the FDP had wanted to keep the budget at the same level as in 1987 (around DM 6 million). Now it decided to double the federal party's campaign budget to DM 12.8 million. This was possible only because a fiscal austerity program had been adopted in the mid-1980s after private contributions to the party had

---

11. Inside de Maiziere's Grand Coalition, the East German Liberals (and Social Democrats) disagreed with the Christian Democrats about some of the modalities of the first all-German Bundestag election, leading the BFD to announce its withdrawal from the coalition on 24 July 1990. It was an ambivalent departure, however, for the Liberal ministers remained in their governmental posts as caretakers. Moreover, the BFD gave parliamentary support to a new series of unification steps that were finally proposed by de Maiziere's government, including the arrangements for an all-German Bundestag election on 2 December, passed on 22 August.

almost dried up in the wake of the Flick Affair. The immediate result had been a much slimmer party central, and the FDP had been able to declare itself debt-free by 1987 (Vörlander, 1990: 266). Financially, it was in much better condition in 1990 than in any recent election year.

The budget allocations looked familiar, as did so much else in the publicity and logistical support supplied by the party headquarters. Most of the budget was to be spent centrally, with the largest sums going to 1) newspaper ads (DM 3.7 million), 2) political posters (DM 3.4 million), 3) administration and service costs (DM 1.3 million), and 4) political meetings (DM 1.2 million).[12] As in the past, however, one large sum (almost DM 1 million) was allocated in equal parts of DM 3,000 among each of the now 328 electoral districts in Germany. This cash infusion, which came with broad conditions regarding its campaign use, had become a tradition in the FDP. It was a new and welcome practice in the East, where there was less likely to be much local funding of party activities.

The campaign planners tried to take advantage of the fact that the six state elections on 14 October came only seven weeks before the Bundestag election. This gave the FDP and other parties an opportunity to start up their electoral machinery early and keep it warm thereafter. This was particularly important in the new Eastern states where the FDP competed under its own name for the first time. The Liberals had counted on their unification congress making a positive impression in the East, as polls suggested had indeed happened, and they hoped that the pre-election conference in Nurnberg would help the FDP win ground in the difficult political terrain of Bavaria.

The Free Democrats had reason to be happy with the outcome in both East and West. After a full eight years of absence from the state parliament in Munich they had finally managed to gain reentry, if by a very slim margin (5.2 percent). In the five new federal states it was even possible to speak of a minor electoral breakthrough, for here the newly unified FDP improved considerably upon the poor showing of the BFD earlier in the year, win-

12. The data was provided by the FDP headquarters, but I have rounded the sums off to the nearest DM 100,000. It strikes a U.S. observer that the cost of TV and radio spots amounted to only DM 570,000 or 4.5 percent of the total budget, largely because advertising space is provided free by the government-owned media.

ning 7.7 percent of the total vote (against 5.3 in March). Of particular importance was the discovery by the small party that it had landed in the role of balancer, something that has become increasingly rare in West German politics at the state level. In three states (Mecklenburg, Saxony-Anhalt, and Thuringia), the FDP entered coalition governments with the CDU. But in Brandenburg something new was tried out – the "traffic light" coalition, with the SPD and the Alliance '90.

The October state elections gave the FDP fresh confidence as well as a flying start for the Bundestag campaign. Following the strategy adopted in the early summer, the FDP now directed much of its energies toward promoting its "functional" argument, which presents the party as a moderating force inside the coalition government. There was nothing new about this argument in the old Federal Republic, but it was taken up with new vigor by the Liberal campaigners who warned against a conservative majority of the CDU/CSU, despite polls that indicated that such an outcome was highly unlikely. Other polls showed that a majority of voters (55 percent of the CDU-supporters and 65 percent of the SPD-supporters) expressed a preference for coalition government (Forschungsgruppe Wahlen, 1990: 69). In the East, the FDP's participation in four of the five new state governments could serve as a fresh and practical example of the Liberal argument, something that was missing in nearly all the older states. Still, the focus was on the balance of power in Bonn, where the FDP had played the role of junior coalition party since 1969.

The second-vote strategy has been a regular part of the FDP electoral arsenal since 1972, and it was used again in 1990. As had sometimes happened in the past, the coalition partner responded with a second-vote campaign of its own, pointing out that "the second vote is the chancellor vote." To a certain degree the FDP's combination of the functional argument with the second-vote strategy placed the CDU/CSU in a bind: by protesting too much, it might bring about the unintended and unwanted effect of raising voters' awareness about ticket-splitting.

The FDP also used every opportunity to personalize its campaign. This was particularly true for its two main issues, foreign policy (including *Deutschlandpolitik*) and economic policy. As in the March and October elections, FDP posters, newspaper ads, and other political commercials exploited Hans-Dietrich Genscher's enormous popularity to help represent the party's claim to achievement and competence in international relations. He was regularly introduced as representing "the Germany that the world trusts." In the FDP's presentation, his policies had been a crucial factor in ending the Cold War, and his steady hand continued to be needed at the foreign ministry in a time of major change in the international order.

Count Lambsdorff was similarly pictured as not only being his party's leader but also its major authority on economic matters. No one spoke as decisively as he did against a tax increase to pay for German unification. Instead, he proposed creating a lower tax region in the East as a way of encouraging investment. Neither of these positions could be maintained very long after the election, however, for it had become evident that huge financial transfers would be necessary to keep the new Eastern states from a complete economic and social collapse. Soon there would also be doubt about another economic position for which Lambsdorff's FDP took considerable credit. This was the principle, adopted in the unification treaty, that restitution of private property should have priority over compensation in cases where such property had been confiscated by the Communist rulers in the former GDR. As could have been expected, this approach eventually encouraged a flood of claims that clogged the law courts and discouraged the productive use and development of disputed property.

As in the past, the FDP directed many of its messages to special interests, both material and ideal. Like the rest of its self-presentation these targeted appeals were always packaged as "liberal" – an honorific, if somewhat vague term in today's German political vocabulary. The party placed special importance on the electoral targeting of the self-employed and professionals through direct mailings and ads placed in magazines aimed at occupational groups and middle-class homeowners. There was also a special effort made to reach such groups in the East, for which the old networks of the Liberal Democrats turned out to be useful. To its middle-class audiences, the FDP presented itself as a defender of individual achievement and property rights, as well as a watchdog against excessive bureaucratization, high taxation, and other statist proclivities.

But the FDP also continued its past practice of attempting to woo voters who could be attracted by civil libertarian or moderately post-material metaphors and slogans. To them it presented itself as a defender of civil rights, individual lifestyles, decentralization, and environment. The FDP stressed more than other parties that a "market economy" would provide the best framework for environmental protection – and it was not above pointing out the experience of Eastern Germany as a kind of negative proof of this proposition.

The FDP had made it a high priority to gain electoral ground in the new states. It invested relatively far more resources of all kinds into this area, by concentrating almost one-third of the centrally sponsored 665 campaign meetings there, for example. The most conspicuous example of this targeting of resources eastward, however, took place in Genscher's home town in Saxony-Anhalt. In the state elections of October the FDP had done remarkably well in Halle, and it was decided to pull out all the stops and go for a direct mandate on the first ballot in the city. There was a very heavy investment of funds into the chosen district, and Genscher made sure to visit.

Electoral Victory

On 2 December 1990 the FDP received 11 percent of the second-ballot vote and thus broke into the double-digit zone in which it would like to have a permanent place. Its success in Eastern Germany (13.4 percent) was particularly welcome after the disappointing of 5.3 percent won by the League of Free Democrats (BFD) in the *Volkskammer* election of March. The all-out effort to win a single-member district in Halle was also crowned with success. With just over one-third of the first vote (34.4 percent), a Free Democrat wound up winning the party's first direct mandate since 1957. The winning candidate was Uwe Lühr, a trained economist who had worked as a high-level administrator in Halle before 1989 and been a city mayor since May 1990. His background was not atypical for a long-time member of the LDP (he had joined the party in 1967, at the age of eighteen). Soon after the election the party leadership selected him as its candidate for secretary general, for which he would be duly elected at the party conference in the fall of 1991.

The FDP won 79 seats in a Bundestag that had been expanded

to 662 representatives. Of these, 62 were elected in the more populous Western electoral region, and 17 in the Eastern area, including the three former Liberal party leaders Rainer Ortleb (LDP), Bruno Menzel (FDP in the GDR), and Jürgen Schmieder (DFP). The share of Easterners in the FDP parliamentary party was 21.5 percent, somewhat lower than their share in the CDU (23.9 percent), yet considerably higher than in the SPD (14.6 percent).

Compared to recent Bundestag elections, the percentage of women in the FDP parliamentary party has grown considerably from 12.5 to 20.3 percent. Of the sixteen women, three were Easterners. Before 1983, a parliamentary party in which women made up one-fifth of the members would have been impressive, but that is no longer the case now that the Greens and the SPD have broken the traditional mold. In 1990 the FDP was only ahead of the CDU/CSU (13.8 percent) in this respect, and both government parties were far behind the Left: the SPD (27.3 percent), the Alliance '90/Greens (38 percent), and the PDS (47 percent).

Among voters, the FDP had improved among all age groups. It continued to do especially well among voters between 35 and 60, where it won 12.5 percent of the vote within the enlarged Federal Republic (Statistisches Bundesamt, 1992b). The party was weakest among voters over 60 (9.3 percent). In the age group 18 to 25 the FDP was supported by 10.6 percent of the voters in United Germany, but here there was another interesting East-West difference: in the new states, the FDP did relatively poorly among these youngest voters. In the West, the FDP received almost as strong support from youth (10.5 percent) as in the electorate overall (10.6 percent) – something that provides the party with a small ray of hope that it can begin to attract the younger voters it had lost after its coalition change in 1982.

In social terms the FDP continued to be a party whose supporters came overwhelmingly from the middle class, both "new" and "old." The Mannheim electoral researchers concluded that in Eastern Germany the FDP had done unusually well among the self-employed (over 20 percent), as well as among people in leading administrative positions (*leitende Angestellte*), from whom it received almost 20 percent of the vote as well (Forschungsgruppe Wahlen, 1990: 69–70).

Although the second vote alone determines parliamentary strength, the FDP was encouraged by a remarkable improvement in its ability to attract both votes. As late as 1987 the FDP received less than 5 percent of the first vote (4.7 percent), an amount that constituted only 52 percent of its share of the second vote (9.1 percent) that year. The difference had been even more dramatic in 1983 (Søe, 1990). In 1990, by contrast, the FDP held on to 7.8 percent of the first vote, and this amounted to 71 percent of its share of the second vote (11.0 percent). There are splittings in both directions, however, so that the FDP in fact received both votes from only 50.6 percent of its second-ballot supporters (Statistisches Bundesamt, 1992b, Heft 4: 21). It is nonetheless intriguing that the percentage of non-splitting supporters of the FDP was much lower in the Western electoral region (45.8 percent) than in the Eastern region. This marked regional gap in ticket-splitting was peculiar to the FDP in 1990, and it supports the impression that its voters in the West have become relatively "tactical" in distributing their two votes (Statistisches Bundesamt, 1992a, Heft 3: 9–10 and 12–13).

Some Conclusions and Reflections

The FDP's electoral victory of 1990 should not obscure the central fact that the FDP's political success was a relative one. Its role as a parliamentary party continues to be contingent on the electoral system of modified proportional representation, without which the German Liberals would be of no political significance. In comparison with the *Volksparteien*, the FDP remains a relatively small "third" party with a very weak core of loyal supporters and therefore dependent on attracting an unusually large number of itinerant votes. Even with their poor performance in 1990, the Christian and Social Democrats together had still received seven times as many votes as the FDP. In fact, the CDU/CSU came much closer to winning a parliamentary majority than its 43.8 percent of the vote suggests: in the expanded Bundestag it had won 48.2 percent of the mandates and was only 13 seats short of a majority, compared to a margin of 26 seats in the smaller Bundestag that had just been dissolved.

Any electoral advance is welcome to such a small party, but the FDP's political significance derives less from improvements in its relatively modest share of the vote than from its strategic position as balancer within the party system. The two may be related, of course, as is the case with the electoral success in 1980, which encouraged the FDP to risk a breakaway from its coalition partnership with the SPD in 1982. It is useful to remember, however, that even an electoral setback can leave the FDP in a pivotal position, such as happened in October 1969, when the party received only 5.8 percent of the vote yet was still able as majority-maker to bring about the first full transfer of governmental power in the Federal Republic.

Ironically, despite its victory in 1990 the FDP has not regained the pivotal position in the Bundestag that it held for almost a quarter of a century, from 1961 to 1983. The Greens' (temporary) exodus from the Bundestag has not led to a restoration of the "two and one-half" party system because two new and smaller contingents (the PDS and Eastern Greens/Alliance '90), both with an electoral base in Eastern Germany, were able to win parliamentary representation. Neither is a likely coalition partner for the FDP. In a curious way, the FDP seems to have become more dependent upon the Christian Democrats for remaining in government office than vice versa. Arithmetically, at least, there is a viable majority alternative for the CDU/CSU. Although another Grand Coalition seems politically unlikely at the time of this writing, it cannot be completely ruled out that the problems connected with unification might not at some point provide a reason for another experiment with inclusive government – similar to the one formed to share responsibility for dealing with the far simpler economic crisis in the late 1960s. Even without such a mid-term coalition change by the Christian Democrats, the FDP still might lose its cherished role as majority-maker and junior coalition partner after the next Bundestag election if right-wing populists succeed in gaining parliamentary representation, thereby reducing the CDU/CSU's strength to such an extent that a "small" coalition with the Liberals would not command a legislative majority. Given the angry mood of the far Right at present in united Germany, this kind of a scenario cannot be ruled out entirely. Such a shift in the electoral and parliamentary balance of power would have a disorienting impact not only on the FDP, but also on the established process of coalition politics in Germany in which the Liberals have played a crucial role for decades.

Such speculative concerns aside, there are more immediate qualifications to the FDP's victory of 1990. The most important political outcome has been the institutional extension of the West German party system, with some modifications, into the East. In uniting itself with the rival Liberal parties of the East, the FDP contributed significantly to this process. The transfer has also been impressive because it could not be taken for granted. Yet as it is still in its initial phase, its stability remains uncertain. A year and a half after the election there are growing signs of estrangement among Eastern voters who may yet seek expression outside the transplanted party system with its convenient absorption of the old bloc parties. The political disillusionment among Easterners may well be more serious than the much discussed *Parteienverdrossenheit* of the West. In confronting potential voter disaffection, the FDP shares the boat with the other traditional parties yet has a lot more to lose if a considerable number of voters begin drifting away from the new political establishment.

There are no regular elections scheduled in the new states until 1994, but there are signs that the political party system of united Germany is not yet firmly in place. One dramatic indicator is provided by the membership losses for the Liberals in the new states – down from about 136,000 to 58,000 in less than two years (see Table 5.1). Analysts had expected a large falling-off after unification, but in some places the drop has been stunning. Genscher's home region of Saxony-Anhalt registered the sharpest fall of all, from about 29,000 registered FDP members to little more than 9,000. Still, polls indicate a considerable backing for the FDP in Eastern Germany and much of the electoral trends in the near future will depend on whether there is enough economic revival in the region before 1994 to give Easterners more hope and faith in the institutions and leaders they have largely inherited. It cannot be ruled out that some voters may shed a seemingly prevailing apathy and make more explicit social policy demands than hitherto.

The FDP finds itself in a different kind of pivotal position. Over the years it has become strongly identified as a *Wirtschaftspartei*, though it has a "social-liberal" tradition as well and there are signs that this end of the political spectrum could be revived within the small party. The new Eastern members of the party tend to have a stronger social orientation than their Western counterparts. Carola von Braun, the leader of the FDP in Berlin and now a member of the party presidium, is the most prominent of several leaders who have begun an attempt to organize and give expression to leftist-liberal views within the party's so-called *Elbe Kreis*.[13] It seems appropriate that she is a Westerner, she who owes her Berlin post to support from party members in the eastern part of the city. The outcome of this social-liberal venture will depend, at least in part, upon whether the Eastern membership figures continue to plummet or stabilize around their present number, already somewhat below the total for the West.

Even before national unification the FDP was aware that it needed to consider far-reaching organizational and programmatic revisions. It also must confront a long-delayed generational shift in leadership. In April 1992 Genscher announced his intention to resign after almost twenty-three years in the cabinet, eighteen of them as Foreign Minister. His replacement, Klaus Kinkel, has surprised many by quickly abandoning his administrative habits and showing impressive political talent. Just two years after becoming a formal member of the FDP, he is already spoken of as a serious candidate to replace Otto von Lambsdorff when the latter's term ends in 1993. There are other candidates in the wings, including the ambitious self-promoter Jürgen Möllemann, a previously unsuccessful candidate, Irmgard Schwaetzer, and the perennial dark horse, Wolfgang Gerhart. Until now, at least, no one has discovered a strong political talent among the Liberals from the East, although a number have been given prominent positions – for example, Rainer Ortleb as minister of education and Uwe Lühr as secretary-general of the FDP. The Liberals have not yet come fully to terms with the partly tainted legacy the LDPD and NDPD acquired at the time of party unification. On the whole the FDP seems to have been less embarrassed than the CDU or SPD by the charges linking prominent Eastern politicians to the repressive practices of the party-and-police state in the GDR, even though the Liberal closet is still not empty of political skeletons. The FDP appears to have been more insistently acquisitive than the CDU in making claims to property that belonged to the formerly privileged bloc parties in the GDR, and there could be still more embarrassments to come, given the present level of criticism of the parties as self-serving institutions in Germany.

13. See the 16 Theses contained in the group's proposal submitted in advance of the 1992 party conference, *Zu den Aufgaben des Liberalismus im zusammenwachsenden Deutschland* (On the Tasks Facing Liberalism in a Uniting Germany).

One of the main problems for the Liberals in "getting their act together" as a party may lie in the fact that they are spread far too thin by the day-to-day politics of governing and electioneering. Ralf Dahrendorf once recommended that the party take another hiatus in the opposition in order to regenerate itself as it had done between 1966 and 1969. Yet this is asking a lot from politicians, especially in a party that is constantly reminded of its political mortality in the never-ending series of electoral bouts. Now that there are 16 states in the Federal Republic, some Liberals have discovered a preference for concentrating the regular state contests on a few dates rather than leaving them spread out as now. Whatever else happens, there will be a short respite because no state elections are planned for 1993. It remains to be seen whether this respite will give the FDP a chance to recuperate and begin some self-reform. The leadership turnover will preoccupy the party, though it could end up providing the impetus for other important changes as well.

It is probably unrealistic to expect the small party to undergo any major transformation. In the past the FDP repeatedly showed itself adept at adjusting to changing political weather and surviving political threats to its existence. On occasion it has even managed to deal with pressing needs for change in its program, strategy and leadership. However, it has yet to show any skill in turning one of its occasional electoral breakthroughs into a broader and more solid base. In mid-1992 there is little evidence that the FDP has found a way to consolidate its gains. The party has enjoyed relatively good standing in the polls since 1990, but in each of the four state elections between January and September 1991 it registered marginal setbacks while still managing to clear the five percent hurdle in all of them (see Table 10.1). In Baden-Württemberg in 1992 the FDP was unable to improve upon its low share of votes of four years earlier. In Schleswig-Holstein, however, it returned to the parliament in Kiel (with 5.6 percent), after spending four years without representation. The return had some symbolic importance for the FDP, as for the first time since 1978 it is represented in all the state parliaments of the Federal Republic. In each of the two state races, however, the FDP lagged behind a right-wing populist party – the Republicans in Baden-Württemberg, and the German People's Union (DVU) in Schleswig-Holstein. Such results are apt to revive the FDP's recurring nightmare of a major shift in the party balance of power mentioned earlier.

The present political uncertainties in German party politics make it seem very likely that the FDP will continue to carry on as before, stressing even more its functional argument as a Liberal coalition party. It is, after all, a party whose importance derives from its special additive character in government. Such a self-presentation need not rely on scare tactics or, as we now know, the construction of a *Buhmann* to take the place of Franz Josef Strauss. The current spate of right-wing activism in German electoral politics might lead the FDP to reassert its civil libertarian role within the coalition. There is reason to believe that a large part of the electorate, including many voters who do not regularly support the FDP, will continue to be comfortable with the special "checks and balances" of coalition government provided by the Liberals. The Free Democrats may rediscover that their well-established functional appeal can be made more effective with the electorate than their search for the as yet elusive new "potential" of unattached voters, who supposedly can be drawn to the small party as best representing their own "liberal" predispositions or life-styles (IPOS, 1991).

The FDP will probably continue to find it difficult to explain to its voters a change of coalition partners. Past experience suggests that many coalition supporters react negatively to what they perceive as betrayal by a small government party. Eventually, however, the change will have to come – and it need not be handled as clumsily as in 1982. The end of a legislative period is probably the most credible time for announcing an intention to change partners, unless a major conflict forces the issue in mid-term. The FDP is itself constrained by the balance of power within the German party system. As a classic small coalition party, it can only shift when and if a new balance makes such a move both arithmetically and politically possible.

References

Ammer, Thomas. 1991. *Die Parteien in der DDR und in den neuen Bundesländer*. Typewritten manuscript, 10 June.

Beerfeltz, Hans-Jürgen. 1991. 'Analyse der Bundestagswahl 1990. *Die liberale Depesche*. No. 2, February, pp. 22–25.

Berndt, Rolf. 1990. *Wiedervereinigung als Organisationsproblem. Gesamtdeutsche Zusammenschlüsse von Parteien und Verbänden*. Typewritten report. Bonn: FDP.

Berndt, Rolf and Hans-Jürgen Beerfeltz. 1990. *Der liberale Wahlkampf in der DDR*. Typewritten report. Bonn: FDP.

Die neue Bonner Depesche and *Die liberale Depesche*. Bonn: FDP. Monthly membership magazine of the Free Democratic Party. The name change took place in September 1990, at the time of the unification congress.

Forschungsgruppe Wahlen e.V. 1990. *Bundestagswahl 1990. Eine Analyse der ersten Gesamtdeutschen Bundestagswahl am 2. Dezember 1990*. Mannheim: Forschungsgruppe Wahlen, Report No. 61.

Friedrich Naumann Foundation. 1990. *Parteien und Wahlbündnisse in der DDR. Programme und Statuten*. Königswinter.

Generalsekretär der FDP. *Informationsbriefe*. (Regular information letters from the party general secretary to FDP officeholders.)

Gerlach, Manfred. 1991. *Mitverantwortlich. Als Liberaler im SED-Staat*. Berlin: Morgenbuch Verlag.

IPOS. 1991. *Liberales Potential in Westdeutschland. Oktober 1991*. Bericht. Mannheim: IPOS.

Kirchner, Emil J. and David Broughton. 1988. "The FDP in the Federal Republic of Germany: The Requirements of Survival and Success." In *Liberal Parties in Western Europe*. Edited by Emil J. Kirchner. Cambridge: Cambridge University Press, pp. 62–93.

Lapp, Peter Joachim. 1988. *Die 'befreundeten Parteien' der SED. DDR-Blockparteien heute*. Cologne: Verlag Wissenschaft und Politik.

Ritter, Gerhard A. and Merith Niehuss. 1991. *Wahlen in Deutschland 1946–1991*, Munich: Verlag C.H. Beck.

Schiller, Theo. 1991. "Die FDP nach dem Beitritt: Gestärkt auf wackligen Beinen." *Die Neue Gesellschaft*. No. 2, pp. 158–163.

Søe, Christian. 1985. "The Free Democratic Party." In *West German Politics in the Mid-Eighties*. Edited by H.G. Peter Wallach and George K. Romoser. New York: Praeger, pp. 112–186.

______. 1989. "'Not Without Us!' The FDP's Survival, Position, and Influence." In *The Federal Republic of Germany at Forty*. Edited by Peter H. Merkl. New York: New York University Press.

______. 1990. "The Free Democratic Party: Two Victories and a Political

Realignment." In *Germany at the Polls. The Bundestag Elections of the 1980s*. Edited by Karl H. Cerny. Durham, NC: Duke University Press.

Statistisches Bundesamt. 1992a. *Wahl zum 12. Deutschen Bundestag am 2. Dezember 1990*. Heft 3. Endgültige Ergebnisse nach Wahlkreisen. Stuttgart: Kohlhammer.

Statistisches Bundesamt. 1992b. *Wahl zum 12. Deutschen Bundestag am 2. Dezember 1990*. Heft 4. Wahlbeteiligung der Männer und Frauen nach dem Alter. Stuttgart: Kohlhammer.

Süss, Walter. 1992. "Streit um Vermögen der DDR-Parteien: Die delegierte Revolution." *Das Parlament*, No. 21, 15 May, p. 9.

Veen, Hans-Joachim, Marcel Bulla, Jürgen Hoffmann, Norbert Lepszy, and Matthias Zimmer. 1990. *DDR-Parteien im Vereinigungsprozess*. Sankt Augustin. Forschungsinstitut der Konrad-Adenauer-Stiftung. Interne Studien, Nr. 20/1990. 24 September.

Vorländer, Hans. 1990. "Die FDP zwischen Erfolg und Existenzgefährdung." In *Parteien in der Bundesrepublik Deutschland*. Edited by Alf Mintzel and Heinrich Oberreuter. Bonn: Bundeszentrale fur politische Bildung.

______. 1992. "Die FDP nach der deutschen Vereinigung." In *Aus Politik und Zeitgeschichte*. Beilage zur Wochenzeitung *Das Parlament*. B 5/92. 24 January, pp. 14–20.

6

Disunited Greens in a United Germany: The All-German Election of December 1990 and Its Aftermath

Donald Schoonmaker and E. Gene Frankland

As a result of the West German Greens' failure to gain representation in the Bundestag on 2 December 1990, the future prospects of the Greens and the allied citizen movements of the East on the national level in united Germany are problematic. Without a superior organization effort from party activists who have been disdainful of the "organizational imperative," the Green party project may well go down in history as a one-generational effort that brought new issues onto the policy agenda and then lost its focus, and eventually its influence. Intra-party wrangling, improved inter-party competition from the SPD, and ineffective coordination with the Eastern Alliance '90/Greens (*Bündnis '90/Grünen*) all contributed to the party's decline. Furthermore, it will probably be noted in history that the New Left postmaterialist Greens lost some of their appeal in the 1990s from their core group of the new middle class when the material issues relating to the reconstruction of Eastern Germany came to the fore. Postmaterialist parties, as organizations, appear to be precarious vehicles for "New Politics" issues, especially when the political maneuvering room to the left of a reform-oriented social democratic party gets smaller, and when economic issues come to dominate the policy agenda.

To get an overview of these prospects for the Greens and their Eastern counterparts, let us start with some impressions of the night of the all-German elections on 2 December 1990. After that, we will review to the recent pattern of party development of the

Greens in the West and the Alliance '90/Greens in the East. Finally, we will move forward to more recent events: the election campaign of 1990, the results of the election and the consequences for the party, the clear signs of reform suggested by the state election-tallies of 1991 and 1992, and the outcome of the national party conference in April 1991. The defeat of the Western Greens in December 1990 appears now to have provided the impetus for a clearer party identity and the possibility of real electoral cooperation with its Eastern counterparts. We shall conclude with comments on the future prospects of the Greens in a united Germany, drawing upon some "theories" that students of politics have offered up about New Left parties.

Election Night

The Greens began the decade of the 1980s by founding a party "unlike the others" in Karlsruhe after often chaotic and tumultuous debates. At the end of the decade, in early December 1990, the voters in the Western part of Germany halted their experiment on the national level. The Greens knew that they were whistling in the dark during the 1990 Bundestag campaign, but they still were *not* prepared for this eviction notice from parliament. The success of Kohl's CDU and the FDP was to be expected, and the defeat of the SPD was not surprising either, as their expected eastern strength never materialized. The ouster of the Greens, however, caused great surprise. While the television anchor on election evening kept pushing for a prediction on the Greens as the returns were coming in, the harried Mannheim pollsters kept asking for more time. By nine o'clock that evening it was clear that the Greens in Western Germany would not get above the 5 percent hurdle needed to gain representation in the Bundestag. The 6 percent won by the Alliance '90/Greens of the East granted them representation. The alternative party of the future was now a non-parliamentary party of the past.

The party that petitioned the Federal Constitutional Court for an electoral law giving special consideration to minor parties of the East lost out, while its Eastern counterpart won eight seats. Sensitivity about the Eastern Alliance '90/Greens autonomy had prevented an all-German Green party from forming that would have given a united Green party enough votes for 5.1 percent or

34 seats in the Bundestag. Although the formal merger of the East Greens and the West Greens did take place on the day *after* the election, as planned, it was under circumstances that neither party could have imagined. Instead of getting ready for new policy ideas, the Bonn staff had a special group meeting with the local unemployment office.

In one fell swoop, a lively New Left opposition party with over 40 deputies – the largest parliamentary representation of all such parties in Europe, with its more than 200 staff members – was virtually eliminated as an alternative political force in Bonn. The interpretations given by Green activists and other political commentators on this debacle were candid and direct. Hubert Kleinert of the Federal Steering Committee complained the Greens had used up their political credit; they had tried to defy the laws of political physics and now the time for a thorough housecleaning (party reforms) among the Greens was at hand. Wolfgang Ullmann, a newly elected deputy from the Alliance '90 noted that, sorry as he was to say it, the *Kasperltheatre* antics of the Western Greens had not served them well. The *Frankfurter Rundschau* lamented the demise of the Western Greens and the degeneration of a party of such great creativity and innovation into self-absorbed factionalists who lost their way in a paper chase (*Schnitzeljagd*). Theo Sommer of *Die Zeit* spoke somewhat cavalierly of the Greens as being the fertilizer on the fields of the classical parties. Walter Momper of the Berlin SPD, in a comment reflecting his disgust with the Alternative List (Green) party in West Berlin, said that the Greens were an *"auslaufendes Modell,"* a phased-out model.

A day after the election, leading moderates Joschka Fischer and Antje Vollmer met the press corps in Bonn and stated that the bill had come due for badly needed organizational reforms. They said that the cold water of this defeat could provide the stimulus for the party to begin the process of renewal, and their suggested reforms hinted at a more pragmatic, centrally-controlled party. As soon as they finished their comments, Jutta Ditfurth, leader of the fundamentalist wing, told the press that such reforms would spell the end of the Green movement-party and its radical democratic tradition. Thus did the reform impulse start on a typically Green note of antipathy toward unanimity.

Are reports on the death of the Greens greatly exaggerated?

While most political analysts attributed the defeat of the Greens of the West to their ambivalence or *Sprachlosigkeit* on the issue of German unity, the reasons for defeat had long term causes as well as short term precipitating effects, and these must be assessed in order to comment on the future of the Greens.

The East German Revolution and the Green Response

1989 began as a year of promise for the Greens of West Germany, but it ended with the issue of German unity confronting them. As we will see, unification unsettled an already unclear political identity and led to its defeat in the December 1990 election, its dismissal from the Bundestag, and, finally, pushed the party to the center and resolved the struggle between the left radicals and the left-center reformers in favor of the latter. ·

The optimism felt in early 1989 by the Western Greens rested on the 11.8 percent vote tallied in West Berlin. This was one of its highest votes ever and led to a coalition with the SPD. In June, the Greens increased their European vote from the 8.2 percent in 1984 to 8.4 percent. On the state level in both North Rhine-Westphalia and Rhineland-Palatinate the party increased its share of the vote from 1984. On both the subnational and supra-national level the party was showing confidence and strength. In contrast, the national party in Bonn was still quarreling, loudly and openly, between the purist *Fundis* (opposition in principle; no coalitions) and the moderate *Realos* (constructive opposition; coalitions if possible). Even with these roiled waters, the public opinion polls still gave the Greens hope for success in the next national election (see Figure 1.1, Party Support in West).

Though the elections in West Germany were quite normal, the local elections in May in East Germany and their aftermath sent shock waves throughout the ruling SED (Socialist Unity Party or Communist Party of East Germany), a clear sign that "normality" on the East side of the Wall was soon to end. When Egon Krenz announced on election evening that 98.85 percent had voted for the National Front's Communist-dominated candidate slate, most East Germans probably barely noticed. Yet, for the first time in the history of the GDR a group of critical dissidents did notice and made outspoken charges of election manipulation and corruption (Knabe, 1989: 14). Because the nomination process for these elections had been controversial, church groups asked citizens to either not vote or vote "No" – both qualifying as acts of defiance with possibly criminal consequences under this regime. The groups also sent election observers to watch the count. There were obvious discrepancies that the groups reported, both in the number of "no" votes and in the participation rate. The 20 percent of votes that the observers counted in these categories did not square with Krenz's 98.85 percent. Manipulated exercises in unanimity were creating bolder critics.

The public outcry of anger and scorn, including ads in newspapers about vote tampering, had built up over two decades of increasing disillusionment with a rigid authoritarian state. These negative feelings, slowly and perceptibly, were eroding the state's legitimacy (Kuehnel et al., 1990: 25). Beginning with the Prague spring of 1968 and continuing on through the forced emigration of Wolf Biermann in 1976, the movement for reform in Poland and Hungary, and the support given *glasnost* and democratization by Gorbachev in the Soviet Union, the forces for change were growing in East Germany.[1]

The Protestant church was an institution of crucial importance for those citizens who refused to conform politically. It provided sanctuary or *Schutzraum* (protective space) for the peace groups, human rights organizations, and ecology groups from which most of the leadership for the citizen movement groups of the fall of 1989 issued (Dähn, 1982; Klessmann, 1991: 61). The SED had assumed that by granting the church some autonomy from state control a safety valve had been created to let off steam. Yet, as became obvious a decade or so later, they had miscalculated their political "physics"; the steam built up and was channeled through preacher-activists like Friedrich Schlorlemmer and Wolfgang Ullmann who became political leaders. The lid finally blew off in the fall of 1989 when the dissidents went public and helped

1. Some of the background information to support the arguments for the loss of legitimacy, especially among critical members of the intelligentsia, comes from interviews with all eight members of Alliance '90/Greens Bundestag delegation in early June of 1991. Those interviewed were Konrad Weiss and Wolfgang Ullmann (Democracy Now), Vera Wollenberger and Klaus Feige (The Greens), Werner Schulz and Ingrid Koeppe (New Forum), Gerd Poppe (Initiative for Peace and Human Rights and Christina Schenk (Independent Women's Group). Deputy Koeppe clearly staked out a dissident role early in 1976 by being the only person in her educational institution who refused to sign a petition against Wolf Biermann's actions. See the extensive interview which she gives in Gaus (1990).

mobilize the street demonstrations that brought down the state.[2]

In the late spring of 1989 those dissidents still constituted a very small minority, yet the unyielding hard line of the German Democratic Republic as compared to the reforms of Hungary and Poland was eroding the Communist party's legitimacy.[3] The Greens of West Germany showed as little interest in the election fraud in East Germany as the East Germans did in the European election, yet fast-breaking events would soon set German-German affairs on a common track that would eventually lead to one Germany and sizable political problems for the Greens.

August began with what one East German observer later called the *Erdrutsch* (earthquake). Hungary had removed border fences with Austria in May, creating an opening in the fortified border that East Germans quickly discovered (Hamilton, 1990: 6). Ignoring the trickle at first, the official party newspaper, *Neues Deutschland*, maintained its hard line – "The Wall will not come down as long as those conditions which led to its building exist. . . . " However, by late August it became clear that East Germany was feeling increasingly isolated from its Bloc allies as the trickle of emigres increased to a steady flow (Boegeholz, 1990: 300–301).

The demonstrations that began in Leipzig in early September created an extraordinary political atmosphere that rapidly led to the "retirement" of party leader Honecker; the breaching of the Wall in Berlin on 9 November; the removal of the Communist party; the "capturing" of the files of the State Security (the *Stasi*); the establishment of a transitional government led by Hans Modrow; and the negotiations with West Germany on future contractual relations. East German citizen movements – the core of the present Alliance '90 – played an historic role in what some have termed the first successful peaceful democratic revolution in Germany. This time the communists could not do what Bertold Brecht had satirically suggested at the time of the mass revolt in 1953 – simply "elect" another people.

2. Schlorlemmer was a leader in the formation of Democratic Awakening before it allied itself with the CDU and consequently became a SPD member. Ullmann was a founder of Democracy Now, one of the citizen movement groups of Alliance '90 and is currently a member of the Bundestag.

3. While the Greens celebrated a solid vote in June 1989 in the Euro-vote, the communist leadership in East Germany announced its support for the suppression of Chinese students in Tiananmen Square and criticized reformer Modrow and Hungary for their support for *glasnost* in the Soviet Union.

Wir sind das Volk; Wir sind ein Volk
(We are the people; we are one people)

The citizen groups that showed such courage in challenging the dictatorial, well-armed state had several aims. They wanted to stop their fellow citizens from emigrating and they wanted constitutional and democratic reforms. The crowds that gathered in early November in numbers up to a half-million shouted, "We are the people." That phrase expressed their right to self-determination, to real elections, to civil liberties. The most influential citizen group, New Forum, embodied this non-violent, democratic and constitutional program. It believed in reforming East Germany into an ideal of democratic socialism, neither capitalist nor SED-socialist. New Forum clearly espoused a two German state position.

When the crowds in late November cried, "We are one people," the citizen movement groups were thrown off balance. They had envisaged a leisurely transitional period during which East Germany could formulate a new constitution based on extensive participation; only after that would some type of arrangement be worked out with West Germany. They had not expected the train toward unity to move at the great speed it did. Although they had been on the cutting edge as the true heroes who overthrew the old regime they were not to be the shapers of the new one. A reformed SED group under Hans Modrow took over in December when the Krenz government simply collapsed. Modrow pulled the citizen movement groups into his government to lend it support, but the great majority of Easterners were not ready for any extended discussions:

> faced with the relentless exodus of tens of thousands of fellow citizens, a crumbling economy, and a catastrophic health care situation, confronted daily with revelations of the Old Guard's systematic abuse of power, and casting an apprehensive glance at the economic disaster afflicting other reformist states in Eastern Europe, the East German people looked quickly for a short-cut to prosperity and democracy. That short-cut became unification (Hamilton, 1990: 13).

The citizen movement groups, especially New Forum, Democracy Now, Initiative for Peace and Human Rights, the Greens, and the Independent Women's Association (all eventually members of Alliance '90/Greens as well as partners of the Western

Greens) had to learn the democratic game of "hardball" politics in short order.[4] They actively participated in the Roundtable discussions with Modrow's government and the bloc parties that the Communist regime had propped up since 1950 (Thyssen, 1990). As soon as the date for free elections of the *Volkskammer* was in sight, however, another dynamic came into play. James Madison says that liberty is to faction as air is to fire, an indispensable element. Capitalizing on the sudden liberty in the newly accessible East, the major West German parties hustled to "empower" their sister parties. But the citizen movements cried foul, cursing the "colonizers" for contaminating their politics with mass advertising, public relations hoopla, and organized "spontaneous" demonstrations. And yet, the citizen groups ended up being drowned out by the tumult and hurly burly of modern West German campaigning techniques.

The Greens of the West were confused by the rapidly changing events on the Eastern side. They cheered the dismantling of the Wall, and identified quite obviously with the dissidents – mainly peaceniks, feminists, ecologists, decentralist democratizers, and human rights activists – who formed citizen movements to help shape a democratic and constitutional German Democratic Republic. But as each day went by in early 1990, and the wasted human and natural resources of the GDR came more clearly to light, they could sense the groundswell for a quick unification, an impatience with constitutional discussion, and dwindling interest in the merits of two Germanies or a loose confederation. The dissident groups and the Western Greens still hoped to avoid a leveraged buyout, or what some were calling an *Anschluss* (annexation), but the Eastern population, about to vote in the first democratic election in fifty-seven years, were listening more attentively to the major parties of the West.

Joschka Fischer of the Hesse Greens said in February 1990 that the Greens had to accept unification, though he had in mind a confederation following considerable time for constitutional discussion. Antje Vollmer, a Green Bundestag deputy, visited Halle

---

4. There were other citizen movement groups working with the groups that eventually made up Alliance '90/Greens, but one group, Democratic Awakening, moved to the right of center, and another, United Left, moved too far too the left and had too many former SED members for the Alliance '90/Green activists.

in the East, but the options she held out were confederation or a plebiscite for a new constitution (*Frankfurter Rundschau* and *Frankfurter Allgemeine Zeitung*, 7 February 1990). The debate within the Western Greens ranged from leftist support for two Germanies to a moderate wing that spoke of honoring the democratic voice of East Germany. The Western Greens extended some support behind the scenes to the citizen movements and the small Green party, but the Eastern sister movements and party clearly wanted little Western help. In the *Frankfurter Allgemeine Zeitung*, Guenter Bannas summarized the views of Alliance '90 and Green groups: They did not want identification with a Western party riddled by factional disputes. They preferred to put their own individual stamp on this decisive election, and they held to the principles of the Round Table – no election campaigners from outside. One subtext to this fear of being "domesticated" (annexed) by outsiders was the feeling by Easterners that technical assistance was acceptable but that attempts to influence policy or provide outside speakers were to be rejected (Bannas, 1990).

The Greens of West Germany shared this distaste for the massive intervention on the part of the Western *Volksparteien* in East German politics. They, too, were perplexed and upset at the tempo with which plans for national unity were moving. Like the Eastern citizen movements, they had long invested much emotional capital in avoiding a unified Germany and they preferred two Germanies, not one Germany expanded by means of, in their eyes, Kohl's power politics and the Deutsche Mark.

The debate among the Western Greens on the national unity question speaks volumes about their identity crisis and subsequent defeat in the all-German December election. Although the Greens inveighed regularly against the taboos of the uptight Bonn Republic, one of their own major taboos was reconstituting the national state. They had earlier pushed to remove the clause for unification from the preamble of the Basic Law and their position over the years had been to advocate two Germanies independent of the major blocs. The Greens were many things to many people, but they were not *nationalists*. They feared the consequences of unification. The issue left the party confused, ambivalent, and discordant. All at once, the Greens' policy positions on de-militarization, bloc dissolution, and the reduction and withdrawal of troops lost much of their edge. The ground beneath the feet of eco-socialists (the group that took socio-economic structural change seriously) began to move when the full consequences of real existing socialism became more widely known (Schily, 1990: 196; Stein and Ulrich, 1991: 75; Horacek, 1991: 98–106). As Ralf Fücks of the Green party Executive Committee put it, Kohl seized the initiative while "The Greens, in contrast, . . . attached themselves to the two state concept and the emergence of the third way, which the economically, politically, and morally ruined East Germany should follow." For many Green activists, the new Germany would become the Fourth Reich. Others argued, openly and publicly, over how the two state concept could work, how the "third way" could be followed, and whether unification should take place, after the public debate had already shifted to *how* it should be done (Fücks, 1991: 33).

The March 1990 *Volkskammer* election cleared the air of the speculations of the Greens (see Table 1.2 in Chapter one). *Das Volk* had spoken and it wanted to be *ein Volk* as soon as possible. The Eastern Greens and the Independent Women's Association had jointly received 2 percent of the vote. Alliance '90 – the citizen groups – received 2.9 percent. The critical issue of the election was the timetable for unity and the parties allied with the Christian Democrats and Free Democrats won a mandate for "the quicker, the better" (see chapters by Kuechler, and Norpoth and Roth in this volume). The election was both a reality check and a wake-up call for the Greens of the West and Alliance '90/Greens of the East. Without the pure proportional electoral system neither the Alliance nor the Greens would have received representation in the *Volkskammer*. With over 93 percent of the citizenry voting, the Alliance for Germany (the major center-right parties of the West allied with their Eastern parties) received 48 percent. The issues on which the Alliance '90 and the Greens had campaigned – constitutional issues, unity via confederation, the plan for ecological restructuring, dealing with the *Stasi* – were at the bottom of the agenda for most East Germans. One major issue dominated this election as it was to dominate the December election: the fast track to German unity (Gibowski, 1990).

In between the Volkskammer elections and the May local elections in the GDR, the Greens in West Germany met for an extraordinary conference in Hagen.

144

The Hagen Conference: The Elusive Search for a Green Identity

The consequences of the 18 March East German election were clear to all political forces, and the message for the SPD and the Greens was unmistakable. There would be no measured pace toward one Germany. There would be few constitutional debates, and the economic disaster of the GDR, which was being daily more revealed, called for massive and quick help from the rich uncle to the West. All of these issues provided the Hagen Conference of late March 1990 with an opportunity for Green party definition in a time of decisive defining moments.

The moderate center of the party (*Aufbruch* or Awakening and the *Realos*), led by Antje Vollmer, stated their case with clarity: The Greens of the West should be primarily an ecological-civil rights party of non-dogmatic leftists, not a leftist-socialist ecological party. Fischer, Ralf Fücks, and Ruth Hammerbacher also advocated an ecological reform party energized by a civil rights platform concerned with Eastern and Western citizen movements and parties. This conception of the party would have a distinct profile and be open to sharing power with the SPD. It would also work in cooperation with the Eastern movements and Green party, while respecting their autonomy.

Vollmer's centrist group lost at Hagen without the leftist-socialists winning, and the political identity of the Greens thus remained muddled in a critical election year. By their choices for the Federal Executive Council and by the leftist clichés regarding capitalism in several resolutions, the Green party delegates left their party unity in an unresolved state. The *Neue Zuericher Zeitung* of Switzerland summed up the significance of the Hagen Conference:

> The party conference in Hagen showed in its totality the contradictions and confusions as a further aspect of the decline of the Greens as a political force in the Federal Republic of Germany. The party has been marginalized further by the unification issue (*Neue Zuericher Zeitung*, 3 April 1990).

Yet the Hagen Conference had made some progress. The Greens said goodbye to the idea of two German states without giving any clear definition about what they wanted instead. They did distance themselves from the PDS (successor to the SED-

Communist party of East Germany), but without enough finality for some Greens. And they did speak forthrightly on the ecological challenge for the new Germany, the problems women faced, the need for a new definition of citizenship (*jus solis* not *jus sanguis*), and the need for multicultural tolerance. Finally, for the first time a Green of East Germany spoke at a West German Green conference. Friedrich Heilmann of East Berlin praised the efforts of the Western Greens but also pointedly noted: "We do not want to be drawn into your factional disputes" (Bannas, 1990).

Heilmann's comments in April proved prophetic about the realistic chances for party coordination or integration between the Greens (West) and what had become Alliance '90/Greens (East). Both groups shared many of the common ideals in the Hagen Protocol, yet there would be precious few Western Greens speaking in the East and vice-versa. The parties would run on separate lists in separate geographical spaces, and though some Eastern citizen movement activists would show up on a party list in North Rhine-Westphalia, that would be the exception and not the rule.

At Hagen they also passed a resolution recognizing the inevitability of unification (Protocol of the Extraordinary Conference of the Greens, Hagen, 30 April to 1 May 1990). Even with this bow toward political reality the Greens were soon to be left at the station for they did not want the fast train to unity even as it was well underway. The Western Greens had inhibitions stemming from their principles of not forcing an alliance with the citizen movements of the East, but that "train" had been boarded by the other parties months ago. It was not until September that a formal arrangement with the citizen movements of the East had been accomplished. In June, a long-time observer of the Greens (Bieber, 1990) summed up their plight:

> The German-German union, in principle accepted unwillingly and in its constitutional form rejected, brings the Greens to the all-German election in the dangerous proximity of not jumping the 5 percent electoral hurdle. A Green-Green alliance would help out in this dilemma, but the eastern Greens are far from this. Many West German positions and styles of doing things don't suit them.

Bieber was incorrect on the second part. A marriage of convenience was worked out for the December election, but his instincts were correct on the question of the survival of the Western Greens.

The All-German Election Campaign

The final party conferences at Magdeburg in the East and Bayreuth in the West in September 1990 did help the party put together a common platform. At Bayreuth, the Alliance '90/Greens agreed to fuse with the Greens of the West after the December election. Thus, all the attempts at an all-German Green party-movement slate came down to this formula: common ideals and goals but separate campaigns in separate spheres. However organizationally distinct the parties, the Bayreuth platform showed great skill in formulating the common tradition of a Green-citizen movement political force.

Bayreuth, a Bavarian town near the East German border, drew together five hundred Green delegates who took the ideas of the Hagen and Magdeburg conferences and cast them into campaign phrases and slogans. The banners in the hall at Bayreuth read: "Without us all will be black/red/gold" (Germany's national colors); "Defeat Kohl"; "The Green/Rainbow Alternative to Deutschland, Deutschland über alles".

The preamble from this conference noted that the citizen movements and the Eastern Greens joined with the Western Greens in criticizing "the traditional parties, their power politics, and the need for a new definition of the 'quality of life'." They described their common task of striving for a society of "solidarity and ecological concern which is democratically radical, constitutional, emancipatory and feminist, nonviolent and multicultural." Calling for imaginative political activity *inside* and *outside* parliament, they pledged to fight the replacement of the command economy of the GDR with an unregulated market economy of glaring inequalities. Speaking for a European Germany, they called for an expansion of the Conference on Security and Cooperation in Europe rather than building up NATO. They concluded with an appraisal of what had brought this common platform about:

> Out of the experiences of our opposition to the one-party dictatorship of the GDR and the corresponding battle against the economically-dominated party democracy of the FRG, we want to join ranks to offer a strong alternative. We will be attentive to the identity of the partici-

pating groups and work together on the foundation of the common program (*Die Gruenen: Wochenzeitung* 39 / 1990).

Promulgated several days before the official celebration of German unity on 3 October the campaign platform of the combined parties/movements of East and West offered a distinct option to the German voters, not only on the unification underway but also on the future of the new Germany.

The prospect of German unification caught many, inside and outside Germany, off-balance. The fragmentation of the Soviet empire in Eastern Europe, the breaching of the Wall, and the rapid psychological transition from *"Wir sind das Volk"* to *"Wir sind ein Volk"* left the Greens (West) on the wrong side of history. Thus the all-German election campaign began with the Greens having very little to say on an issue that dwarfed all the others. The unification issue was the dominant theme, and the Greens represented a position that was out of touch with many of their supporters. As the Mannheim Group noted: "The rejection of German unity by the Greens had no majority in its own electorate. On the contrary, 66 percent of the Green electorate were for it even if enthusiasm was not that of the flag-waving CDU" (Forschungsgruppe Wahlen, 1990a: 72).

Attempts to substitute the endangered climate of the planet and fears of the ozone hole (the thrust of the Green electoral campaign) for the public's concerns about unification left the Western Greens in a hole of their own. The Greens' chances for success were further reduced when their major competitor, the SPD, chose Oskar Lafontaine as its Chancellor candidate. Lafontaine aimed right at their new middle-class constituency with issues that the Greens had popularized since the early 1980s. In other words, he moved the SPD to the left, reducing "the hunting ground" (Panebianco, 1988) of the Greens. Finally, as noted above, the Greens remained constant to their principles of recognizing the autonomy of the citizen movements and Greens in Eastern Germany. They refrained from the kind of organizational takeovers the major parties had engineered. Moreover, they petitioned the Federal Constitutional Court to allow for smaller parties to gain representation by getting 5 percent of the vote in either East or West, instead of the new Germany being the single electoral area. Running independently from their Eastern German counterparts showed them to be true decentralists, and not very far-sighted strategists.

The state elections in Bavaria and the elections to the new state parliaments in the five new Eastern *Länder* in October 1990 gave mixed messages to the Greens of the West. The Bavarian Greens had no trouble gaining representation in the state parliament, although their percentage of votes dropped from what it had been four years previously, while environmental issues had gained in salience with the voters. Still, they had won 6.4 percent of the votes, outpolled the FDP, and showed that local organization and a position not too far from the center would be rewarded. The state elections in the East brought slightly larger percentages for the Alliance '90/Green parties, except in Mecklenburg-West Pomerania where the citizen movement and the Greens could not develop a workable alliance. With well over 6 percent of the vote, they received no seats there. However, the clearest signal that emerged was that the parties promoting a faster track to unification were still favored by a large majority of Easterners. The tempo of unification was *the* major issue in the East and West (Norpoth and Roth in this volume).

The Bundestag campaign of the Western Greens exhibited some of that peculiar amateurism that had been their trademark for over a decade, though in this election the appeal fell flat. Their slogan, "Everybody talks about Germany, we speak about the weather," as a way of asserting the priority of environmental issues over the fixation on unification was an example of their being too clever by half. The public opinion polls indicated quite starkly the importance of the economic and constitutional issues surrounding German unity. The Greens' use of a whistle-stop train tour throughout Germany to call attention to the climate catastrophe and the ozone hole was an example of focusing on the wrong topic at the wrong time. Ineffective use of the media, inadequate "showcasing" of their leading party personalities, and continual wrangling by various party members made this campaign a forgettable one for many Green supporters. It was not enough to inveigh against Deutschmark nationalism; a much more specific critique was expected by the voters. On the Eastern side, the true amateurs, Alliance '90/Greens, were at work in their first Bundestag campaign. Outspent, outorganized, and overwhelmed by the role that the media played in electoral politics, the Eastern party played a plucky game but their ideas regarding how the new Germany should come to be collided with the wishes of their countrymen. Though they did manage to garner the votes needed to clear the 5 percent hurdle, their best effort had yielded them only eight seats.

Green party activists knew that the election would be close. In September one of the reliable public opinion polls had the Western Greens at only 5.3 percent, though the October and November polls were somewhat more encouraging. The feeling was that the "Perils of Pauline" (the silent film series where the star is always rescued from a doomed fate at the last minute) would end with Green Pauline once again being rescued. In retrospect, the party had its liabilities: a relatively small core of voters, a large group of floating voters, a dearth of outstanding personalities, and a lack of clarity on *the* issue of the campaign. One miracle too many was being requested. This time the train was unification and Pauline was under the wheels.

The Election Results

The Greens ended up with only 4.7 percent of the vote in Western Germany. They had failed to jump the 5 percent hurdle and therefore received no seats (see Table 1.3). The pollsters were wrong for several reasons. First, almost a quarter million former Green voters did not turn out in 1990, and these non-voters did not show up in many polls. Second, the Greens' core electorate is probably no more than about 3 to 4 percent of the electorate (Wiesenthal, 1991: 157), which means that many Green voters are floating voters who may change their votes at the last minute, and in December 1990 many switched from Green to SPD. Although the SPD lost badly in the election, especially in Eastern Germany, they did steal 600,000 votes away from the Greens.

An overview of what occurred in the election on the Western side is that the Greens lost votes in all age categories (Forschungsgruppe Wahlen, 1990b). They got a decreased share of younger and first voters (one-third less from the 18 to 24 age cohort of 1987 and an even greater loss in the 25 to 40 group, many of who had defected to the SPD). The Western Greens continued to do very poorly with voters over fifty. On the Eastern side, the distribution of the Alliance '90/Greens votes by age showed a very high percentage of the younger age categories, yet one-third of their voters were over fifty. In terms of occupation and education, both

Alliance '90/Greens and Greens (West) parties drew heavily from the more educated, salaried white-collar class in the public sector. Very few votes came from workers and independent businessmen. Both parties had the highest percentage of student voters. However, it is also clear that the SPD and the other parties had cut into this traditional category (see Norpoth and Roth in this volume).

In the early 1980s the Green voters had slightly more male voters than female. This has reversed itself over the years, with the percentage of females continually increasing over that of males in Western Germany and the gap between female and male being considerably greater in Eastern Germany. In Western Germany, the Greens lost most decisively in what had been their urban university strongholds of 1987 (Forschugsgruppe Wahlen, 1990b). It is here that massive hemorrhaging – 6.0 to 9.1 percentage points – drained the life from the party.

A puzzle in this election is that the Greens received more first votes (5.5 percent) than second votes (4.8 percent) in Western Germany. The second vote is the decisive one that allocates seats proportionally to smaller parties that have not won any district seats with the first vote. Since the Greens have always had a stronger second vote, none of the possible explanations are encouraging for them. It could mean that former supporters gave them a useless symbolic first vote, but then voted for the SPD or the FDP. It could mean that some voters – especially in the more leftist city-states of Bremen, Berlin and Hamburg – gave their second vote to the PDS (where the PDS won, the Greens lost proportionally) after casting their first vote for the Greens. Since former Green voters should know how the electoral system works, one conclusion is that giving the party a useless first vote is like damning with faint praise. It also shows the high number of split ticket voters among those who voted Green. This indication of a lack of party loyalty remains a major problem for the Greens in the uncertain future. Significantly, the smallest deviation from the second vote occurred in Hesse, a *Land* where the Greens have worked on party discipline.

The Western Greens lost more than seats in the Bundestag; over 200 staff people in Bonn also lost their positions. *Die Zeit* pointed out (Drieschner et al., 1990) that this *Denkfabrik* (think tank) had offered high quality research and analysis on a wide variety of public policy issues, from the innovations of the eco-tax to how the Federal Republic should adapt to the changing role of NATO, the European Community, and the Conference for Security and Cooperation in Europe. Furthermore, the severe reduction in public financing for the party foundations will undercut support for traditional Green projects. That, in turn, will put a further damper on the declining Green networks in many urban areas.

Postlude: Further State Elections and the 1991 Conference on Party Reform

The national election has not been the *coup de grace* that Walter Momper of Berlin said it would be. Rather it appears now to have been a form of shock therapy that has galvanized the party in a very tangible way. The results of state elections in the two years following the national election show that Greens on the state level have responded positively to the threat to their survival.

One of the first tests was the *Land* election in Hesse on 20 January 1991 in which the Hesse Greens put their *Realo* approach on the line. There is ample evidence to suggest that the defeat on the national level merely reinforced the tactics that the *Land* party had been already planning. This technique included a very disciplined and structured campaign plan, special attention given to getting out the first voters and youth vote, more care given to media policy – including placards and posters that played up the personality of the party leader, Fischer – and portrayal of the Greens as thoughtful reformers. Fischer and his party cohorts used the December Bundestag debacle to portray the election as a test of the future destiny of the party. Hesse, he claimed, would set the style for party reforms needing to be implemented by the Greens at large.[5]

The campaign strategy succeeded for a variety of complex and unexpected reasons. The Greens were aided by the interjection of the Gulf war issue into the campaign, which allowed them to mobilize their younger voters in demonstrations against the pos-

5. Interview of 28 November 1990 with *Land* deputy and leader of the Greens in Hesse. Fischer spoke as a state party leader who realized the narrowness of the margin that might keep the Greens in the Bundestag, but his main energies were focused on the January election in Hesse. He also made no secret of his difficulty in getting enthusiastic about German unity, a fact that Ralf Fücks notes (1991).

sible involvement of Germany in the conflict. Though their share of the vote (8.8 percent) was down from the previous 1987 *Land* election (9.4 percent), they did win a higher share than in the all-German election of December (5.6 percent). The most significant demographic factor was the increase in the youngest age cohort vote from the last *Land* election and, obviously, from the national election vote (Forschungsgruppe Wahlen, 1991a).

This trend reversal reflects both the voter mobilization campaign and the appeal of the centrist reforming stance, as opposed to the polemical fundamentalist style that had characterized some other state-level Green parties. The bravado pose of the past with which the Hesse Greens had talked about possible coalitions with the SPD was gone, replaced by a more moderate approach. The strategy is clear: build upon the generational core and make the special effort necessary to broaden the traditional constituency.

The reformist impetus was reinforced by the results of the Rhineland-Palatinate election of 21 April 1991, where the new low-profile, moderate Green party did better than anticipated by winning 6.5 percent of the *Land* votes. This represented a higher portion of the votes than the Greens had managed there both in December 1990 (4 percent) and in the 1987 *Land* election (5.9 percent). The Forschugsgruppe Wahlen (1991b) attributes these gains mainly to pro-SPD tactical voters who favored a Red-Green coalition. However, the victorious SPD ended up opting for the FDP as its junior partner.

The Hesse victory was seen as an important turning point, especially for the pragmatic forces in the party that looked forward to the moderates' organizational reforms. Yet, it is still an open question whether the Greens can change those "marks of origin" that many have come to see as distinguishing the party. The reforms agreed on at the Neumünster party conference in 27–28 April 1991 eliminated rotation completely, reduced the size of the Federal Executive Committee, increased the role of elected state party leaders and parliamentarians in federal decision-making, and set up dual chairs with a Green from the East and a Green from the West. But for want of a two-thirds majority the party did *not* change the rule forbidding the simultaneous holding of a party office and an elected office. However, it is very likely that individual *Land* organizations will soon accomplish this through their own reforms.

The spring series of *Land* elections ended on a positive note with the Hamburg election of 2 June 1991. The Hamburg Greens (GAL) had come completely unglued over the last couple years as a result of factional in-fighting. In the aftermath of the Greens' December 1990 debacle, local party activists did a remarkable job of piecing the coalition back together (minus radical ecologists and far leftists) in time to contest the state elections. Though the Greens' share of the Hamburg votes in 1991 (7.2 percent) was about the same as in the 1987 state election, it represented an improvement over the December results (5.8 percent). A rival Alternative List, the supporters of the fundamentalist views of Jutta Ditfurth (who had resigned from the Green party after the Neumuenster reforms), won a mere 0.5 percent, the same percentage as did the PDS's Left List. While most of their votes in earlier years would have gone to the Greens, the departure of the far leftists clarified the political profile of the Hamburg Greens.

The Bremen election of September 1991 continued the electoral successes of the Greens on the state level. The Greens increased their share of the vote to 11.4 percent (1.2 percent more than 1987). They became part of the governing *Ampelkoalition* (traffic light coalition) with the SPD (red) and the FDP (yellow), and they received the important ministries of Environmental Protection, Energy, and City Planning, as well as Culture, Youth, and Integration of Foreigners. This was the first coalition of these three parties in Western Germany, and it corresponds to a similar coalition in Brandenburg on the Eastern side. In their analysis of the election, the Forschungsgruppe Wahlen stated that a good share of the voters had seen the Greens as a constructive opposition in the past with a track record of realistic and diligent political work (Forschungsgruppe Wahlen, 1991c).

Two trends are worth underscoring in the Bremen election. The Greens, as in Hesse, slightly improved their vote in the youngest age category, but their increases in the 25 to 35 cohort were greater and still greater in the 35 to 45 group. A generational core is definitely there – the platform upon which the Greens must build – and reform politics appears to pay better dividends across the board than radical demands. The impact of this type of politics is clear. In Bremen, the Greens' suggestion that the inner city be free from cars was accepted in the coalition negotiations. And the critical issue of the widening of the Weser river will be discussed with an eye on environmental consequences (*Die Tageszeitung*, 10 December 1991).

Finally, the two state elections of 1992 in Baden-Württemberg and Schleswig-Holstein attest to the remarkable recovery made by the Greens from the national defeat of 1990. In Baden-Württemberg in early April the Greens achieved their best vote ever there. 460,000 voters (9.5 percent) supported the moderate *Realo*/eco-libertarian politics in this *Land* with its diverse economy and traditional center-right CDU politics. An indication of the Greens' position on the ideological spectrum is the coalition negotiations that the CDU conducted with the Greens before settling on the SPD and a grand coalition. These coalitions negotiations were looked on with scorn by the national party in Bonn, which feared a loss of credibility, but the *Land* party considered the negotiations to be their own affair (Forschungsgruppe Wahlen, 1992a).

The state election in Schleswig-Holstein can be called a success story only in a relative sense. Since their founding the Greens have never cleared the hurdle into the state legislatures of Saarland and Schleswig-Holstein. A powerful SPD party apparatus dominated in both states by a powerful personality, Lafontaine or Engholm, kept poorly organized Green forces below the 3 percent level. In the election of April 1992, however, the Schleswig-Holstein Greens garnered 4.9 percent of the vote and came within 397 votes of entering the *Landtag*. The Greens had more than doubled their 2.1 percent of 1988, the important factors being a solid vote among younger voters and a greatly improved party organization (Forschangsgruppe Wahlen, 1992b). The six state elections since December 1990 are positive signs for the Green project in Western Germany.

Green politics on the state and national level has moved in a pragmatic direction. Professionalization, greater attention to the media, and more time spent on organizational tasks seems to be paying off since these changes went into effect after December 1990. Yet whether the Greens are simply reaping a bonus from an increasing distrust of the major parties, as public anxieties about unification's social and economic costs have mounted, is not easy to discern. We now shall step back a bit from recent electoral politics to consider some speculations about the Greens' future based on certain "structural" constraints.

Speculations on the Future of the Greens in a United Germany

Students of politics are not good at hitting moving targets, and the pace of change in Central and Eastern Europe since 1989 should make any would-be Cassandra cautious. Yet it seems clear that the Greens will go nowhere as a national party if they cannot recruit more active members and better mobilize a core electorate. These have become increasingly difficult tasks in recent years – even for conventional parties. A number of scholars have noted the special inhibitions regarding organizational work characterizing supporters of "left-libertarian" parties as Kitschelt (1989) terms them. Left-libertarians show more loyalty to ideas and issues than to specific parties,[6] and their intellectual sophistication predisposes them to voting tactically rather than strongly identifying with a party. Inglehart, who describes these voters as "cognitively mobilized nonpartisans," observes:

> While electorates are becoming more politicized, their behavior is becoming less constrained by established organizations. . . . The rise of the West German Greens, for example, reflects both the emergence of a postmaterialist constituency whose outlook is not captured by the existing political parties and the emergence of a growing pool of voters who are politicized but do not feel tied to established parties. (Inglehart, 1991: 369).

The problem is that they don't feel attached to parties in general. But in endeavoring to become the counter-model to the established parties, the Greens soon found themselves awash in spontaneity, self-emancipation, amateurism, and a type of free-wheeling individualism that made collective action difficult. And as noted earlier, the alternative networks for the Greens in the West have declined since the early 1980s (Zeuner, 1991). Because these grassroots groups provided many of the active workers of the Greens (Pappi, 1989), the consequences of reduced movement support are serious. These informal semi-institutionalized groups just can not be counted upon to provide the same long-term support that the trade unions or the churches did for the mass parties during their formative decades. Recruiting party activists and maintaining a loyal core in the electorate (safely above the 5 per-

6. Kitschelt expands on Eldersveld's use of the term, "stratarchy": a decentralized, loosely coupled, disjointed system with elite fragmentation and a great deal of autonomy among suborganizations and weak commitment mechanisms.

156

cent threshold) will be challenging tasks for the Greens in the years ahead. The key target for both jobs is a middle class that has expanded due to greater educational opportunities. Yet neither the Greens nor the other parties can count on these new middle-class voters to be "captured" loyalists. Still a plus for the Greens, at least in Western Germany, is their clearly defined generational base of voters that is now between 35 and 50 years old. These are the 68ers who came of age in the heady days of the late 1960s and during the expansion of the participatory repertoire in the 1970s. However, the December 1990 results indicated that this cohort is vulnerable to poaching by the other parties, particularly the SPD. The Greens' prospects with the over-50 cohort and the under-35 cohort can be described as "dismal" and "uncertain" respectively. In late 1990, at least it looked like the Greens were candidates for going down in history as something quite unusual: a generational party that could not extend its convictions to a wider share of the electorate.

In the East, the organizational problems of the Alliance '90/Greens groups, which are still more movements than parties, seem even more formidable. The chances of their being largely absorbed by the major parties in the socio-economic turmoil of the next several years cannot be ignored. The active memberships of these movement-parties have already shrunk to a few hundred, their financial resources are strapped, and the appeal of their civil rights, feminist, and ecological platforms during a *Wiederaufbau* (rebuilding) period is likely to have little resonance.[7] These movements in the East developed in an atmosphere of fear and anxiety, protected somewhat by the Church, where the opportunity to expand on styles of opposition and dissent was definitely limited. Forty years of Communist party rule in East Germany gave little encouragement to a "silent revolution" of the type that Inglehart has described as having happened in the West. It is therefore premature to talk of any core Green voters – much will depend on how the SPD reorganizes itself in the East, and how the fragile movement-parties differentiate themselves from the large *Volksparteien*.

7. Interviews with Alliance '90/Green party workers in Berlin, Dresden, Leipzig, Halle, Rostock, and Schwerin in June 1991 suggested that membership figures are very low, the issues on the agenda are predominantly economic ones rather than the concerns for democratization, a new constitution for Germany, or civil rights. Many of these party workers, especially the officials for New Forum, have a longing for the old days of the movement and are clearly suspicious of the political party as an organizational form.

Our guess is that the competition from the SPD will become more intense for the Greens, East and West. The new generation of SPD leaders – Lafontaine, Engholm, Schroeder – favor a post-materialist/materialist mix of policies that is quite different from that of Vogel or Rau. They would be just as content to absorb the Greens as to be in coalition with them, if they can manage it. (The SPD is in a bit of a squeeze between its trade-unionist core and its new middle-class supporters.) One scenario sees the shrinkage and absorption of the Greens, first on the national level, then in most states, and after a still longer period of time, on the local level. Thus, little hope is held out for the courageous Eastern neophytes bucking well-heeled and well-organized party machines while articulating issues that will be secondary in importance for the foreseeable future.

The scenario of Rainer-Olaf Schultze (1990) is quite different. He sees a German party system of some differentiation with strong left- and right-wing voices, reactions against central control and the market, and a series of policy problems where the *Volksparteien* are given plenty of competition. Throughout Germany, he sees decreasing party loyalty and increased issue-voting sparking a vigorous debate between Left and Right (Schultze, 1990: 147). But the poet and dramatist Bertold Brecht always saw the big fish eating up the small fish. Especially now, determinism of the Brechtian or Marxist variety should not seem convincing. Can the small Green party learn anew how to outmaneuver the big parties, as it did in its earlier years, in a united Germany?

Conclusion

Joachim Raschke (1991) has written a stimulating book about the West German Greens in which he analyzes the nature of the long-term crisis that contributed to their defeat in 1990 and suggests very specifically how the Greens and their Eastern counterparts need to strike out on a new beginning. His catalog of needed repairs does not have to be spelled out in detail, but at the top of his list is their establishing a clear identity. The signs are that the Greens have worked through their dogmatic switch from the anti-system leftists of the late 1960s and that they will now go forward as a party of the reform Left – concentrating on ecological and civil rights issues (Fücks, 1991; Stein and Ulrich, 1991) while continuing to push for democratization in society and polity. The latter two issues are crucially important in working out a long term relationship with the Alliance '90/Greens of the East. The special problems of the East also suggest that ecological concerns must be re-thought to take into account the scarce resources there. The West German Greens' perspective had presumed a post-materialist affluent society. The balance between ecology and economic development – between materialist and post-materialist demands – obviously needs adjustment given the problems in the new Germany.

As has been noted earlier, the Greens recognized the need for organizational reform and the party conference in Neumuenster in April 1991 brought tangible results. A question still on the table is whether the Greens *and* their Eastern allies are ready to compromise principles that raised movement techniques to the status of an untouchable myth. Keeping in touch with the grassroots and working out reliable connections with new social movements is good politics, but not at the expense of dispersing power so that no central direction and no clear political profile emerges. Democracy, as Raschke and earlier theorists (e.g., Dahl, 1991) have noted, includes accountability *and* governance. An egalitarianism that leads to pluralistic stagnation can be just as bad as an headstrong oligarchy.

Critics of the Greens have suggested that a certain measure of professionalism is vital for a modern political party, and especially so for a "framework" party in which expertise in communications, long-range planning, policy development, membership recruitment, and coordination are so crucial. The Green party worker at the headquarters on Colmantstrasse in Bonn who boasted on the eve of the all-German election that the Greens have never used marketing research or pollsters in a campaign should be praised for his principles but advised to consider more seriously the demands of party competition.

Are the "marks of origin" so decisive – as de Tocqueville and Panebianco (1988) seem to suggest – that adaptation is not possible? The leopard may not change its spots, but if it wants to survive it reviews its techniques. The Greens have been doing that. Kitschelt's study (1989) of the Greens' organizational dilemma detected a change from recruiting by ideological reflex to professional criteria. In many ways the factional problems of the Greens have been reduced by the early attrition of right-wing activists and the more recent departure of left-wing activists. The skeptics regarding the Green party experiment – and they have some solid arguments – tend to see the party as being a generational flash in the pan because of its inability to renew itself beyond its core of '68ers. However, the state elections of 1991–1992 suggest that organizational work can remobilize young voters, although it means doing a different type of party work than in the previous decade.

In conclusion, working out a healthy and mutually sustaining relationship with the Eastern Alliance '90/Greens will be the litmus test for the long range success of the Greens. With representation in thirteen of sixteen *Land* parliaments, coalition participation in three, thousands of seats in local councils, and access to a sizable amount of state funds (Müller-Rommel, 1991), the Greens and their allies have the potential to offer the constructive criticism and long range suggestions on the formidable policy challenges that the new Germany confronts. Political systems with massive over-institutionalized parties, tied to powerful economic interests, need a less institutionalized and more cheeky adversary with some autonomy from the dominant economic interests. Raschke (1991) notes that the big parties are like the massive tankers and that they have the power but need the tugboat to help them change course. The Greens did that for the SPD in the 1980s as the FDP did it for the CDU. Perhaps if the Greens and Alliance '90/Greens can promote the civility in their party organization that they seek for German society as a whole, they will develop a more stable organization and a more loyal electorate. The Greens have always talked about *Lernprozess* (the learning process). Now it is up to them to apply the lesson before school is out.

References

Bannas, Guenter. 1990. "Doch Präger wollen die DDR-Grünen ihren Wahlkampf," *Frankfurter Allgemeine Zeitung*, 7 March.

Bieber, Horst. 1990. "Grüne am Abgrund." *Die Zeit*, 22 June.

Bögeholz, Hartwig. 1989. "Der Umbruch: Zur Chronologie der Ereignisse in der DDR." In *Aufbruch in eine andere DDR*, ed. Hubertus Knabe. Reinbek: Rowolt.

Dähn, Horst. 1982. *Konfrontation oder Kooperation? Das Verhältnis von Staat und Kirche in der SBZ/DDR 1945–1980*. Opladen.

Dahl, Robert. 1991. *Democracy and its Critics*. New Haven: Yale University Press.

Drieschner, Frank et al. 1990. "Wie die Zukunft aus dem Parlament verschwand." 14 December. Hamburg: *Die Zeit*.

Frankfurter Allgemeine Zeitung. 1990. Antje Vollmer's remark in Halle, 7 February.

Frankfurter Rundschau. 1990. "Müssen Deutsche Einheit Akzeptieren," 7 February.

Fücks, Ralf. 1991. "Ökologie und Bürgerrechte: Plädoyer für eine neue Allianz," in *Sind die Grünen noch zu retten?*, ed. Ralf Fücks. Reinbek: Rowolt.

Gaus, Guenter. 1990. *Deutsche Zwischentöne: Gesprächsporträts aus der DDR*. Hamburg: Hoffmann und Campe, pp. 79–94.

Gibowski, Wolfgang. 1990. "Wahl der DDR-Volkskammer vom 18. März 1990," *Zeitschrift für Parlamentsfragen* 21: pp. 3–22.

Die Grünen: Wochenzeitung 39/1990, "Ungeahnt politikfähig: Bundesdelegierten- versammlung der Grünen in Bayreuth ein Erfolg."

Forschungsgruppe Wahlen e.V. 1990a. "Wahl in den neuen Bundesländern: Eine Analyse der Landtagswahlen vom 14. Oktober 1990." No. 60, Mannheim: Forschungsgruppe Wahlen e.V.

Forschungsgruppe Wahlen e.V. 1990b. "Bundestagswahl 1990: Eine Analyse Der Ersten Gesamtdeutschen Bundestagswahl am 2. Dezember 1990." No. 61, Mannheim: Forschungsgruppe Wahlen e.V.

Forschungsgruppe Wahlen e.V. 1991a. "Wahl in Hessen: Eine Analyse der Landtagswahl vom 20. Januar 1991." No. 63, Mannheim: Forschungsgruppe Wahlen e.V.

Forschungsgruppe Wahlen e.V. 1991b. "Wahl in Rheinland-Pfalz: Eine Analyse der Landtagswahl vom. 21. April 1991." No. 64, Mannheim: Forschungsgruppe Wahlen e.V.

Forschungsgruppe Wahlen e.V, 1991c. "Wahl in Bremen: Eine Analyse der Bürgerschaftswahl vom 29. September 1991." No. 66, Mannheim: Forschungsgruppe Wahlen e.V.

Forschungsgruppe Wahlen e.V. 1992a. "Wahl in Baden-Württemberg: Eine Analyse der Landtagswahl vom 5. April 1992." No. 67, Mannheim: Forschungsgruppe Wahlen e.V.

Forschungsgruppe Wahlen e.V. 1992b. "Wahl in Schleswig-Holstein: Eine Analyse der Landtagswahl vom 5. April 1992." No. 68, Mannheim: Forschungsgruppe Wahlen e.V.

Hamilton, Daniel. 1990. *After the Revolution: The New Political Landscape in East Germany*. Washington: American Institute for Contemporary German Studies.

Horacek, Milan. 1991. "Die Mauer im Kopf: Grünen und Osteuropa," in *Sind die Grünen noch zu retten?*, ed. Ralf Fuecks. Reinbek: Rowolt.

Inglehart, Ronald. 1990. *Culture Shift in Advanced Industrial Society*. Princeton: Princeton University Press.

Jung, Matthias. 1990. "Parteiensystem und Wahlen in der DDR: Eine Analyse der Volkskammerwahl vom 18. März 1990 und der Kommunalwahlen vom 6. Mai 1990." In *Aus Politik und Zeitgeschichte*, 29. Juni 1990. Bonn: Bundeszentrale für politische Bildung.

Kitschelt, Herbert. 1989. *The Logics of Party Formation: Ecological Politics in Belgium and West Germany*. Ithaca: Cornell University Press.

Klessmann, Christopher. 1991. "Opposition und Dissidenz in der Geschichte der DDR," in *Aus Politik und Zeitgeschichte*, 25 January 1991. Bonn: Bundeszentrale für politische Bildung.

Knabe, Hubertus. 1989. "Die deutsche Oktoberrevolution." In *Aufbruch in eine andere DDR*, ed. Hubertus Knabe. Reinbek: Rowolt.

Kuehnel, W., J. Weilgohs and M. Schulz. 1990. "Die neuen politischen Gruppierungen auf dem Wege vom politischen Protest zur parlamentarischen Interessenvertretung: Soziale Bewegungen im Umbruch der DDR-Gesellschaft." *Zeitschrift für Parlamentsfragen* Heft 21: pp. 22–37.

Müller-Rommel, Ferdinand. 1991. "Stabilität durch Wandel: Die Grünen vor und nach der Bundestagswahl 1990." In *Neue soziale Bewegungen in der Bundesrepublik Deutschland*, ed. Roland Roth and Dieter Rucht. Frankfurt: Campus Verlag, 2nd expanded edition.

Neue Züricher Zeitung, "Party Conference in Hagen: Continuing Factional Strife of German Greens: No Clear Distancing from Left Socialists and PDS," 3 April 1990.

Panebianco, Angelo. 1988. *Political Parties: Organization and Power* (translated by Marc Silver; published in Italian in 1982). Cambridge: Cambridge University Press.

Pappi, Franz Urban. 1989. "Die Anhänger der neuen sozialen Bewegungen im Parteiensystem der Bundesrepublik." In *Aus Politik und Zeitgeschichte*, 23 June. Bonn: Bundeszentrale für politische Bildung.

Raschke, Joachim. 1991. *Krise der Grünen: Bilanz und Neubeginn*. Marburg: Schueren Presseverlag.

Schily, Otto. 1990. "Irgendwann reisst halt der Geduldsfaden." In *Die Grünen: 10 bewegte Jahre*, ed. Michael Schroeren. Wien: Ueberreuter.

Schultze, Rainer-Olaf. 1990. "Wahlverhalten und Parteiensystem." In *Der Bürger im Staat* Heft 3. Stuttgart: Landeszentrale für politische Bildung.

Stein, Tine and Ulrich, Bernd. 1991. "Die Kohorte frisst ihr Kind: Die 68er und der Niedergang der Grünen." In *Sind die Grünen noch zu retten?*, ed. Ralf Fücks. Reinbek: Rowolt.

Wiesenthal, Helmut. 1991. "Die Wähler und 'ihre' Partei: Notizen über eine Beziehungskrise." In *Sind die Grünen noch zu retten?*, ed. Ralf Fücks. Reinbek: Rowolt.

Zeuner, Bodo. 1991. "Die Partei der Grünen. Zwischen Bewegung und Staat." In *Die Bundesrepublik in den achtziger Jahren*, ed. Werner Suess. Opladen: Leske & Budrich.

7

From SED to PDS:
The Struggle to Revive a Left Party

Henry Krisch

OF ALL THE GERMAN POLITICAL PARTIES involved in the politics of the tumultuous years 1989 to 1991, there was one party that in its background, nature, and goals was different from the others, and for which the experiences of these years posed the most fundamental challenges. That was the Party of Democratic Socialism (*Partei Demokratischer Sozialismus*), PDS.

As the legal and, what is more important, political successor to the *leading party* of the former German Democratic Republic (GDR),[1] the PDS faced a bouquet of thorny tasks. It had to adapt itself to the change from a Leninist ruling party to being one of a number of parties competing within a democratic, constitutional, political, and electoral framework. It had to articulate its understanding of how it related to its predecessor, the Socialist Unity Party of Germany (*Sozialistische Einheitspartei Deutschlands*, SED). Finally, it faced a dual task in attempting to woo popular support: it had to make itself credible to an East(ern) German population that had become highly critical of the SED while at the same time finding an effective appeal to potential left-wing voters in West(ern) Germany.

Given these numerous and daunting tasks, it is hardly surprising that the PDS has had, at best, limited success in all of these areas, or that its future role in German politics, especially in the period after the 1994 federal elections, remains unclear.

---

1. The relevant passage in Article 1 of the GDR Constitution read, "The German Democratic Republic is a socialist state of workers and peasants . . . under the leadership of the working class and its marxist-leninist party" (Verfassung 1984: 9). The latter portion of the passage quoted was removed from the constitution at a session of the GDR legislature, the *Volkskammer*, on 1 December 1989.

163

The SED and the Unification Process

During a two year period beginning in the summer of 1989, the SED underwent a startling change in its role in society. From a position of great power as a Leninist-type ruling party it sank to a marginal role at the fringes of German politics. Even in the former East Germany, as we shall see, the PDS retains only limited importance as an opposition force.[2]

The outward signs of this reversal of position were numerous and inescapable. Within two months, beginning in mid-October 1989, the same SED leadership that had dominated GDR politics for almost two decades was driven from all of its party and state offices. Indeed, several of its members were either under indictment or threatened by legal action. Party membership dropped from 2.3 million in the summer of 1989 to 180,000 in October 1991 (Table 7.1). Those who remained in the SED after October 1989 often did so only to pursue their goal of the total transformation or even dissolution of the old party. Such people left in waves of resignations throughout this period when the SED and then PDS did not change radically enough to suit them. Finally, the SED's political downfall paralleled the formal loss of its constitutional standing as a ruling party.

Moreover, during 1990 the party, while struggling for survival and re-definition, also had to engage in four critical election campaigns within an eight month period: the 18 March *Volkskammer* elections, the 6 May local elections, the 14 October state elections, and finally, the all-German national elections on 2 December. Thus the attempted transformation and revitalization of the SED/PDS took place during an almost continuous process of public appraisal and judgment of the party and of the party's continuing need to appeal to an aroused electorate. It is symptomatic of the party's difficulties that its share of the vote (in Eastern Germany) dropped from over 16 percent in March to just over 11 percent in December (Table 7.2). It merits noting that this electoral performance is on a par with the records of other one-time "fraternal" parties in other East European countries. Some evidence suggests that attitudes and behavior originally evoked by the East German political system may continue to influence life in

2. There is extensive literature about all aspects of the SED. A good introduction as of the mid-1980s is in Spittmann (1987); a comparative treatment of the last phase of SED development is Krisch (1989).

Table 7.1. SED/PDS Membership, 1989–1991.

TIME	MEMBERSHIP
Summer 1989	2,300,000
End of 1989	1,400,000
End of January, 1990	1,000,000
Late-February, 1990	650,00
Early-May, 1990	450,00
End of May, 1990	345,000
End of 1990	284,000
End of May,1991	250,000
October 1991	180,000

SOURCE: *Der Spiegel* 22 (27 May 1991), pp. 53–56; Frankfurter Allegemeine Zeitung (8 January 1991 and 8 October 1991); Kuppe and Ammer (1990: 8–10).

Table 7.2. Number of PDS Voters in 1990 Elections in Eastern Germany

ELECTION	DATE	NUMBER OF VOTERS	PERCENTAGE
Volkskammer	18 March	1,892,381	16.4%
Communal	6 May 1990	1,183,000	14.6
Landtag	14 October 1990	885,000 (1,055,000)[1]	11.6
Bundestag	2 December 1990	1,002,814 (126,000)[2]	11.1

SOURCE: Kuppe and Ammer (1991: 27: 27–9, 55).

1. Including votes for Berlin in East Berlin in boroughs on 2 December 1990, since the Berlin state elections were held 2 December.
2. In Federal Republic (West).

Eastern Germany, despite the lack of a pre-communist national heritage available to people in the other formerly communist countries (Focus, 1990; *Electoral Studies*, 1990).[3]

Within the SED/PDS during this 1989–90 period there was a struggle to overthrow the existing intra-party regime, thereby making the SED a viable instrument for a reformed socialism. This process began with shifting attitudes within the party during the final years of the GDR, reaching its public climax during and after a special SED party congress in December 1989.

In the official world of the SED leadership, the fall of 1989 was to be marked not by the collapse of the regime, but by a celebration of the GDR's fortieth anniversary and its concomitant validation of SED control. One of its chief ideologues declared that there was "absolutely nothing" to indicate a need for correcting the SED's course or deviating from its policies, for which there was no useful alternative (*Volk* , 1990a: 37–9).

Indeed, the SED leaders had been growing more anxious about ideological unrest within the party for several years, particularly under the influence of Gorbachev's reforms in the Soviet Union. At the last "old" Central Committee Plenum in June 1989, Politburo spokesman Joachim Herrmann had warned of unnamed forces at work seeking to propagate such ideas as "bourgeois pluralism" in the socialist states, and to do away with socialism under the pretense of renewing it (Herrmann, 1988).[4] Herrmann was merely echoing Honecker's provocative comments at the prior CC meeting (Honecker, 1988), wherein the leader had denounced the "screeching of hysterical philistines" (*Gequäke wildgewordener Spießer*) who, by urging imitation of Soviet reforms want the GDR to "march into anarchy." Comparing the record of the SED favorably with that of the CPSU, Honecker left

3. Thus in the first post-communist elections in Hungary and Czechoslovakia, the successor party equivalents of the PDS received roughly 10 percent and 13 percent respectively. Polish elections were not held under comparable circumstances; in Bulgaria, the renamed communist party polled over 40 percent. In a survey conducted in 1990, younger East Germans tended to think of themselves as "East German" rather than just "German"; they would have preferred a reformed GDR rather than complete unification. (Times/Mirror Center, 1991). All this suggests that the performance of the PDS, and the persistence of "GDR" attitudes, are comparable in intensity and persistence to parallel phenomena in the other East European countries.

4. In this connection he specifically deplored developments in Hungary; a month earlier, the Budapest government had opened its border with Austria.

little doubt that the burgeoning hopes among party rank and file members (as well as the GDR population at large) for a Gorbachevian reform in the GDR would not be met.

The nervous calls for greater ideological militancy and steadfastness reflected a half-acknowledged concern over the ideological disarray within both the party and society. As two West German analysts have pointed out, it remains unclear even after two years, when, and to what extent, the SED leadership realized that the internal crisis and the erosion of the "socialist camp" added up to a systemic crisis for the GDR (Suckut and Staritz, 1991: 1038).

Some former leaders, after the event, claimed to have anticipated trouble arising from the leadership's increasingly stubborn rejection of change, but no individual or group of party leaders took any initiatives until the fall of 1989.[5] Meanwhile, party members at middle and lower levels, who had to defend and justify ever more unpopular policies, were themselves prompted to rebel (Suckut and Staritz, 1991: 1039).

Even though the party's leaders might not have recognized it, the last years of the GDR saw an erosion of the ideological consensus among SED members. This was especially the case for attitudes toward *perestroika*. At the end of 1988, young people (students, apprentices, and young workers) questioned by the Leipzig Institute for Youth Research and *who were SED members*, supported Gorbachev's policies "strongly" by 90 percent ("very strongly" 55 percent) (Friedrich, 1991: 28). This was at the very time when such regime policies as the ban on postal distribution of the Soviet press digest *Sputnik* had aroused the opposition of large numbers of party members, especially intellectuals. This falling away from the SED banner was especially significant among younger people. In May 1989, for example, an astonishing 87 percent of apprentices said they could not imagine themselves as SED members. Furthermore, 56 percent were "slightly or not at all" persuaded of the validity of Marxism/Leninism (Friedrich and Griese, 1991: 146). It is not surprising, therefore, that throughout the year preceding the December 1990 elections, the PDS had lower levels

5. For example, Hans Modrow, the Dresden *Bezirk* party leader who had been kept out of the Politburo by Honecker and his circle, later remarked about his speech to the 1988 7th CC plenum, that although members had commended him for his daring, he now knew that he had said all too little, and that that he did say had been insufficient. Therefore, Modrow concluded, his personal responsibility remained very great (Modrow, 1989).

of support among young (18 to 24 year old) voters than among the electorate at large (Friedrich and Förster, 1991: 703).

By October 1989 the brittle shell of the East German regime began to crack. It did so under the impact of several developments, all of them critical, with which the regime could not deal effectively. These included the flight of East Germans to the Federal Republic by way of Hungary and West German embassies in Eastern Europe, the increasing pressure from the Soviet Union to embark on domestic reforms, the rising citizen activism culminating in the formation of alternate political groups, and the apparent paralysis of the leadership in the face of these problems.

Although it is not our purpose to deal with the tumultuous events of late 1989,[6] we can track the SED's reaction to these events. This reaction occurred on two levels. At the Politburo level, a cabal was organized that led in mid-October to Erich Honecker's removal as general secretary (he also lost his state offices). Honecker's two closest Politburo collaborators, Gunter Mittag and Joachim Herrmann, were also removed from office. The latter duo had been responsible for policy in two areas, the economy and the media, areas of particular concern to party members and GDR citizens alike. In 1988–89, Mittag had in fact become the second most powerful member of the leadership.

The leaders of this revolt were Politburo members Günter Schabowski, the former Berlin party chief, and Egon Krenz, the Politburo and Secretariat member responsible for security. Both men had become increasingly uneasy over the absence of a positive regime response to the flight of East Germans. Krenz was also aware he had fallen out of Honecker's favor.

The first outward sign of the impending change in leadership appeared in the Politburo statement of October 11, in which the SED declared that the causes for mass flight must be sought "also among us," and that building socialism required the contributions of all. The party could not be indifferent to the flight of people who had grown up, lived, and worked in the GDR. This reversal of existing policy failed to evoke a response from Honecker, leading to his dismissal a week later.

6. There has been an enormous outpouring of books and articles on the events of that autumn, ranging from (at the time) semi-legal photo journalism to accounts by Politburo members. Three vivid accounts in English are: Darnton (1991); Borneman (1991); and Gleye (1991).

In the crucial Politburo session of 17 October, Honecker found very few supporters; in the next day's Central Committee session, regional party leaders were only too glad to be rid of the incubus of Honecker's leadership. This was especially true of those who, like Dresden's Hans Modrow, had been excluded from policy making circles (Schabowski, 1990: 71–111; Krenz, 1990: 11–17, 204–7; Bortfeldt, 1990: 10–12). By prior arrangement, Egon Krenz assumed Honecker's state and party positions. For the moment no other changes were made.

This change of leadership at the pinnacle of the party ignited a much wider desire for change in the party's membership base. In the words of two West German scholars, the palace revolution was promptly followed by a revolt of the masses. ("*Auf der Palastrevolution folgte daher prompt der Aufstand der basis*") (Suckut and Staritz, 1991: 1045). Already in the summer months of 1989, 14,000 members had left the SED (Bortfeldt, 1990: 9). This was the crest (for the moment!) of a wave of resignations that had begun in 1988, according to Politburo member Erich Mückenberger. Mückenberger was then head of the Party Control Commission, which reported to the General Secretary. Although technically not responsible for membership issues, Mückenberger nevertheless felt constrained to bring these resignations to the attention of the leadership. He was very disturbed when "people who have been in the party for 20 or 30 years, comrades with whom one has fought many a good fight" resigned in disgust (Kirschey, 1990: 59). Partly because of this, the SED had a net membership loss in 1988. The losses were concentrated in seven of the 15 Bezirke, with the top three being Leipzig, Karl-Marx-Stadt, and Dresden – all centers of mass unrest in 1989! (*Neues Deutschland*, 1989).

Mückenberger's reports open a window into the internal condition of the SED, and provide us with indices of the growing chasm in outlook between the party's central bureaucracy and the great mass of the membership in the years immediately preceding the revolutionary events of 1989. For example, the numbers of internal disciplinary proceedings instituted against members, and of penalties leveled, including expulsion, all rose sharply after 1987. Growing numbers of party members, some in responsible positions (*Leitungskader*), did not return from visits to West Germany. This breakdown of party discipline, moreover, clearly had a political impetus. Actions that led to censure of members included being provocatively against the party's line and using Soviet press materials to argue for pluralism. It is therefore hardly surprising that 81 percent of those expelled from the SED in 1988 were judged to have sinned against the "unity and purity" of the party (Bortfeldt, 1990: 4–7).

The unrest among the party membership took on political meaning in the aftermath of the October leadership change. Many party members had joined for career reasons; for them, the loss of the party's privileged status, especially in relation to filling state positions, was a reason to leave the party (Suckut and Staritz 1991: 1038–9). For others, the turmoil of the autumn led to passivity and resignation – many local party organizations simply ceased to function. For a minority of committed but reform-minded members, the last quarter of 1989 was their long-awaited opportunity to reform the party.

This effort took two main directions: the formation of reform groups ("Platforms") within the party, and the call for a special ("extraordinary") party congress. The SED leadership under Krenz at first reacted to events in familiar fashion – promising reforms, engaging in public relations (especially "dialogue sessions" between party leaders and the public), and gradually replacing old leaders. A new Politburo, with a mixture of old and new members, was elected in early November.

In addition, similar changes were introduced into the state machinery. For example, the *Volkskammer* selected a non-SED chairman in a contested election. In early November, the entire GDR cabinet resigned and was replaced by one headed by a leading SED reform figure, Hans Modrow.

It was during these weeks in the winter of 1989–90 that a significant change took place in how the public, including ordinary party members, viewed the SED. Remarks made at the SED special party congress in December gave a sense of ordinary members' attitudes. A skilled worker referred to Honecker as "this fellow who, partly because we allowed it, could make himself an Emperor and trample 17 million people in the dirt." Another delegate complained about feeling afraid and isolated at work because he was known as a loyal SED member. A machinist declared that if the delegates wanted plain speaking, he would tell them how his colleagues spelled out the initials SED:

S–Sauwirtschaft, E–Egoismus, D–Diebstahl! (Messed-up economy, egoism, theft) (*Neues Deutschland*, 1989: 4).

Public discontent with the SED was fueled by the party's seeming reluctance to press for fundamental reforms, and the revelations about the luxurious life style of party leaders. The SED yielded on many issues, but always grudgingly and often after public pressure. This convinced many party members (and citizens) that only a complete overhaul of the party would make it a useful instrument of reform (Bortfeldt, 1990: 17–19).

When the Central Committee met on 8–10 November (the famous meeting at which the opening of the borders was somewhat inadvertently announced), it resolved to convene a "party conference." The party headquarters building was surrounded that evening by a throng of party members, called out to demonstrate by the party organization of the GDR Academy of Sciences. The crowd demanded a special party congress; Krenz demurred, saying the leadership could not change its mind in response to crowd pressure. Later that evening, after receipt of many messages demanding a congress, the leadership hastily convened another Central Committee session at which it was decided indeed to convene a special party congress for mid-December.

As the struggle to shape this congress intensified, the position of the Krenz leadership grew ever weaker. Partly to forestall a drive for dissolution of the SED, the entire Politburo and Central Committee resigned on December 3 (all the regional (*Bezirk*) and many district (*Kreis*) secretaries had resigned or been forced out of office over the preceding month). A special commission was set up to prepare the party congress; one of its leading figures was the later SED and PDS chairman, Gregor Gysi (Bortfeldt, 1990: 25–7; Falkner, 1990: 1752–4).

The special party congress that met in Berlin on 8–9 and 15–16 December 1989 was certainly unlike any that had preceded it. Instead of well-ordered proceedings and material comfort, the 2,753 delegates in the Dynamo sports arena had plain food, long, quarrelsome, and intense sessions; there was easy access for outside observers (Bortfeldt, 1990: 22–6).

This meeting marked the zenith of efforts made by SED dissidents to break with the old party. They wanted to establish a leftist and socialist party that would be credible precisely because it would have no connection with the SED. The main political struggle was between the congress organizers (the preparatory commission) and an upstart caucus of Berlin reformers, the WF Platform.[7]

The crucial issues were whether to make a fresh organizational start by formally dissolving the SED, what name to give the party, the party's structure, and what stance the party should take toward the SED's past record. The "official" draft program and the WF Platform statement are quite similar in their positions on most issues of foreign or economic policy. The differences are in the nuances, and turn on the source of political authority in the GDR. The WF group wanted power to emerge from popularly elected, local action groups; it sought to insure that any new party (or state) structures created would have to respect the power of the revolutionary movement. (For the text, see Falkner 1991: 33–4.) The WF demanded a new start in practice (*faktische Neugründung*) as well as in theory; this would have amounted to a refounding of the party.

After prolonged and stormy debate in a closed, late night session, the majority at the congress supported the official preparatory commission when it voted down a resolution calling for the SED to be dissolved. The same view prevailed in the question of the party's name, and so, for another month, the party sported a double name: SED/PDS. Only in January, and after further resignations and loss of popular support, was the "SED" dropped.

The congress's programmatic documents called for the transformation of the SED into what was variously called "a Marxist socialist party" and a "modern socialist party." This party was to be internally democratic, concerned about the mass of the GDR population, about the environment, dedicated to peace, and prepared to accept a democratic, pluralist political order. The congress approved a call for the GDR to find a "third way" between Western capitalism and Stalinism, a call that has remained a regular feature of party doctrine and of its chairman's speeches. Finally, it upheld the independence of the GDR, while allowing

---

7. "WF" stood for *Werk für Fernsehelektronik* (tv electronics factory); representatives of the factory's party organization, plus a group from the social science faculty of Humboldt (Berlin) University were linked through Thomas Falkner, a newly elected head of the party organization at GDR Television. The election of a rank-and-file reformer as local party head gave this and other reform groups immediate access to national television, especially the morning newscasts. For details, see Falkner (1990).

for cooperation that would perhaps lead to confederation with West Germany.

This decision to maintain a degree of continuity between what had been the SED and what became the PDS foreshadowed the position of the PDS in German political life during the electoral year 1990 and beyond.

The failure of the delegates at the special congress to break more decisively with the old party was due in part to tactical and concrete considerations that seemed weighty at the time. For example, both Gysi and Modrow called for a strong party that would give Modrow's reform government the necessary support. Moreover, as the legal successor to the SED, the new party would be able to dispose of at least some of the old party's considerable property holdings.

Although these may have seemed compelling reasons in December 1989, they soon lost their force; indeed, they became burdens for the party. Modrow's government provoked a storm of criticism when it called for the establishment of a new security agency to replace the Ministry for State Security, the hated *Stasi*. It was first forced to share its authority with a "Roundtable" at which all parties and a variety of social-political groups were represented, and then (in late-January 1990) to join as a coalition government of national unity.

There was, however, a deeper reason for the failure to break with the old party. Thomas Falkner, himself as WF leader an advocate of such a course, acknowledged that many delegates (even among WF supporters) were people for whom the party represented a style of life. They "longed for a strong and active party leadership of respected people, whom one could follow in peace and without losing one's self respect" (Falkner, 1991: 37). Such delegates were happy to respond to Hans Modrow's impassioned appeal "not to let the party break apart or go under, but rather to make it clean and strong!" (Parteitag, 1990: 5). As we will see, this issue remains a current problem for the PDS.

The party that emerged from this turmoil of transformation was sufficiently different from the old SED as to be a plausible contestant in the forthcoming democratic elections. Its new party statute eliminated all references to democratic centralism, replaced the Politburo-Central Committee system with an Executive (*Vorstand*) of 101 members, and an elected chairman. The newly elected chairman, Gregor Gysi, received 93.5 percent of votes cast. A series of Commissions replaced the former Departments of the Secretariat.

In a radical break with Leninist tradition, the new structure allowed for the formation of "platforms" and interest groups through which the leadership hoped to appeal to reform-minded elements in West Germany, as well as to keep reformist members within the party. To an extent, this strategy has succeeded, especially with regard to feminist interest groups and a "leftist" platform; thus 17 of 54 members at-large elected to the party executive in January 1991 were from interest groups (Kuppe and Ammer, 1991: 17–19). However, some of these groups either disbanded or left the party when their particular programs were not adopted. By spring 1991 only one platform of the five founded at the end of 1989, the radical *Kommunistische Plattform*, remained in existence (Phillips, 1991: 12; Bortfeldt, 1991a: 12; Falkner, 1990: 45).

The First PDS Campaign

Ironically, the continuing disintegration of the PDS was halted, at least temporarily, by the need to campaign in the GDR's first (and last) truly free election. Indeed, for the whole of 1990 internal party affairs became secondary as the PDS struggled to attract voters in three GDR elections (national, local, regional), as well as in the all-German election in December.

A constant factor throughout the year was the PDS' increasing dependence on the energy and personality of its chairman, Gregor Gysi. He was the son of a highly placed SED functionary; his family background – partly Jewish and connected to the anti-Hitler resistance – made him a typical product of the GDR's founder generation. Gysi had become the head of the GDR trial lawyer's association and had gained a reputation as an energetic defender of GDR dissidents. He proved to be a charming and indefatigable party leader.

It was an ironic twist of fate for a party seeking to become more democratic and membership-oriented that it was soon identified, by friend and foe alike, with its new chairman. The campaign for the March elections set the tone for the year. Gysi was a tireless campaigner, willing to engage in such stunts as parachuting from airplanes. He was pictured in campaign literature as "the man with the broom," sweeping the party and the country clean.

The PDS gained an initial advantage from the organizational skills of many SED administrators. Its campaigns were imaginative and professionally run; there were slick slogans and posters ("Take it Gysi," and "We're the new bunch"). On the other hand, it was the only party other than the *Bundnis '90*, that did not receive help from a West German sister party.

In the March election the PDS received 16 percent of the vote and 1.8 million votes (Roth, 1990: 372–4; Kuppe and Ammer, 1991: 27–9, 55). The party ran most strongly in Berlin and in the North of GDR; it ran second in the *Bezirke* of Berlin, Neubrandenburg, Rostock and Dresden. Analyses of the vote showed that the PDS was the party of bureaucrats and intellectuals. Its best showing was among intellectuals (including almost half of East Berlin intellectuals), chief administrators, and office and service personnel (*Angestellte*). It was not a workers' party, finishing a distant third in the competition for workers' votes (Table 7.3). In June 1990 the PDS' deputy chairman, André Brie, flatly declared that the working class as a socio-cultural entity had been destroyed by the Nazis; the party would be better served by appealing to new social movements that mobilized people seeking a life style going beyond that of a society dominated by capital (*Neues Deutschland*, 1990).

Table 7.3. Party Preference by Social Group in the GDR, May 1990

	WORKERS	SALARIED EMPLOYEES	INTELLECTUALS	PEASANTS	STUDENTS
CDU/CSU	46.5%	35.0%	27.5%	57.6%	63.6%
SPD	31.6	31.1	25.8	27.3	27.3
PDS	14.3	24.3	33.0	15.2	9.1
New Forum	7.6	9.7	13.7	—	—
Total	100%	100%	100%	100%	100%

SOURCE: Fischer and Wittich (1990: 4).

The PDS and Unification

Once the East German electorate had signaled the population's basic commitment to rapid unification, the focus of politics both within the party and in electoral competition came to be the effort to define the PDS role in the democratic party spectrum of all-German politics. This problem still dominates PDS affairs today and its resolution will determine whether the PDS remains an enduring force in German politics.

In general, the PDS fervently espoused the Eastern cause. It opposed moves toward rapid unification, warned of the social and economic consequences of a West German takeover, and generally played on the nostalgia and sentiment for the "old cause." During the March campaign, for example, carrying the GDR flag was almost the equivalent of carrying a PDS banner. As mentioned above, it had clearly become the party of those who were skeptical about unification and identified themselves as GDR citizens (rather than as "Germans").

Generally, East German voters supported parties that reflected (and aroused) the voters' own hopes and fears. A survey of opinion in the spring of 1990 showed that of East Germans pessimistic about the future, almost three quarters (73 percent) supported the PDS (Adler and Kretschmer, 1990).

Given this voter base, the future election performance of the PDS would depend in large measure on how the process of unification, which dominated German life in the summer and fall of 1990, was received by the people of the one-time GDR. Survey results indicated a generally favorable view of unification in principle; already in early 1990, a majority of PDS voters were not opposed to unification "at a slow pace." Moreover, although Eastern Germans approved of democracy in theory, far smaller numbers approved of democracy as actually practiced in the Federal Republic.

Thus the PDS faced a dilemma concerning unification. While its main constituency was feeling at the very least cautious toward unification, by early 1990 most East Germans favored it. The party leadership presumably decided to secure its electoral base by opposing most steps toward unity. In doing this, the PDS was certainly more credible than it would have been as a suddenly ardent supporter of unification; it could not, however, expect a great deal of support for this position.

Consequently, the PDS deputies in the *Volkskammer* voted against the treaty on economic and social unity, which established the German currency union, as well as the state treaty in

August 1990. While it continued to warn of the negative consequences of unification, its campaign themes of protecting the heritage of the GDR, especially in social policy, showed that it did not seriously expect any other outcome but the unity that did arrive on 3 October.

The PDS and the October State Elections

In the state elections of October 1990 the PDS lost votes in each of the five newly reconstituted *Länder*, when its vote is compared to that of the March elections. In each state the PDS finished either third or fourth among the five parties that gained Landtag seats. In the three *Länder* of Mecklenburg-Western Pomerania, Brandenburg, and Saxony-Anhalt, the PDS exceeded its national average of 11.6 percent. The PDS reacted to these election results by expressing satisfaction that it would now be represented in all the state legislatures, despite the drop in its vote totals since March (*Neues Deutschland*, 1990a).

State elections for Berlin were held concurrently with the national elections in December, rather than in October. Here the PDS received 9.2 percent of the vote city-wide; behind this total lay two very diverse figures: 1.1 percent in West Berlin and 23.6 percent in East Berlin. The PDS' 23 seats were the third largest bloc in the Berlin assembly, but here, as in all the other new federal state legislatures, the PDS members were effectively declared to be unfit (*nichtkoalitionsfähig*) for being part of a governing coalition.

The Bundestag Campaign

For the national election of 2 December the PDS sought an arrangement with like-minded groups in the Federal Republic. This proved to be difficult, as the Greens would not enter into arrangements with the PDS. The PDS, for its part, did not want to be associated with the West German Communist party (DKP), which had been an instrument of the old SED. The solution was the creation of an electoral alliance, the *Linke Liste*, with which the PDS could set up joint slates.

After a great deal of haggling, during which the PDS' still rather hierarchical style clashed with the disorganized political style of its putative Western partners, it was decided that these electoral associations would form the basis for post-election party organizations rather than an expansion of the PDS to the Western states. Because of the West German parties' law, this conversion took place in the fall. Consequently, PDS meetings became quite lively as West German radicals began appearing at meetings, shocking old SED members with their style of discussion (Süß, 1990).

In September 1990 the PDS and its Western partners agreed upon an extensive and detailed election program (Wahlprogramm, 1990). Most of the specific recommendations in this program, on such issues as women's rights, ecology, social policy, and participatory democracy, are heavily borrowed from familiar West German left-wing notions. The program declares that the PDS and the Linke Liste favor a socialist alternative to capitalism, although in its details this position does not go much beyond workplace democracy and a variety of property ownership forms. This program, however, hardly differs from those of the SPD or the Greens. There is no mention of class struggle, but much talk of global as well as life-style issues. PDS election slogans stressed the party's new image, and its claim to play a left opposition role, proclaiming that "Everyone wants to get into the government - not us!" (*Alle wollen in die Regierung. Wir nicht*). PDS leaders clearly saw that highlighting these issues was important if the party wished to attract new, and especially Western, voters. At the same time they realized that such campaign materials must have seemed strange for much of the old rank and file (Süß, 1990).

The PDS' prospects for the December elections were dimmed by a scandal over the party's finances (*Neues Deutschland*, 1990b). It was discovered that the PDS Treasurer, Wolfgang Pohl, and the head of the party's finance commission, Wolfgang Langnitschke, had secretly arranged to transfer some DM 107 million to the accounts (in several countries) of a Soviet firm. The investigation of this affair brought on a series of nocturnal police raids on PDS headquarters in Berlin. After initial denials, the PDS admitted that this illegal transfer had indeed taken place.

The affair had multiple and damaging effects on the PDS' election chances. It reinforced the image of the party as incorrigibly wedded to old ways of exercising power. Its enemies, especially in West Germany as well as among the veterans of the GDR citizens movements, saw in this affair a clear sign that the party's supposed renewal had made little if any real progress. Within the PDS itself, the affair disheartened many members who had clung to the hope of a renewed party. Many left the party at this time; others remained but with considerably lessened enthusiasm for the party.

Still more discouraging to PDS supporters were the motives of the officials responsible, and the light this shed on the party. What had apparently moved them to take this action was the fear that the PDS would be declared illegal; the funds were to enable the party to operate in the underground. The idea that the renewed PDS was to operate transparently, and be a normal party within the German polity, and not a party of systemic opposition, was apparently a hard lesson to learn.

The most important date of the campaign for the PDS was probably 29 September. On that date the Federal Constitutional Court ruled in favor of a suit brought by the PDS, Greens, and Republikaner calling for a revision in the electoral law. The court's ruling held that a party or electoral alliance could obtain seats in the Bundestag by receiving 5 percent of the vote in either one of two electoral districts (the districts corresponded to the Western *Länder* and the new Eastern *Länder*, respectively).

The PDS campaigned for the national election much as it had earlier in the year. The program and slogans, as have been described, were those of March and October. The focus of the campaign was still on Gysi. On a visit to Munich, Gysi's campaign was a "star turn" in a skeptical if not hostile setting (*Neues Deutschland,* 1990c). Vainly did Gysi exhort PDS campaigners to appeal more directly to voters; in the aftermath of the October scandal over party finances, the necessary energy seems to have been lacking. Speaking to the PDS Vorstand only a few weeks before the election, Gysi chastised those who longed for "a socialist oasis in an otherwise hostile capitalist environment" (Süß, 1990).

The results of 2 December showed that the PDS had remained a regional force. This was indirectly acknowledged before the elections by Gysi himself, who in his election eve appeal called for a heavy PDS vote so that the people of the former GDR would have some representation in the Bundestag. In the former East Germany, the PDS performed quite respectably, especially when one considers its troubles (financial scandals, internal disputes) during the year past. In the five states of Eastern Germany, the PDS received 9.9 percent of the vote. In Berlin electoral district 261, it elected Gregor Gysi, one of the two deputies (other than CDU/CSU and SPD candidates) to receive a direct mandate.

In the former Federal Republic, however, the PDS suffered a disaster; its percentage of the total vote was unpleasantly comparable to the usual DKP vote. The PDS did best in the West in Hamburg and Bremen (1.1 percent each); that success was qualified by the fact that in both states the PDS ran behind the Republikaner.

In the Bundestag itself, the PDS has been hampered by the fact that the small size of its delegation prevents it from attaining *Fraktion* status, and the opportunities that go with it. Here the Constitutional Court came to the rescue again. Ruling on a complaint from both the PDS and Bündnis '90, it decided the two groups could have expanded "group," if not Fraktion, status (for details on the PDS activities in the Bundestag, see Phillips, 1991: 9–10). The PDS also benefited from the German law on party finances, receiving DM seven million to defray its campaign expenses (*Süddeutsche Zeitung*, 1990).

After the Election

In the aftermath of a year of hectic and almost constant political change, the PDS entered 1991 facing a period of normality and a host of problems that remained after the electoral frenzy had abated. One such problem was its relation to Western leftists. The continuing friction between the PDS and its allies surfaced at the PDS' second congress, held in two stages in January and June 1991 (Bortfeldt, 1991a and 1991b). One deputy party leader position was reserved for a Western German; a struggle between two West German woman candidates prevented either one from getting the needed majority.

In general, the party has tried to be open to like-minded persons, seeing itself as a constituent part of the Left. The PDS now acknowledges a great range of intellectual inspiration, including revisionists, utopians, and others. Somehow the differences in political style are nonetheless a great obstacle (Phillips, 1991: 18–20). These developments have made both PDS members and potential Western German allies doubtful as to the PDS's future in former West Germany. Manfred Coppik, a former left-wing SPD Bundestag member, writes bluntly that, "the project of an autonomous western development for the Linke Liste/PDS has failed. Without close dependence on the East-PDS, all that would develop in the West would be a sectarian handful" (Coppik, 1991: 120).

A further source of tension is the still unresolved issue of the PDS' relation to its SED past. In the aftermath of the January session of the 2nd PDS congress, a Berlin delegate, Harald Wolf, pointed out that the finance scandal of fall 1990 had demonstrated that the PDS is too preoccupied with preserving its property and continuity. It wishes to expand its existing structure to the West, rather than be transformed into a genuinely all-German party (Wolf, 1991). Other participants in that same post-congress discussion pointed out that the PDS still has the "culture" of the old SED – desiring unity and harmony at the expense of conflict, passively waiting for the word for a clear line from party leaders.

When one turns to policy issues it is very hard to find what is new and different about the PDS. Gehrke and others had made a great point in early 1991 of the PDS being the party most adamantly against the Gulf War, calling for no military call-ups or no German troops sent abroad. Besides renewing the call for a new constitution, the PDS' current policy profile, like its 1990 election platform, offers little that is new.

The overwhelming weight of party membership remains in the East. Even there, almost one-fifth of the membership is from Berlin and its immediate surroundings – and most of them are from Eastern Berlin (Gysi, 1991). Fewer than one in ten members are under 30 years of age; over one half are retired (Spiegel, 1991). Socially, the largest group of PDS members come from the intellectual and administrative groups (many of whom, not coincidentally, live in and around Eastern Berlin). Many members are in the party to make a statement about their personal identity as "left," caring people, rather than from any ideas about using the party as a tool for affecting policy (Chrapa, 1991: 110; Fischer and Wittich, 1990: 8).

What then is the future of the PDS? Where is its place on the political spectrum? For mild social reform, there is the SPD. For participatory and ecological policies, there are the Greens and Bündnis '90 (now a formal party). All of these have better credentials in espousing their causes than the one-time *Staatspartei*. A massive radicalization of German society in a leftward sense might give the PDS a "revolutionary" opening, but this hardly seems a likely prospect.

An obvious role for the PDS is as a regional interest party – an Ossie CSU. Even assuming that the social integration of the former GDR goes very slowly, the constituency for an Ossie party is likely to exclude all those in the East who are economically successful and politically cosmopolitan. That would leave the PDS as the party of a shrinking constituency fighting a rearguard action; such a role would probably mean the end of the PDS in time.

Of course, the PDS may not survive the 1994 Bundestag election, when there will presumably not be a special 5 percent district. In that event the PDS, now at 8 percent in its Eastern bailiwick and well below 5 percent nationally, will likely disappear as a parliamentary force. Its members will, in large numbers, retire from active politics. Its leaders, especially the reform-minded ones, will find places in the Green or Bündnis '90 parties or, quite likely, in extra-parliamentary social and civic action groups.

The attempt to fashion a leftist opposition party out of the dead mass of a Leninist state party, always a difficult and problematical undertaking, will be seen, despite several years of strenuous effort, to have failed.

References

Adler, Frank, and Albrecht Kretzschmer. 1990. "Wer sympathisiert mit welcher Partei?" *Neues Deutschland.* 15–16 September, p. 10.

Borneman, John. 1991. *After the Wall.* New York: Basic Books.

Bortfeldt, Heinrich. 1990. *Von der SED zur PDS- Aufbruch zu neuen Ufern?* Berlin: Kommission Politische Bildung des Parteivorstandes der PDS.

______. 1991a. "Die PDS und ihr zweiter Parteitag," *Deutschland Archiv* 24, (March): pp. 268–73

______. 1991b. "Der zweite Parteitag der PDS- zweite Tagung," *Deutschland Archiv* 24, (September): pp. 936–40.

Chrapa, Michael. 1991. "Empirisches zur PDS-Ergebnisse eine parteisoziologischen Untersuchung," *Utopie kreativ* 12 (August): pp. 108–13.

Coppik, Manfred. 1991. Traditionen und Perspektiven einer Partei des demokratischen Sozialismus, *Utopie kreativ* 16 (December): pp. 115–20.

Darnton, Robert. 1991. *Berlin Journal 1989–1990*. New York: Norton.

Electoral Studies 1990. Special issue on East European and Soviet elections of *Electoral Studies*, vol. 9 (December).

Falkner, Thomas. 1990. "Die letzten Tage der SED. Gedanken eines Beteiligten," *Deutschland Archiv*, vol. 23 (November): pp. 1750–62.

______. 1991. "Von der SED zur PDS. Weitere Gedanken eines Beteiligten," *Deutschland Archiv*, 24 (January): pp. 30–51.

Fischer, Evelyne, and Dietmar Wittich. 1990. "Zur sozialstruktur des politischen Verhaltens im Gebeiet der ehemaligen DDR," *Informationen zur soziologischen Forschung* 26.

Fitzmaurice, John. 1990. "Eastern Germany," *Electoral Studies* 9: pp. 327–36.

Focus, U.S. Department of State. 1990. *Focus on Central and Eastern Europe* 20, 20 July.

Förster, Peter and Günter Roski. 1990. *DDR zwischen Wende und Wahl*. Berlin: LinksDruck Verlag.

Friedrich, Walter. 1990. "Mentalitätswandlungen der Jugend in der DDR," *Aus Politik und Zeitgeschichte*, Beilage zur Wochenzeitung *Das Parlament*, B 16–17.

Friedrich, Walter and Peter Förster. 1991. "Ostdeutsche Jugend 1990–II. Teil," *Deutschland Archiv*, 24: pp. 701–14.

Friedrich, Walter and Hartmut Griese, ed. 1991. *Jugend und Jugendforschung in der DDR* Opladen: Leske + Budrich.

Gleye, Paul. 1991. *Behind the Wall: An American in East Germany, 1988–89*. Carbondale, IL: Southern Illinois University Press.

Gysi, Gregor. 1991. "Gysi spricht von Spaltungstendenzen in seiner Partei," *Frankfurter Allgemeine Zeitung*, 8 October.

Hermann. 1989. "Aus dem Bericht des Politbüros . . . ," *Neues Deutschland* (June 23): pp. 3–9.

Kirschey, Peter. 1990. *Waldsiedlung Wandlitz- die geschlossene Gesellschaft*. Berlin: Dietz Verlag.

Krenz, Egon. 1990. *Wenn Mauern Fallen*. Vienna: Paul Neff Verlag.

Krisch, Krisch. 1989. "The SED After Two Congresses: Party Policy in the Gorbachev Era," in David Childs et al., *East Germany in Comparative Perspective*. London and New York, Routledge.

Kuppe, Johannes and Thomas Ammer. 1991. *Von der SED zur PDS Bonn*. Gesamtdeutsches Institut, 1991.

Land elections. 1990. "Alles dreht sich um die Einheit," *Die Zeit* (October 26): p. 4.

Modrow, Hans. 1989. "Speech at 10th CC Plenum," *Neues Deutschland* (10 November).

Neues Deutschland 1989. 11 January 1989.

Neues Deutschland 1989. Special party congress debates 8–17 December.

Neues Deutschland 1990a. 24, 26, 27–28 October.

Neues Deutschland 1990b. 29, 30 October, 3–4 November.

Neues Deutschland 1990c. "Die rote PDS im blau-weißen Münchener Löwenbräukeller," 28 November.

Parteitag 1990. *Außerordentlicher Parteitag der SED/PDS*. Berlin: Dietz Verlag.

Phillips, Ann. 1991. "Transformation of the SED? The PDS One Year Later," *Berichte des BOIS* 42. Cologne: BOIS

Programm 1990. "Für eine starke linke Opposition- Wahlprogramm der Linken Liste/PDS," *Neues Deutschland* (September 27): pp. 8–10.

Times-Mirror Center. 1991. *The Pulse of Europe*. Times-Mirror Center for the People and the Press, Washington D.C.

Roth, Dieter. 1990. "Die Wahlen zur Volkskammer in der DDR. Versuch einer Erklärung," *Politische Vierteljahresschrift* 31: pp. 369–93.

Schabowski, Günter. 1990. *Das Politbüro*. Reinbeck bei Hamburg: Rowohlt.

Spiegel 1991. *Der Spiegel* 22 (27 May): pp. 53–6.

Spittmann, Ilse, ed. 1987. *Die SED in Geschichte und Gegenwart*. Köln: Verlag Wissenschaft und Politik.

Suckut, Siegfried and Dietrich Staritz 1991. "Alte Heimat oder Neue Linke? Das SED-Erbe und die PDS-Erben," *Deutschland Archiv* 24 (October): pp. 1038–52.

Süddeutsche Zeitung 1990. 4 December.

Süß, Walter. 1990. "Sozialistische Oase in der Krise," *Das Parlament*, 48, (23 November): p. 4.

Verfassung 1984. *Verfassung der Deutschen Demokratischen Republik*. Berlin, Staatsverlag der DDR.

Volk, Micha et al. 1990a. *"Wir sind das Volk!": Die DDR im Aufbruch*. München, Heyne.

Wahlparteitag 1990. *Wahlparteitag der Partei des Demokratischen Sozialismus*, (24–25 February). Berlin: Dietz.

Wolf, Christina. 1991. Letter in *Neues Deutschland*, 15 February.

III. THE CAMPAIGN AND THE VOTERS

8

The Campaign in the Media

*Holli A. Semetko and Klaus Schoenbach**

THE DECEMBER 1990 BUNDESTAGSWAHL was a landmark election, the first national election in unified Germany. It also marked the first time since 1933 that East Germans could cast their votes in free national elections. Moreover, it was the first election campaign aimed at two very different electorates, one living in relative wealth and abundance while the other was impoverished, surrounded by reminders of economic failure. How did the media cover this important event? What were the major political issues in the press and on television? How visible was the general election campaign in the news? Were the chancellor candidates and the main political parties successful in obtaining coverage?

Journalists from Western and Eastern Germany brought very different traditions to the job of reporting the election campaign. In the West, with its tradition of a free press going back more than 40 years, journalists cast a critical eye on political life and were at least free to offer strongly worded assessments of the political parties and the government as they had done in the past (see e.g., Schoenbach and Wildenmann, 1978; Krueger, 1978; Mathes and Freisens, 1990). They also had decades of experience in reporting

*This is part of a larger study of the media in the 1990 German national election campaign. We are grateful to a number of institutions for making this study possible. These include our home institutions, particularly the Office of the Vice-President for Research, Rackham Graduate School, the department of communication, and the Center for Political Studies at the University of Michigan in Ann Arbor; and the Institute for Journalism and Communication Research of the Academy for Music and Theater in Hanover; as well as the Forschungsgruppe Wahlen in Mannheim, and the *Bundespresseamt* in Bonn. The German Marshall Fund of the U.S. provided a fellowship for the first author to be in Germany to conduct the study. We are also especially grateful to ZDF, and in particular Mr. Klaus Bresser and those who produce the main evening news program *"heute"*, for giving Dr. Semetko access to conduct her observations and interviews during the election campaign.

on election campaigns. In the communist German Democratic Republic (GDR), however, with its tightly controlled press, journalists were expected to either passively take up and report or even praise government activity. Criticism of domestic political leaders was virtually non-existent and journalists were expected to follow the "party line" in evaluating foreign countries and foreign politicians. Moreover, they had no previous experience in reporting on free election campaigns. Because of these very different reporting traditions, we also ask: Were there important differences in the coverage of the campaign in the Eastern and Western media? We address these questions by drawing on a content analysis of fifteen newspapers and five main evening television news programs. In this chapter, we compare the political coverage in the press and on television news in Eastern and Western Germany during the two-month period before Election Day. This is the "hot phase" of the general election campaign, when the political parties' campaigns were fully underway, with regular rallies, advertising in the press and on television, and many posters on display in the streets.

Before turning to our findings, we describe the key features of Germany's media system during the first national election campaign.

The German Media System

Germany's media system has changed considerably in recent years, first with the introduction of commercial radio and television in the Federal Republic in 1984, and then with German unification in 1990. Since the fall of the Berlin Wall in 1989, the Eastern media landscape has come to resemble the Western system. State control ended, party-owned newspapers and magazines were sold or handed over to (mostly West German) commercial companies, and new radio and TV stations as well as newspapers and magazines were founded.

The Print Media

In 1991 there were 1,673 different editions of daily newspapers in Germany with 158 different editorial staffs – 119 in the West, 39 in the East (Media Perspektiven, 1991: 42). Shortly after the Wall fell in November of 1989, however, nearly twice as many independent newspapers had existed in the German Democratic Republic. There were the communist provincial newspapers, the newspapers published by other political parties, and the newly founded newspapers published by Western companies and by groups of East German journalists. The number of newspapers declined fairly rapidly, however, though the formal structure of the press in the East continues to resemble the one before the Wall came down. The former communist SED (Socialist Unity Party) provincial newspapers still account for more than 90 percent of the circulation of all newspapers in the former GDR, though nearly all of these newspapers are now owned by Western publishing companies. Interestingly, since unification, the staffs of these provincial newspapers have hardly changed. In many cases the chief editors were promoted from within and not imported from the West (Schneider, forthcoming).

The German press – both in the East and in the West – is mostly a provincial one. There is no heavy concentration of prestige press in the nation's capital city, Berlin, unlike London or Paris, for example. The "prestigious" national circulation German newspapers originate in Frankfurt (*Frankfurter Allgemeine Zeitung* and *Frankfurter Rundschau*), Bonn (*Die Welt*) and Munich (*Süddeutsche Zeitung*). There are only eight tabloids in Germany and only one of these, the *Bild*, has a large national circulation of more than 4 million.

In the Western part of Germany almost half (49 percent) of the counties and larger cities (containing 36 percent of the Western German population) have only one local newspaper. On the other hand, in only 10 percent of the counties and cities are there more than two local newspapers available (Schütz, 1989).

Der Spiegel is Germany's weekly newsmagazine. Three national weekly newspapers (*Die Zeit, Deutsches Allgemeines Sonntagsblatt, Rheinischer Merkur*) are known for their political analysis. One of the illustrated weekly magazines, *Stern*, also contains some political coverage.

Political parties have almost no role to play as owners of newspapers and magazines in Germany – both in the East and the West. This does not mean, however, that the print media are completely neutral in political terms. Many of them lean more or less openly toward a specific political party or at least a political ideology (such as free enterprise or the social responsibility of the state). The vast majority of the newspapers support conservative views – particularly on economic issues.

The Electronic Media

After World War II, the Western Allies tried to prevent any possibility of a revival of the centralized control over national broadcasting that had been utilized so effectively by the Nazis. Accordingly, the new constitution, or Basic Law of the Federal Republic, gave jurisdiction over the organization of radio and television to the states rather than to the federal government.

The British public service model heavily influenced the system that finally emerged when the Western allies handed power over to German authorities (see Head, 1985: 151 ff.). Nine broadcasting stations were in operation in the Federal Republic until 1983 and all were confined to either a specific state, a large area within a state or a combination of states, depending on how the Western allies defined their zones in 1945. These stations usually broadcast up to four different radio services or channels each. In Eastern Germany, however, the system was highly centralized. Prior to 1991, there were only two nation-wide television channels and four nation-wide radio services.

Only by means of inter-state treaties did the West German broadcasting corporations become national in scope. In 1954 the first television channel of the Federal Republic (incorporated as *Arbeitsgemeinschaft der Rundfunkanstalten Deutschlands*, or ARD) started as a joint enterprise of all the state radio services. These services still contribute programs to the national network in amounts proportional to their respective financial standing. In 1963 a second television channel (*Zweites Deutsches Fernsehen*, ZDF) was added – a new corporation, but again one based on a treaty among the West German states. Finally, in 1965 all stations of the Federal Republic (some of them independently) began to broadcast third channels in five different regions. Prior to 1983, therefore, the average West German had a choice between three to four television channels. These public service channels are supported by license fees paid by those who watch television, and also receive partial support from advertising aired on a very restricted schedule.

Since the mid-1960s, on the other side of the Wall, the Eastern audience had access to two East German-based television channels (DFF1 and DFF2) as well as at least one West German channel that broadcast from the nearby border. For most East Germans, the West German television services were much more important sources of information about politics and world events (Hesse, 1988, 1990). After the Wall fell, however, the audience ratings for DFF1 went up and the channel's news broadcasts came to be seen as more credible. Television reporters in the East appeared to adjust fairly quickly to the new openness in the coverage of politics. In the new *Bundesländer*, at the time of the 1990 general election campaign, the two Eastern German television channels (DFF1 and DFF2) and the four central radio services remained in operation and most people in the new *Bundesländer* could also receive the signals from ARD and ZDF. During the campaign then, the majority of Easterners turned to the East German channel, DFF1, and at least one of the public service channels, ARD or ZDF, for television news. The broadcast media landscape in the new *Bundesländer* has changed considerably since the 1990 election, however, with DFF1 and DFF2 replaced by a broadcast media structure resembling that existing in the old *Bundesländer*.[1]

Prior to November 1989, the broadcasting services in the GDR had been strictly state-controlled. Those in the West, however, were and still are "publicly controlled" and this carries an important political implication that is not true of public service broadcasting in the U.S. Each "publicly controlled" channel has a broadcasting council that sets general policy. State laws specify how the broadcasting councils should be "representative" of the public. Some of the members of the broadcasting councils are members of the state parliaments and their numbers reflect the proportion of political power at the state level. The majority of

1. In the Eastern part of Germany a two-tiered broadcasting system has emerged since unification. The old centralized broadcasting system has been restructured along the model in the West, with authority at the state level. The old West German "nation-wide" public service channels can now be received everywhere in the East. In addition, the three southern states of the former German Democratic Republic (Saxony, Saxony-Anhalt and Thuringia) jointly formed a new broadcasting station, the Central German Broadcast System (MDR). Brandenburg remained on its own, and Mecklenburg-Western Pomerania joined the (Western) North German Broadcast System. Only the MDR offers its own programming, whereas in the northern part of the former GDR, the broadcast services contribute to programming on existing television channels. The former four radio channels have been replaced by six publicly controlled ones, originating in the East. The first licenses for commercial radio were issued as early as 1990.

council members, however, are representatives of recognized interest groups (such as youth organizations, women, workers, employers, or churches). Traditionally, in the council decision-making process the representatives of interest groups take sides on the basis of their party affiliations or sympathies. As a consequence, controversies in the broadcasting councils are not, for instance, between churches and youth organizations but between liberal delegates of the churches and of the youth organizations on the one hand, and between conservative council members of the same organizations, on the other (see, e.g., Kepplinger and Hartmann, 1989).

In early 1984 the state parliaments passed legislation permitting the first West German private radio and television stations (cf. Humphreys, 1990). The decision to permit private ownership of broadcast channels was officially celebrated as progress in media diversity. Conservative state governments spearheaded the move toward private TV and initiated the creation of new private channels in part because they believed the public channels exhibited a "leftist" political bias. The new channels are funded entirely by advertising. Five of the new television stations are German-based commercial organizations: RTLplus, SAT.1, Pro7, Tele 5, and Kabelkanal. These and other private TV channels, as well as the more than 150 commercial radio stations, are not controlled by the old broadcasting councils and are therefore less likely to be the object of political parties' criticisms and oversight.

By early 1991 66 percent of Western households could receive – mostly via cable – RTLplus, 62 percent could view SAT.1, Pro7 was available to 27 percent, and Tele 5 to about 30 percent. Kabelkanal began broadcasting only in the spring of 1992.

German broadcasting is obliged by state laws and Constitutional Court decisions to be an instrument of information, to assist its audience in forming opinions, to contribute to education, and to offer entertainment. The entertainment portion of broadcasting services has increased in the last decade. The new channels are more dependent on ratings than the old public service channels. Consequently, the Constitutional Court of the Federal Republic allowed the new private channels to offer less than the public service channels in the way of information and educational programming. Nevertheless, in response to competition from the new private channels, the public service channels increased their share of entertainment programming in their schedules. Entertainment took up 62 percent of ZDF's programming in 1990, up from 58 percent before the introduction of commercial broadcasting (ZDF, 1984 and 1991). On ARD, entertainment accounted for 45 percent of programming before the private channels came on the air in 1983, and 51 percent by 1990 (ARD, 1984 and 1991).

Media Coverage of the Political Parties

The political parties have made greater efforts to present themselves within the regular news coverage of the media in recent years. There are obvious cost advantages to using the news and documentary programs rather than paid advertising as vehicles for informing electors. News coverage may also provide additional credibility to politicians' statements.

In Germany, as in many countries, one way for politicians to achieve more frequent media coverage is to stage events that appeal to journalistic news values. These so-called "pseudo-events" may include political rallies, press conferences, travels abroad, and the like (Boorstin, 1963; Radunski, 1980).

Some of the media outlets in the Federal Republic facilitate politicians' attempts to gain coverage by giving them opportunities to express their views directly. In past national election campaigns, for example, ARD and ZDF have broadcast a series of debates between the top candidates and other politicians for which journalists often only supply the cues (cf. Baker and Norpoth, 1990; Baker, Norpoth and Schoenbach, 1981). Some newspapers also provide political parties with a certain amount of space to be filled with information of the parties' own choosing (see, e.g., Bauer, 1989).

Explicit endorsements of political parties or candidates by mass media, however, are somewhat looked down upon in Germany. Even the most politically outspoken newspapers rarely directly ask their readers to vote for specific parties or candidates. Politicians have made light of the electronic media's legal obligation to provide their audience with politically balanced coverage. Radio and television news producers are often pressured by party managers and candidates who complain regularly about unfair coverage. As both the laws and the respective court decisions are not entirely clear as to what "balance" really means, tradition provides some direction. What is now widely accepted as a model of balance in the coverage of politics concerns the time devoted to a political party or its politicians in the entirety of a station's programming, rather than within each individual program. Political parties often monitor the amount of time they receive in broadcast programs to ensure that their time share is not less than their opponents'.

Another way to encourage balanced coverage is confined to public broadcasting only and apparently unique to German public service broadcasting: the parties have a say in the hiring of TV and radio managers, reporters, and editors. Party affiliation is a predominant criterion for filling many of the top positions in German public service broadcasting corporations. In practice, this means that if one important post is occupied by a card-carrying Christian Democrat or by someone with at least some sympathy for that party, a second important post will eventually be filled by a Social Democrat. The broadcast councils, discussed earlier, in which representatives of interest groups take sides along party lines is another source of influence in the promotion and hiring process. The council members often have a say in the decision to hire or promote people to key positions in public broadcasting.

The amount of time on public television channels devoted to politicians seems to have dropped in recent years, however, both in the news and in other information programs. Although there is still the fear of pressure from the parties, there is greater fear of losing ground in the new and competitive marketplace. Public television channels now increasingly try to keep politicians from all parties from using TV as a platform, and strive to avoid presenting politicians in program formats that viewers might find dull or uninteresting.

Political Coverage in the 1990 Election Campaign

The final two months preceding the December 1990 national election were marked by significant and unprecedented events. The most important of these was the political unification of the Federal Republic of Germany and the German Democratic Republic on 3 October 1990. This was followed by state elections on 14 October 1990, when each of the five new *Bundesländer*, as well as Bavaria, went to the polls.

All coverage of German politics in fifteen newspapers and on the main evening news programs of five television channels were content-analyzed from 1 October to Election Day, 2 December 1990. Our analysis was deliberately not restricted to campaign coverage only. Instead, all political coverage mentioning German politicians was coded, except for that in the local news sections of newspapers, and included news articles, commentaries, and cartoons. The fifteen newspapers consisted of eleven from the old *Bundesländer* with the highest circulation, and four newspapers in the new *Bundesländer*. The newspapers included in our study, along with their circulation and ownership, are presented in Table 8.1. In addition, all reports concerning German politics, German political parties, or politicians were analyzed on the main evening television news programs of the public service channels ARD and ZDF, the two widely available private channels RTLplus and SAT.1, as well as on the Eastern channel, DFF1.

Subjects of Political Coverage

What were the main subjects of news stories during the final months before the first national election in unified Germany? It is perhaps surprising that in the West German media, at least, foreign affairs issues were the most important issues in the news during the election campaign (Table 8.2). Developments in the Gulf accounted for approximately half of these foreign affairs stories. The other half consisted of Germany's relations with the Soviet Union, Poland, the U.S., East-West relations in general, the EEC, NATO, and defense.

"East German issues" were the next most important issues in the Western media. These included the financial scandals of the PDS, the successor party of the former SED, as well as the GDR's past and its particular economic problems. Less often mentioned were law and order, the environment, the future of the GDR's army, the cost of housing, culture and the arts, taxes, and health care.

Among the Eastern media, the issues referring to the new *Länder* were understandably at the top of the agenda. Foreign affairs issues nevertheless received a substantial proportion of the coverage in the East and ranked second in order of importance.

Taking together the coverage of the Landtag elections of 14 October and the Bundestag (national) election, the campaigns were the main topic of approximately 15 percent of political cov-

Table 8.1. German Newspapers used in Content Analysis of Political Coverage (October–December 1990)

	1990 CIRCULATION (IV/1990)	1990 PUBLISHER OWNER
EAST		
Freie Presse, Chemnitz	607,000	Treuhandanstalt[1]
Leipziger Volkszeitung	372,000	Treuhandanstalt[2]
Sächsische Zeitung, Dresden	523,000	Treuhandanstalt[3]
Volksstimme Magdeburg	420,000	Treuhandanstalt[4]
WEST		
Augsburger Allgmeine	361,500	Presse-Druck- und Verlags GMbH/Guenter Holland
Berliner Zeitung, Berlin*	286,800	Axel Springer-Verlag
BILD-Zeitung, (Hamburg)*	4,339,400	Axel Springer-Verlag
Express, Köln*	310,300	Verlag M. DuMont-Schauberg
Frankfurter Allgemeine Zeitung	385,900	Frankfurter Allgemeine Zeitung
Hannoverische Allgemeine Zeitung	409,300	Verlagsgesellschaft Madsak
Nürnberger Nachrichten	349,000	Nürnberger Presse Druckhaus Nürnberg GmbH
Rheinische Post, Düsseldorf	397,000	Rheinisch-Bergische Druckerei- und Verlagsgesellschaft
Süddeutsche Zeitung, Müchen	383,400	Süddeutscher Verlag
Südwestpresse, Ulm	369,200	Verlag Neue Presse-gesellschaft GmbH
Westdeutsche Allgemeine Zeitung	655,000	Westdeutsche Allgemeine Zeitungsverlagsgesellschaft E. Brost & J. Funke GmbH

*Tabloid.
1. In December 1990 to Medien Union Ludwigshafen/Die Rheinpfalz.
2. In summer 1991 to Verlagsgesellschaft Madsack (50%) and Springer-Verlag (50%).
3. In summer 1991 to Gruner+Jahr (60%) and Social Democratic Party (40%).
4. In summer 1991 to Heinrich Bauer-Verlag.

196

Table 8.2. Main Subjects of the Political Media Coverage

	NEWSPAPERS[1]			TELEVISION NEWS [2]		
	EAST	WEST	TOTAL	EAST	WEST	TOTAL
Election Campaign	19%	18%	18%	15%	15%	15%
Landtag	(9)	(6)	(7)	(9)	(10)	(10)
Bundestag	(10)	(12)	(11)	(6)	(5)	(5)
Foreign Affairs	15	21	20	20	28	26
Domestic Affairs	13	18	16	14	15	15
East German Issues	36	19	24	33	21	24
Unification	8	9	9	8	8	8
Environment	1	3	3	1	2	2
Immigration	1	2	2	1	1	1
Economy	2	3	3	3	3	3
Social Welfare	2	4	4	1	2	2
Other	2	4	2	4	5	4
Total	100%	100%	100%	100%	100%	100%
Number of Stories	2,562	7,587	10,049	389	1,126	1,515

1. For definition of East and West German newspapers see Table 8.1.
2. Eastern TV news on DFF1; Western news on ARD's "Tagesschau," ZDF's
   "heute," SAT.1's "Blick," and RTLplus' "Aktuell."

erage in television news stories and 18 percent of newspaper articles. There were no major differences between East and West media on this point. Interestingly, however, the *national* election campaign itself was rarely the main subject of a story on the evening television newscasts in the final eight weeks before Election Day. It accounted for only five percent of stories on television. Although there was more attention paid to the national campaign in the press, it was nevertheless the main subject of only 11 percent of stories.

Politicians and Parties in the News

During the "hot phase" of the election campaign, the parties of the government continued to govern and to attract a great deal of media attention. Based on a study of all political coverage in the press and on television, it is clear that the parties of government benefited from better coverage, a "Regierungsbonus" (cf. Kepplinger, 1982; Krueger, 1978). They were the main political actors in approximately two-thirds of all press and television stories, in comparison with about one-third for all the opposition parties (Table 8.3). The governing Christian Democratic Union (CDU) and its politicians alone were the main actors in 29 percent of press and television stories, in comparison to about 20 percent for the SPD, the main opposition party. This "Regierungsbonus" was apparent in all media outlets: the parties of government were always more visible than the opposition parties.

Helmut Kohl also enjoyed a "Kanzlerbonus," that is, a bonus for the incumbent chancellor candidate. He was the main actor in approximately three to six times as many stories as his challenger, Oskar Lafontaine, the Social Democrat (Table 8.3).

Table 8.3. Main Political Actor in the Political Media Coverage

	NEWSPAPERS			TELEVISION NEWS		
	EAST	WEST	TOTAL	EAST	WEST	TOTAL
Helmut Kohl	9%	11%	11%	10%	12%	11%
Christian Democratic Union	35	27	29	29	28	29
Christian Social Union	7	9	8	6	7	7
Free Democratic Party	8	9	9	9	7	7
Other Government	5	5	5	4	8	7
Total Government	**64**	**61**	**62**	**58**	**62**	**61**
Oskar Lafontaine	2	3	3	1	2	2
Social Democratic Party	15	22	20	21	18	19
SPD/Greens	—	—	—	—	—	—
Greens/Bündnis '90 (the Eastern Greens)	4	4	4	5	4	4
Party of Democratic (Socialism)	8	6	6	7	7	7
Total Opposition	**29**	**35**	**33**	**34**	**31**	**32**
Parliament	3	2	2	2	4	3
Other	4	2	3	6	4	4
Total	**100%**	**100%**	**100%**	**100%**	**100%**	**100%**
Number of Stories	2,541	7,501	10,042	389	1,125	1,514

SOURCES: see Table 8.1.

All in all then, the opposition parties were not well positioned for getting into the news in the press or on television during the final eight weeks before polling day. There were no significant differences between the media in either part of the country on this point.

Evaluations of the Main Political Actors

Visibility is no longer a bonus if the coverage about a political party or politician is negative. The vast majority of stories in the press and on television in fact did not contain any explicitly positive or negative evaluations of the main political actors. The reports were instead what we have labeled in Table 8.4 as "straight, neutral, descriptive."

In comparison with TV news, newspapers contained more stories with directional evaluations of the main political actors (Table 8.4). This is due to the greater proportion of "commentary" or "editorial" pieces in the press (about 10 percent), whereas these types of stories were rare on television news programs (less than one percent). Western newspapers were more likely to offer directional evaluations than Eastern newspapers, and included more "commentary" stories (cf. Kaase and Schrott, 1991).

It is worth distinguishing between "hard news" stories (*Nachrichten*), "news analysis" stories (*Reportagen*), and "commentary" stories (*Kommentare*) that are required to be labeled as such. The hard news stories, which are based on events taking place in the last 24 hours, both in the press and on television were overwhelmingly neutral: 98 percent in the Eastern press and 95 percent in the West contained no directional (that is, clearly positive or negative) evaluations. In commentaries, however, which are the equivalent of signed columns or editorials, the Western newspapers offer significantly more directional evaluations than the Eastern press. Eastern newspapers were more cautious in their commentaries, where criticisms and praises are to be expected: only 17 percent of these articles contained evaluations of the main political party in the story, compared to 37 percent in the West. Differences also emerged in "news analysis" stories, which often contain information from different points in time and may concern motives or expectations. Only 8 percent of news analysis stories in the Eastern press contained directional evaluations, in comparison to 20 percent in the Western newspapers.

Table 8.4. Reporters' Comments About the Main Political Actors in the Political Media Coverage

	NEWSPAPERS			TELEVISION NEWS		
	EAST	WEST	TOTAL	EAST	WEST	TOTAL
Straight/Neutral/ Descriptive	95%	88%	90%	96%	96%	96%
Positive	2	4	4	1	2	1
Negative	3	6	5	3	2	2
Mixed	—	1	1	—	—	1
Total	100%	100%	100%	100%	100%	100%
Number of Stories	2,542	7,503	10,045	389	1,125	1,514

SOURCES: see Table 8.1

The Campaign in the News

Only a small portion of the stories about German politics – 5 percent of television news stories and 11 percent of newspaper articles – had the national election campaign as their *main subject*. The percentage roughly doubles once we broaden our definition of campaign news to include all stories that at least *mentioned* the national election campaign: it climbs to about 11 percent of stories on television news programs (N=166) and 19 percent of newspaper articles (N=1,969). In most media outlets the majority of these stories appeared in November, with their number increasing as election day drew nearer.

But the news as presented during the election campaign in Germany was not what viewers in the U.S. or Britain would normally expect from their media during election campaigns – with colorful political rallies and politicians on the campaign trail meeting voters or kissing babies. In German television news, these types of stories were far from common. In fact, we found almost no coverage of "pseudo events" of this kind or campaign events staged primarily for the television news cameras. Instead, stories that mentioned the campaign were often educational, clarifying the complicated election procedures and the electoral system. Some concerned the expected or possible results, though opinion poll coverage was rare. Other stories dealt with the substance of the speeches or statements made by politicians on the campaign trail. A number of stories that only *mentioned* the campaign had as their *main subject* issues that were not directly related to the politicians' campaigning activity – such as the cost of unification (particularly in the East); the local government crisis in Berlin; or the internal squabbling of the parties. These were also the most common subjects of newspaper stories in which the campaign was mentioned. In sum, the content of news stories mentioning the campaign, particularly on television, was quite different from what viewers in the U.S. or Britain would be exposed to in an election campaign. The hoopla associated with campaigning was hardly visible, the opinion polls were not featured prominently, and the rallies and speeches on the campaign trail were for the most part not covered in television news.

The *"Regierungsbonus"* and *"Kanzlerbonus"* remained in the stories that mentioned the campaign, although some qualifications need to be made. The parties of government continued to be the main political actors more often than the opposition parties, accounting for approximately 61 percent of campaign stories on television, compared to 34 percent for the opposition. For the press as a whole, the government parties were the main political actors in 57 percent of stories in comparison to 39 percent for the opposition parties. In short, the Regierungsbonus was just as evident in campaign stories as in political coverage as a whole. The Kanzlerbonus, however, was less evident. Helmut Kohl was the main actor more than twice as often as Oskar Lafontaine, but this is a substantially smaller bonus than exists in political coverage in general. There were also important differences across media outlets in the coverage of the chancellor candidates.

An interesting difference between the television news programs on the public service channels (ARD and ZDF) and the private channels (RTLplus and SAT.1) emerged from the figures in Table 8.5. There was no Kanzlerbonus in campaign stories on ARD and ZDF. In other words, Helmut Kohl was just as likely as Oskar Lafontaine to appear as the main political actor in stories mentioning the campaign. This suggests that an effort was made by the public service channels to provide balanced coverage of the chancellor candidates in the context of the election campaign. Subsequent analysis of the amount of time devoted to politicians' statements on television news also shows that the incumbent did not maintain such a strong advantage over the challenger, which

Table 8.5. Main Political Actors in Stories Mentioning the Election Campaign

	NEWSPAPERS			TELEVISION NEWS		
	EAST	WEST	TOTAL	EAST	WEST	TOTAL
Helmut Kohl	13%	13%	13%	19%	12%	14%
Christian Democratic Union	21	23	22	12	23	20
Christian Social Union	6	9	8	12	9	10
Free Democratic Party	8	9	9	14	10	11
Other Government Actors	5	3	4	9	5	6
Total Government	**53**	**57**	**57**	**66**	**59**	**61**
Oskar Lafontaine	6	10	9	2	7	5
Social Democratic Party	12	17	16	14	10	11
Greens/Bündnis '90 (the Eastern Greens)	9	7	7	7	11	10
Party of Democratic Socialism	14	5	7	9	8	8
Total Opposition	**41**	**39**	**39**	**32**	**36**	**34**
Parliament	4	1	2	2	5	5
Other	2	3	3	—	—	—
Total	**100%**	**100%**	**100%**	**100%**	**100%**	**100%**
Number of Stories	439	1,530	1,969	43	123	166

SOURCES: see Table 8.1.

also suggests that special efforts may have been made by the public service channels to provide "balanced" coverage of the candidates. On the private channels, however, Helmut Kohl was clearly more often the main actor than Oskar Lafontaine in stories mentioning the campaign.

The visibility bonus, however, was not a bonus in terms of valence or tone. The vast majority of television stories mentioning the campaign – 91 percent – was predominantly straight or neutral, with only a handful containing explicitly positive or negative evaluations about one or both of the main actors. In other words, the Kanzlerbonus did not result in explicitly favorable coverage (Table 8.6).

Table 8.6. Reporters' Comments About the Main Political Actors in Campaign Stories

	NEWSPAPERS			TELEVISION NEWS		
	EAST	WEST	TOTAL	EAST	WEST	TOTAL
Straight/Neutral/ Descriptive	90%	79%	82%	84%	94%	91%
Positive	2	7	6	9	3	4
Negative	7	11	10	7	2	4
Mixed	1	3	2	—	1	1
Total	100%	100%	100%	100%	100%	100%
Number of Stories	439	1,531	1,970	43	123	166

SOURCES: see Table 8.1

A Kanzlerbonus did emerge in newspaper stories mentioning the campaign, although there was some variation among newspapers. Newspaper stories mentioning the campaign contained more directional evaluations than the political coverage as a whole, largely because of the greater number of "commentary" stories mentioning the campaign. Negative evaluations were in general more common than positive evaluations in such stories.

Conclusions

The 1990 campaign followed a year of tremendous changes in Germany, the most significant of which were monetary and political unification. Despite these important internal developments, political coverage during the "hot phase" of the election campaign focused heavily on foreign affairs issues, in particular on the crisis in the Gulf. This may be a reflection of the unusual circumstances of the time, but it may also reflect a generally greater emphasis on foreign affairs in German news media in comparison to the news as presented in other countries. Issues concerning developments in the new *Länder* were also heavily covered in the news and, understandably, media in the new *Bundesländer* placed somewhat greater emphasis on these issues than on foreign affairs.

How visible was the general election campaign in the news? In the media in both parts of Germany, the national election campaign was rarely the *main subject* of political stories on television, and it was only slightly more often the main subject of articles in the press. By expanding our definition of campaign news to include all stories in which the election campaign was at least *mentioned*, we still found an average of less than one "campaign" story per channel per day on television, and two per day in each newspaper during the two months preceding Election Day. Unlike Britain where the newspapers and television programs are virtually saturated with campaign news, the German 1990 national election campaign, during its "hot phase," was only occasionally visible in the news media.

Although the political parties regularly held rallies and the chancellor candidates were often campaigning in towns and cities, these activities were rarely reported in the main evening television news programs. This general lack of emphasis on the campaign in the main evening news bulletins appears to be at least in part a consequence of editorial decisions, with newscasters assuming that stories merely about campaign events are not "hard news" and do not deserve coverage in the main evening news program. Those involved in producing ZDF's main evening news program "heute," for example, who were interviewed as part of this study, believed the program should cover the issues of the campaign when they were "newsworthy", but that the program should not serve as the transmitter of staged campaign events or "party propaganda".[2] Cameras were rarely sent to the campaign rallies held by the chancellor candidates because nothing "new" was expected to be likely to emerge from the set speeches.

The German television news producer's response to the politicians' campaigning activities is thus completely unlike that of the British or the U.S. television news producer. ITN and the BBC, for example, in 1992 as in previous elections, sent camera crews and reporters along with the party leaders every day and covered all the party rallies. Film from these events was broadcast almost every day of the campaign.[3] U.S. network news, moreover, is very concerned about obtaining colorful visuals that are often provid-

2. These comments come from interviews with newspeople at ZDF's "heute" program conducted by Holli Semetko on 19 November 1991.

3. Semetko conducted observation and interviews with those producing News at Ten at Independent Television News (ITN) in London in March and April 1992, during the British general election campaign.

204

ed by the politicians' rallies and speeches on the campaign trail. Camera crews are sent to follow the candidates and are present at all the campaign rallies. The German television news producer, however, is less preoccupied with having colorful visuals and more concerned with the substance of the story.

In the media in both parts of Germany, the parties of government were the main actors in political stories far more often than the opposition parties. Moreover, the incumbent chancellor, Helmut Kohl, was the main actor in many more stories than his challenger, Oskar Lafontaine. Although the Regierungsbonus and the Kanzlerbonus were not as great when we focus only on the stories explicitly mentioning the campaign, they nevertheless do exist in most media outlets. The only exception was the public service television channels – ARD and ZDF – where the Kanzlerbonus disappeared and both candidates were equally likely to be the main actor in campaign stories. The bonus was maintained on the private channels' coverage of the campaign, however. In this respect, the public service channels in Germany appear to be more like their British counterparts in attempting to provide balanced coverage of the leading contenders in the race, whereas the private channels may be more like the commercial U.S. networks, relying primarily on news values in making judgments about the selection of stories in election campaigns (cf. Semetko et al., 1991).

Due to their more frequent use of "commentary" pieces, newspapers contained more evaluations of the political actors than did television news. Nevertheless, the vast majority of political stories in the East and West German media were predominantly descriptive and did not contain any explicitly positive or negative evaluations of the main political actors. The Regierungsbonus and the Kanzlerbonus are therefore largely bonuses of visibility and should not be understood to refer to a favorable or unfavorable tone in the coverage. This was also found to be the case in television coverage of the 1987 campaign (Mathes and Freisens, 1990).

German television news coverage of the campaign is thus quite different from that in the U.S. or Britain where, in the general elections of the past ten years, the main evening news on the BBC and on ITN, the commercial channel, was saturated with news from the campaign trail (Semetko, 1991; Mathes and Semetko, 1991). Incumbents in the U.S. and Britain also have the advantage of being seen "governing" during election campaigns, although some effort is made by the news media to depict the incumbent or the incumbent party as contending for power during the final stages of an election campaign; most news about the president or prime minister, moreover, is often matched by a similar amount of coverage of the opposition parties or candidates. In Germany, however, this was not the case in 1990 – a major hindrance to the opposition party's ability to communicate to voters via the news media. Whereas campaign events in the U.S. and Britain provide an important opportunity for generating coverage in the news media, in Germany these are largely not covered by television news programs. They are also ignored by many of the current affairs programs that often take the form of panel discussions or issue-specific investigative reports.

Despite the great similarities between the Eastern and Western media's coverage of politics during the campaign, we nevertheless found more caution in the East. This was most apparent in the "commentary" and "news analysis" stories in the Eastern newspapers that, although rare in comparison to number of such stories run in the Western press, contained far fewer evaluations of the main political parties or candidates.

This study of the news coverage of the 1990 national election campaigns hopes to provide a baseline and a set of content analytic variables by which we can assess changes in the news and information worlds in the old and new *Bundesländer* in future national elections. The 1994 national election will be the first national campaign covered by the new broadcast media in the new *Bundesländer*. Future research can assess whether the content of German election campaign news is changing in response to this more competitive media environment.

References

ARD (Ed.). (1984). *ARD-Jahrbuch 84*. Hamburg: Hans-Bredow-Institut.
ARD (Ed.). (1991). *ARD-Jahrbuch 91*. Hamburg: Hans-Bredow-Institut.
Baker, Kendall L., and Helmut Norpoth. 1990. "Television Debates and Press Coverage in the 1980 and 1983 West German Elections." In Karl H. Cerny, ed., *Germany at the Polls: The Bundestag Elections of the 1980s*, Durham, NC: Duke University Press, pp. 167–86.

Baker, Kendall L., Helmut Norpoth, and Klaus Schoenbach. 1981. "Fernsehdebatten der Spitzenpolitiker im Bundestagswahlkampf 1972 und 1976," *Publizistik*, 26: pp. 530–44.

Bauer, Michael. 1989. *Regulierter Journalismus: Spielregeln Lokaler Wahlkampfberichterstattung*. Munich and Muelheim: Publicom.

Boorstin, Daniel. 1963. *The Image*. New York: Atheneum.

Head, Sidney W. 1985. *World Broadcasting Systems*. Belmont, CA: Wadsworth.

Hesse, Kurt-Rolf. 1990. "Cross-Border Mass Communication from West to East Germany," *European Journal of Communication*. 5: pp. 355–72.

______. 1988. *Westmedien in der DDR: Nutzung, Image und Auswirkungen bundesrepublikanischen Hoerfunks und Fernsehens*. Cologne: Verlag Wissenschaft und Politik.

Humphreys, Peter J. 1990. *Media and Media Policy in West Germany*. Providence, RI: Berg.

Kaase, Max and Peter Schrott. 1991. "Media Coverage of the 1990 German National Election Campaign: A Comparison of East and West German News." Paper presented at the American Political Science Association meetings, Washington, DC.

Kepplinger, Hans Mathias. 1982. "Visual Bias in Television Campaign Coverage," *Communication Research*, 9: pp. 432–46.

Kepplinger, Hans Mathias, and Thomas Hartmann . 1989. *Stachel oder Feigenblatt? Rundfunk- und Fernsehräte in der Bundesrepublik Deutschland*. Frankfurt: IMK.

Krueger, Udo Michael. 1978. "Publizistisch bedeutsame Tageszeitungen im Bundestagswahlkampf 1976," *Publizistik* 23: pp. 32–57.

Mathes, Rainer, and Uwe Freisens. 1990. "Kommunikationssstrategien der Parteien und ihr Erfolg." In Max Kaase and Hans-Dieter Klingemann, eds., *Wahlen und Wähler*. Opladen: West-deutscher Verlag, pp. 531–68.

Mathes, Rainer and Holli A. Semetko. 1991. "Foreword: A Comparative Perspective on Television and Election Campaigns," *Political Communication and Persuasion* 8, pp. 139–44.

Media Perspektiven. 1991. *Daten zur Mediensituation in Deutschland*. Frankfurt.

Radunski, Peter. 1980. *Wahlkaempfe. Moderne Wahlkampffuehrung als politische Kommunikation*. Munich and Vienna: Olzog.

Schoenbach, Klaus, and Rudolf Wildenmann. 1978. "Election Themes and the Prestige Newspapers." In Karl H. Cerny, ed., *Germany at the Polls*. Washington, DC: American Enterprise Institute, pp. 169–93.

Schütz, Walter J. 1989. "Deutsche Tagespresse 1989," *Media Perspektiven* 7: pp. 748–75.

Schneider, Beate. forthcoming. *Strukturen, Anpassungsprobleme und Entwicklungschancen der Presse auf dem Gebiet der neuen Bundesländer*.

Semetko, Holli A. 1991. "Parties, Leaders and Issues: Images of Britain's Changing Party System in Television News Coverage of the 1983 and 1987 General Election Campaigns," *Political Communication and Persuasion* 8, pp. 163–81.

Semetko, Holli A., Jay G. Blumler, Michael Gurevitch, and David H. Weaver. 1991. *The Formation of Campaign Agendas: A Comparative Analysis of Party and Media Roles in Recent American and British Elections*. Hillsdale, NJ: Lawrence Erlbaum.

ZDF (Ed.). (1984). *ZDF Jahrbuch 1983*. Lengerich: Kleins.

ZDF (Ed.). (1991). *ZDF Jahrbuch 1990*. Lengerich: Kleins.

9

Unification and Electoral Choice

*Helmut Norpoth and Dieter Roth**

A YEAR AFTER THE FALL OF THE WALL, the policy of quick unification was vindicated by resounding margins at the polls on both sides of the old border. CDU/CSU and FDP savored a triumph over an SPD that had embraced the prospect of unification with more caution than passion. In the Western part, where past results provide a baseline of comparison, the SPD took its worst drubbing in 25 years. Moreover, the Western Greens, with their hostility to unification, plummeted below the critical level of electoral support and wound up expelled from the halls of power. The votes of the newly enfranchised Easterners did remarkably little to disturb the broad outline of the partisan division in the West. They provided a faithful duplicate of the Western pattern, marred only by spots of support for the former communist party (PDS). All in all, the first national election in almost 60 years left little doubt that "unity is now being ratified by the people" (Johannes Gross, as cited in Schmemann, 1990).

It is fair to remind ourselves, however, that few reasonable people would have wagered much on such an outcome a little more than a year before the election. Indeed, who even predicted with any assurance that East Germans would be able to vote in a free election in the foreseeable future, let alone in a unified Germany? The 1990 Bundestag election had been scheduled long before, without any East German participation in mind. The collapse of Communist rule on the other side of the Wall, among other things, buried all campaign scripts prepared by the West German parties for just another election in the "old" Federal Republic.

*We thank the Zentralarchiv für empirische Sozialforschung in Cologne for making available the data of the 1990 West German Panel Study (ZA Nr. 1919). The data were collected by the Forschungsgruppe Wahlen in Mannheim. Neither of those institutes, of course, is in any way responsible for the analysis and interpretations of these data.

209

These parties suddenly had to stake claims on an issue that had lain dormant in public consciousness for decades. While some were glad to seize on this opportunity, others despaired at this unwelcome intrusion. The German election of 1990 affords a fascinating glimpse at how political parties redesign their campaigns in the face of an explosive new issue on their doorsteps. (For detailed accounts of the parties' actions and reactions, see the previous chapters in this volume.)

In this atmosphere of uncertainty it was not at all clear which kind of unification policy would lead to success. What suggestions, if any, did public opinion offer to politicians looking for directions? Something a party intent on winning elections could ignore only at its peril? How much did the general public care about this issue? And were popular demands East of the border compatible with those in the West? As will be shown below, the unification issue offered electoral rewards that were far more tantalizing than tangible.

In this chapter we will examine how the issue of unification intruded on voter perceptions of political leaders and parties during the election year. It makes sense to conduct the analysis of voting in 1990 as a two-part exercise. We know a good deal, comparatively speaking, about the typical forces impinging on the decisions of West German voters (on the 1987 vote, see Berger *et al.*, 1990). Long-term partisan loyalties, for example, largely constrain short-term perceptions of the political world. In such an electorate any issue, even one as potent as unification, takes electoral shape within a system of partisan coordinates. Most issues may bend and stretch those coordinates but only rarely will an issue break them or create new ones. By contrast, new voters like the ones in Eastern Germany face their first electoral decision without firm partisan attachments or other helpful guideposts of some standing. Like their first vote, the study of such voters is a venture into terra incognita.

To examine the partisan choices of German voters East and West we have relied on surveys conducted by the Forschungsgruppe Wahlen. Of particular value for the understanding of West German voting is a panel survey that interviewed the same respondents in late 1989, right after the fall of the Wall, again in mid-1990, when the prospect of unification was still uncertain, and once more after the date of unification but before the first nationwide election in December. For the Eastern electorate, our main data source is the "Political barometer" survey conducted in late-August of 1990.

The Western German Electorate

In the year-and-a-half preceding the 1990 election, partisan feelings among the West German public waxed sharply for some parties, and waned for others (see Figure 1.1 in Chapter 1). A newcomer (the Republicans), who had threatened to disrupt the electoral balance, vanished almost without a trace (Roth, 1990a). At the same time, the major opposition party squandered what appeared to a commanding lead over the CDU/CSU. In early 1989, when German unification was either the stuff of dreams or nightmares, if people cared at all, the electoral prospects of the CDU/CSU looked dim. The public's mood had turned sour over the record of the Kohl government on a number of issues, from unemployment to immigration.

Nobody can be sure that Chancellor Kohl would have lost the election without unification, for parties in government often prove adept at recovering from midterm popularity deficits and few political leaders have confounded their detractors more successfully than has Chancellor Kohl. Moreover, the booming economy was expected to help his government ward off electoral bust, the high rate of unemployment notwithstanding. But neither the economic asset nor Kohl's legendary skill at recovering from adversity would have been enough, most observers agree, to prevent defeat this time.

The Electoral Stamp of Unification

It is difficult to miss the electoral potential of the unification question for the West German electorate. This issue easily met some key conditions for swaying partisan preferences (See Campbell *et al.*, 1960: ch. 8). It acquired an immense salience early in 1990, overshadowing such familiar issues as unemployment, the environment, housing, and asylum rights. Judging from spontaneous responses to the question of what people considered to be the most important problem facing the Federal Republic, there is no denying that the unification issue preoccupied the Western public during the election year.

It is rare to see an issue rise so suddenly to the forefront of public concern and retain its salience for such a long time. Only major wars and economic calamities typically have the potential to do so. In the case of the unification issue, the basic policy question seemed simple enough: being for or against unification. The distribution of public opinion was so lopsided as to make unification almost a non-controversial issue. Supporters of unification outnumbered opponents by a huge margin among the Western public. In the May/June survey, 78 percent said they favored unification, compared to 8 percent opposed; 14 percent said they did not care. No political party could hope to gain voter support by opposing unification, and hardly any dared to with a loud and clear voice.

Yet the skewed distribution of public opinion in no way shut off debate. Unification was an elusive goal. Few would have disputed Chancellor Kohl's private estimate in late-November 1989 that "even if unity were reached by the end of the century it would still be a stroke of luck" (Teltschik, 1991: 52). By what means should unification be achieved? As always, questions of means provoked considerable controversy, and people disagreed on whether it would be best to pursue a crash course of action or a wait-and-see approach. In the May/June survey, 51 percent expressed a preference for the slow path, compared to 27 percent in favor of the fast track. The prospect of unification by no means convulsed a lot of people in fits of patriotic ecstasy. Instead the median voter appeared most comfortable with a government that would take its time with the business of unification. It is hard to see why a party advocating a slow approach to unification should have much to fear at the polls (Downs, 1957).

In translating a policy preference into a partisan choice, a voter must, of course, recognize which of the parties takes the preferred policy position. Very often, this is easier said than done since parties cloud their policy offerings in a fog of ambiguity. As for unification, there seems to be little doubt that the federal government pressed for a faster pace than did the SPD, let alone the Greens, who opposed unification and wanted to talk about the weather instead. To put it in personal terms, Chancellor Kohl was driving hard to achieve unification quickly whereas chancellor candidate Lafontaine sounded unenthusiastic about unity. Although neither one of those alternatives commanded a majority among the

212

Western public, the SPD, with its cautious attitude, may have had a stronger claim than the CDU/CSU.

Indeed, when asked whose unification policy they preferred, respondents in the May/June survey leaned by a slim margin to Lafontaine over Kohl. Whatever his true feelings about unification, the SPD's chancellor candidate captured the support of most voters inclined to a slow unification pace. Thus, the unification issue was doing little, if any, harm to the SPD at that time. Despite the salience of unification, opinions on unification policies provided no hint in May and June that this issue would help the CDU/CSU do well in the December election. What kind of change in opinion might have secured help between then and election day?

We can safely dismiss the possibility that many Westerners came to believe that it was Kohl rather than Lafontaine who preferred a slow approach to unification. If anything, it was Kohl who almost single-handedly turned up the speed of the unification train, from his 10-point plan to personal diplomacy with Gorbachev. Yet the more intensely Kohl pursued unification, the more obvious it should have become that this was not the policy that most Westerners preferred. In the meantime, of course, voters may have come to regard Lafontaine less as an advocate of slow unification than as one who did not care about it altogether. No doubt Lafontaine had great difficulty warming to the prospect of unification and could barely bring himself in his campaign speeches to express any joy over it, unlike other leading figures in his party, especially former Chancellor Willy Brandt.

The key to unification, however, was not in the hands of Lafontaine. His ability to sway opinion on this issue was limited compared to the chancellor. In mid-July, Kohl reached a spectacular breakthrough in his negotiations with Gorbachev that paved the way toward unity (for an inside witness account, see Teltschik, 1991: 319–332). This breakthrough is an example of what Mueller (1973: 208) calls a "rally-round-the-flag" event that typically boosts the popularity of U.S. presidents. To qualify as a "rally point," an event must meet three criteria: 1) It is international; 2) involves the country as a whole and particularly the government leader; and 3) it must be specific, dramatic, and sharply focused. (Mueller, 1973: 209).

The spectacular chain of international events stemming from

the summit with Gorbachev in mid-July to the signing of the unification treaties in mid-September sharply boosted the popular standing of Chancellor Kohl. Asked again in October/November as to whether they favored Kohl or Lafontaine with regard to unification, the same respondents who had given a slight edge to Lafontaine in May/June now strongly favored Kohl over Lafontaine, as shown in Table 9.1. This is a remarkable change of mind that left its imprint on voter preferences. Monthly surveys taken by the Forschungsgruppe hint that this shift occurred in the early summer. Between June and August, the CDU/CSU took a lead in voter support over the SPD that it did not relinquish until election day (see Figure 1.1 in Chapter 1).

One might suspect, from an issue-voting perspective, that Kohl improved his popular standing between May and October largely among voters who favored his policy of rapid unification. But as Table 9.2 documents, he gained only 2 percentage points in this group. Instead, those in favor of taking one's time with unification streamed to Kohl in much larger numbers (+12 percent). Their reasoning may have been that Kohl had achieved the desired goal, never mind the means by which he did it. Many Westerns were probably quite unsure in early 1990 as to whether they wanted a rapid or a slow pace of unification. In the face of

Table 9.1. Support in West German Public for Kohl or Lafontaine with Regard to Unification Policy, 1990 (a)

	MAY/JUNE	OCT./NOV.	CHANGE
Favor Kohl's policy	35%	44%	+9
Favor Lafontaine's policy	40	30	-10
See no difference	11	12	+1
Favor neither policy	14	14	0
Total	100%	100%	
(N = 1,402)			

a. The question in the May/June survey asked respondents which policy they supported at the time, whereas the question in the October/November survey asked them which policy they had supported before unification was achieved. The table is based on the May/June respondents who were reinterviewed in October/November.

SOURCE: Forschungsgruppe Wahlen 1990 West German Panel Survey.

uncertainty, caution seems to be the natural response. Whatever preferences respondents expressed about future policy were not a matter of deeply held convictions. If unification could be achieved quickly and without a major international upheaval, most supporters of slow unification would probably not raise objections. When unification was reached, it did not seem to matter much anymore how it had been done. What mattered was that a goal that had been popular all along had been reached.

At the same time, it is apparent from Table 9.2 that respondents who did not care about unification also flocked to Kohl at a considerable rate (+8 percent). Perhaps they felt warmer about unification now that it had become a fact of life. Most puzzling in Table 9.2, however, is the finding that outright opponents to unification increased their esteem for Kohl most sharply between May and October (+18 percent). Whatever the motive for their conversion, it was the added support of opponents, the indifferent, and doubters of his unification policy that the chancellor needed to overtake Lafontaine in his standing among the Western public. That kind of cross-policy change of opinion smacks of a typical rally effect.

It is worth noting that voters did not only change their mind on unification policy, but also their recollection. A good number of respondents who in May/June of 1990 supported Lafontaine's unification policy reported in October/November, when they were reinterviewed, that they had supported Kohl's policy all along. When people forget that they changed their mind it is safe to conclude that their mind was not really made up in the first

Table 9.2. Changing Support for Kohl's Unification Policy by Respondent's Own Opinion on Unification

Opinion on Unification May/June 1990	Change of Support for Kohl (%) May/June –Oct./Nov. 1990
For fast unification	+2
Take time with unification	+12
Don't care about unification	+8
Against unification	+18

Source: Forschungsgruppe Wahlen 1990 West German Panel Survey.

place. In hindsight, that lowers the electoral risk faced by politicians who chart a course of policy not backed by the median voter.

Economy and Environment as Issues in 1990

There are few elections in recent memory in which the economy has not been on voters' minds. Its electoral potential is easy to spot when problems like unemployment or inflation rank high in public concern. Even when neither of these issues worries the electorate, the economy still merits attention. An economy in good health naturally does not show up among the problems voters want to see solved by government. In 1990, the Western German economy enjoyed just the kind of robust health that would make a government look forward to an election. In agreement with the indicators of economic growth, the vast majority of respondents in May/June rated the state of the economy as good (72 percent) and saw more of the same, if not better times ahead (68 percent). Although economic optimism faded slightly between May and November, the consensus view on the economy was still favorable.

However flattering this sentiment was for the parties in government, there were some thorns in the rosy picture. The highly favorable opinion about the economy in mid-year did not presage an electoral landslide for the Kohl government. Worse, it did not even seem to guarantee bare electoral survival. One might suspect that the CDU/CSU and its ally in government, the FDP, simply did not receive sufficient praise from voters for the state of the economy. Table 9.3 shows what the public thought of the incumbent government as compared to a SPD-led alternative in relation to economic matters. Six months before the election, voters gave the CDU-led government the edge on the economy overall as well as on prices, whereas views about unemployment favored the opposition somewhat. Yet for all their favorable economic ratings, the governing parties stared at electoral defeat then.

Other factors must have diminished the electoral potency of the economy in 1990. With Lafontaine as its chancellor candidate, the SPD's issue weapon of choice in the 1990 election was the environment, the trademark issue of the Greens. This strategy promised electoral returns, and not simply at the expense of the Greens. By the end of the 1980s the environment ranked at or near

216

the top of the list of important problems cited by the Western public. A healthy environment appeared to be displacing economic well being as the dominant goal in FRG politics. In addition to this new weapon, the SPD would also rely on issues of social policy in attacking the Kohl government, especially housing.

On the issues of the environment and housing, the Western public preferred an SPD-led government by wide margins in May/June of 1990 (Table 9.3). This gave the SPD and the Greens formidable weapons of their own in an election campaign not dominated by unification. In such a campaign, to put it starkly, they had to convince the electorate to let its worries over the environment and social welfare overcome its good feelings about the economy. In the first half of 1990, the strategy seemed to be working. But by November it no longer was.

Between May and November, as Table 9.3 also shows, the opposition's lead on the environment was cut in half; on housing, it evaporated; and on social security, a close division gave way to a lead for the governing parties. In a broad sweep covering a variety of issues, the opposition parties lost ground in popular evaluations as the governing parties gained ground. It is far-fetched to imagine that voters had a different reason for every one of the many issues in which they raised their estimate of the Kohl government relative to the one led by Lafontaine. The swing toward the governing side was simply too uniform. It shifted the balance of partisan opinion on every one of the issues probed, including three not shown in Table 9.3 (law and order, relations with the Soviet Union, and relations with the U.S.).

The uniform swing in public opinion across the issue board suggests that a common factor was at work. It is conceivable that this factor was the election campaign, creating a surge back toward the governing parties among erstwhile disenchanted supporters. But the surge in 1990 surpassed the typical backswing allowed for in FRG election campaigns (Goergen and Norpoth, 1991). What is more, as can be gleaned from Figure 1.1 in Chapter 1, it commenced long before the opening of the campaign. The surge, we strongly suspect, was the work of the strongest short term force in the 1990 election, leading a significant segment of the electorate to expect better things across the board from the governing parties. The glowing ratings of the Kohl government in the wake of unification appears to have persuaded these voters

Table 9.3. The Lead of the Governing Coalition over an SPD-led Government in West German Evaluations of Issues, 1990 (a)

ISSUE	MAY/JUNE	OCT./NOV.	SWING
Economy	+12	+23	+5.5
Prices	+10	+17	+3.5
Unemployment	-5	+6	+5.5
Environment	-21	-8	+6.5
Housing	-12	+1	+6.5
Social Security	-1	+8	+4.5

a. Entries in the table columns headed May/June and Oct./Nov. show the percentage of respondents who said that the government of CDU/CSU and FDP would be better at handling a given issue minus the percentage saying an SPD-led government would handle it better. The swing measures the net change between middle- and late-1990.

SOURCE: Forschungsgruppe Wahlen 1990 West German Panel Survey.

that the governing parties also held the better cards on other issues as well.

The Popular Appeal of Leaders

In German federal elections, the campaign slogan, *"Auf den Kanzler kommt es an"* (What matters is the chancellor), has a certain ring of truth. The incumbent chancellor has typically surpassed his challenger in popular support and led the governing parties to electoral victory. In the end, the 1990 election confirmed this rule, although not before threatening to prove itself the exception.

Throughout 1989 and most of the first half of 1990, Kohl trailed Lafontaine by enough of a margin to raise the challenger's hopes of ousting the chancellor. In May of 1990 he still led Kohl by 10 percentage points (Figure 9.1). Yet by October Kohl had overwhelmed Lafontaine in the contest of chancellor approval, maintaining an almost 20-point lead until the election. This sweeping reversal of the popular standings of the two main chancellor aspirants turned the 1990 election into a personal triumph for Helmut Kohl, who took special pride in carrying his electoral district in Ludwigshafen for the first time ever.

The change is also evident in the new appraisal of Kohl's personal qualities. In May/June, he did not strike most respondents as

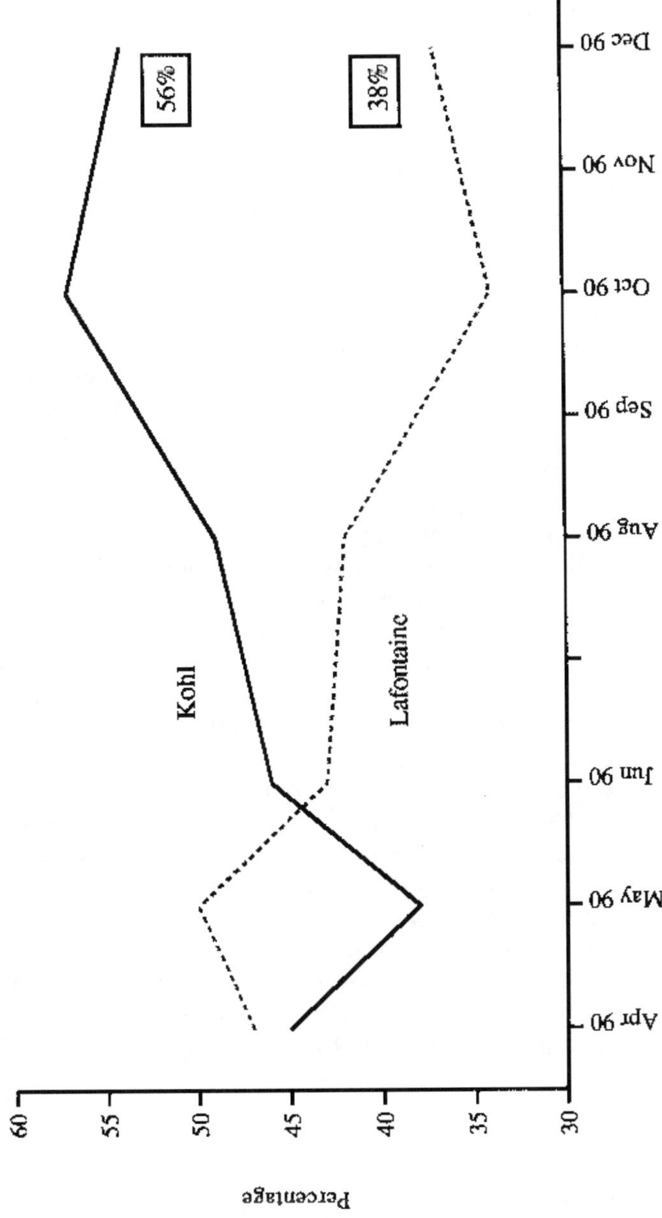

Figure 9.1. Chancellor Preferences of the West German Public, April–Dec. 1990.

SOURCE: Forchungsgruppe Wahlen Monthly Surveys.

being especially forceful or capable of leadership, let alone credible or honest. But in the reinterviews in October/November, respondents gave him substantially higher marks, especially for leadership. This was the domain where Kohl's reputation improved the most and where the gap between chancellor and challenger widened the most (57 percent for Kohl, 21 percent for Lafontaine). Leadership capability ranks among the most salient qualities of chancellor candidates in the mind of the Western public. Thus Kohl managed to convince a large number of Westerners who seemed dubious earlier that he possessed a highly treasured quality.

There is little reason to believe that this was a foregone conclusion of the election campaign. Kohl had been chancellor for almost eight years, and he was hardly a novice with undefined qualities. Only a major event or action testing his mettle as a leader would be likely to sway the public's view of him. It is difficult to see how Kohl could have gained public recognition as a forceful leader in 1990 without his breakthroughs in achieving unification. If there were other successes, they escaped the attention of the general public and most commentators.

Yet even at the peak of his popularity, Kohl could not match, let alone surpass, the personal appeal of his foreign minister, Hans-Dietrich Genscher. On a scale ranging from a low of -5.0 to a high of +5.0, Genscher averaged 3.1 in the October/November survey, compared to 1.5 for Kohl and 1.0 for Lafontaine. The most prominent member of the FDP has established himself as a man above the parties, who had no enemies. In 1990 Genscher enjoyed favorable ratings, on the average, among supporters of all the different parties. Social Democrats liked him just about as much as did Christian Democrats, whose opinion of him barely lagged behind the opinion of his own Free Democrats. Even among Green loyalists, more Greens liked than disliked him. With so little malice toward Genscher, voters proved most charitable to the FDP at the polls in 1990, giving it one of its best years ever. Still Genscher did not lead his party to a first-place finish, for personal popularity is a currency of only limited convertability in German elections.

The Eastern German Electorate

Making sense of the decisions of East German voters presents an incomparably more daunting challenge than is true for voters in the old Federal Republic. Much of our explanatory leverage in electoral analysis comes from laying present results side by side with past results. Patterns established in the past provide us with a map and compass for contemporary electoral journeys, and we tend to attribute significance to a particular factor in a given election to the extent that the result departs from previous ones. In the case of East Germany, there is no such electoral trail of any use.

What is more, unlike newly eligible voters in an established electorate, East Germans entered the electoral process in 1990 without the preparation afforded by the usual forms of partisan socialization. Deprived of the experience of a competitive party system for nearly sixty years, East Germans had few opportunities to form partisan attachments. It is doubtful that more than a handful learned about the party of their 1990 choice from mom or dad at the dinner table, or from membership in labor unions or churches.

It is not clear what short term force could be expected to make the strongest impression on voters held so loosely, if at all, in the grip of partisan allegiances. In the broadest sense, we tend to group short term forces under the headings of candidates and issues. The East German electorate might make an inviting target for a "political leader [who] is endowed by the voters with such an extraordinary measure of personal support at the polls that his latitude for personal decisions becomes rather large" (Converse and Dupeux, 1966: 292). This would seem the hour of the charismatic leader. On the other hand, it might be the case that "a voter in a new society will evaluate the contending parties in terms of their promised changes in his welfare" (Fiorina, 1981: 66). In their first election, such voters would be in a position to cast their vote purely as a matter of future policy, assuming they comprehend enough of politics to engage in such rational behavior.

Partisanship

While opportunities to forge lasting partisan attachments in East Germany were undoubtedly limited, most East Germans did not live in a partisan vacuum. Aside from the Communist Party (SED, now the PDS), there existed parties like the (Eastern) CDU and Liberal Democrats. However subservient those parties were to the ruling SED, they may have provided potential objects for voter attachments. In contrast, having been annexed in East Germany after 1945 by the Communists, the SPD could provide no visible object of partisan allegiance to citizens there for almost half a century. It may seem far-fetched to suggest that this disadvantage had something to do with the poor electoral showing of the Eastern SPD in 1990, but it should not be dismissed out of hand.

More plausible, though, is the likelihood that the partisan feelings of East Germans related not to parties in their midst, but to those West of the border. Being heavily tuned into West German television, many East Germans must have felt quite at home in the party politics of the Federal Republic. Indeed, given how remote politics is for most people in Western democracies, many Easterners may have been as familiar with those parties as were their Western contemporaries.

Short of forging an outright identification with one of those parties, East Germans probably had their favorites among the Western parties. In a survey taken by the Forschungsgruppe in August of 1990, just a few months after the first free election, practically every East German respondent picked one of the four well-known West German parties when asked which one she liked best. In a fledgling electorate, a flood of responses like, "don't like any of them," or "not sure about which one I like best," or even "don't know enough about them" would not have been at all surprising. Yet hardly anybody offered any of these responses. Far from groping uncomfortably with the problem of sorting out the various political parties of another political system, East Germans seemed surprisingly sure-handed in their choices.

This is also the impression conveyed by the aggregate picture of party support (Figure 1.2 in Chapter 1). From March to December of 1990, the CDU held a steady lead, broken only once, over the SPD. Were it not for the presence of the PDS, it would be easy to mistake this chart for one pertaining to the Western German electorate. This similarity, however, may warrant the disclaimer prefacing works of fiction: all resemblances to real characters is purely coincidental. In the Eastern case, the serenity of the aggregate surface masks massive turbulence underneath. Asked about which party they intended to vote for in the next election, barely one in two Eastern respondents of the August survey preferred the same party they had voted for in the March election. Easterners were changing their partisan preferences more frequently in

222

four months than voters in established democracies typically do in four years. This should not be surprising. An electorate lacking stable partisan attachments is easily swayed by the flow of events and conditions. Under those circumstances, a party can quickly make an electoral fortune, and just as quickly lose it, depending on how well it is able to ride the prevailing winds.

The Unification Issue

These short term forces may involve an issue that is so pressing, with perceptions of competing party positions are so clear to the public, that electoral consequences seem a foregone conclusion. Consider the question of unification. Surveys taken at the time of the *Volkskammer* election in March of 1990 showed that East Germans favored unification with West Germany by a margin of 20 to 1. Being so much more lopsided than in the West, the distribution of opinion gave the unification question an even greater electoral potential in the East.

In the simple case of a two-party system, the party that best succeeds in aligning itself with the most favored side in voter perceptions can hope to reap a rich electoral harvest at the expense of the other party, which can come to be seen as aligned with the less favored side. In the more diverse party system that emerged in Eastern Germany, any issue's impact will have to be shared by several parties. That is what happened in the *Volkskammer* election, where the several parties championing unification had to split the lion's share of the vote (Roth, 1990b: 383).

On the other hand, a voter's desire for unification would not explain why he or she chose the CDU as opposed to the FDP (BFD) or the SPD, all of which supported unification. As in the West, opinion on the policy of unification was divided in Eastern Germany. Surveys showed that among voters who wanted rapid unification, 75 percent chose the CDU (plus its allies), which had proposed such a course of action (Roth 1990b: 383). Media postmortems of the *Volkskammer* election pointed to a mandate for quick unification as advocated by Chancellor Kohl and his party.

Although the CDU alliance captured the bulk of voters favoring quick unification, it must also be noted that in March a majority of East Germans still preferred a slow pace of unification. This sentiment, however, was poorly translated into partisan votes.

The SPD arguably staked the strongest claim for voters favoring slow unification, but failed to carry the big bulk of these votes; the CDU captured nearly as many, and the PDS (no friend of unification with the West) took a sizable share as well. Thus, the link between unification preferences and partisan choices in March was quite tenuous. We suspect that East Germans were neither firm in their opinions on unification policy nor clear about the positions taken by the various parties. For an electorate grappling with voting decisions in a free election for the first time in their lives, neither of those features should come as any surprise.

There is a considerable body of evidence that suggests Eastern opinion on unification policy was not firmly cast but responded quickly to changing conditions. The currency exchange on July 1, for example, was hugely popular. By August, as the survey of the Forschungsgruppe Wahlen shows, Easterners had set aside their cautious attitude about the pace of unification and now could not wait to see it happen as soon as possible: 55 percent wanted it "at once" and another 31 percent wanted it "this year." Easterners now sounded desperate for unification. The surge of opinion in favor of quick unification would seem to herald an electoral boom for the party most closely identified with such a policy, and without much doubt the CDU should have been the beneficiary of this development at the expense of the SPD. Indeed, when asked whether they supported Kohl's or Lafontaine's unification policy, Easterners leaned toward Kohl by a 4 to 3 margin, as shown in Table 9.4. While this was reassuring for Kohl, it is not the margin he might have expected in view of widespread clamor for immediate unification.

It appears that many Easterners failed to make the proper connection between their own issue preference and the candidates' positions. This suspicion is confirmed by the finding that shows barely half of those favoring unification "at once" expressed support for Kohl. The sizable group of voters wanting unification "this year" actually gave a slight edge to Lafontaine, who certainly had not campaigned for unification to take place in 1990. One can only conclude that voters were not quite sure about the positions taken by the leading politicians on this issue. Almost one of every five Easterners admitted as much by saying that they saw no difference between Kohl and Lafontaine on unification. Uncertainty and confusion about policy stands were bound to dilute

Table 9.4. Support in East German Public for Kohl or Lafontaine with Regard to Unification Policy, August 1990 (a)

Favor Kohl's policy	40%
Favor Lafontaine's policy	31
See no difference	19
Favor neither policy	9
No opinion	1
Total	100%
(N)	(1,105)

SOURCE: Forschungsgruppe Wahlen Politbarometer East, 16–27 August 1990.

Table 9.5. Support in East German Public for Kohl or Lafontaine with Regard to Unification Policy by Evaluations of Progress Made, August 1990

	UNIFICATION HAS GONE		
	BETTER	AS EXPECTED	WORSE
Favor Kohl's policy	61%	44%	28%
Favor Lafontaine's policy	19	28	40
See no difference	16	18	21
Favor neither policy	4	9	10
Total	100%	99%	99%
(N)	(217)	(368)	(465)
Proportion of All Respondents	20%	33%	42%

SOURCE: Forschungsgruppe Wahlen Politbarometer East, 16–27 August 1990.

whatever electoral potency unification might have possessed as a policy question.

At the same time, with every step taken in its direction, unification had palpable consequences for Easterners, giving rise to satisfaction but also disappointment. The verdict on the progress of unification was decidedly a mixed one. By August, the balance actually tilted toward the negative side. Twice as many people thought that unification had been going worse than expected (42 percent) as thought that it had been going better than expected (20 percent). To be sure, a good number felt it was going as expected but we can only guess how many of them thought it was going as "good" as expected rather than as "bad" as expected.

No matter how desirable the goal, misgivings of this sort cut sharply into Eastern support for Chancellor Kohl. As Table 9.5 shows, within the sizable group that expressed negative feelings about the unification process ("worse than expected"), barely one in four said they supported Kohl's policy. On the other hand, voters with a positive reaction ("better than expected") voiced support for Kohl over Lafontaine by a wide margin. Apparently respondents who felt it was going as expected meant mostly as "good as expected," since far more of them picked Kohl than Lafontaine. Overall, attitudes of the East German public about unification favored Kohl over Lafontaine, but not by a wide margin. The advocate of speedy unification received by no means the overwhelming support from a public that was so impatiently demanding it.

The Appeal of Leaders

One might suspect that voters suddenly thrust into the electoral arena might be easily swayed by political leaders with a strong personal appeal. Though not known for any charismatic qualities in the past, Chancellor Kohl rallied large and enthusiastic crowds in his forays into East Germany soon after the fall of the Wall. By giving his blessing to the Eastern CDU, he saved that party from being repudiated as a former lackey of the hated communists. It is hard to imagine that the Eastern CDU would have made a respectable showing by itself in a free election of a genuinely sovereign East Germany.

Attributing to Kohl a profound influence on the political choices of East Germans, nonetheless, is not the same as crediting him with any personal magic. Did he win people over with the sheer force of his personality or did they like the message he was bringing? When asked to rate political leaders on a scale running from most unfavorable (-5) to most favorable (+5), East Germans gave Kohl a meager rating of 0.7, on the average, in August. While Kohl impressed a majority of the public, one-third of the respondents expressed a negative opinion of him. This is not the rating of a charismatic leader. What is more, Kohl was by no means the most popular politician among the Eastern public. Although rated more favorably than his major rival, Lafontaine (0.3), he fell way short of the popularity claimed by Genscher (2.9). Indeed, if personal ratings point to any charismatic leader in 1990, it would have to be the head of the FDP. As in the West, Genscher was far and away the most popular politician in East Germany. His personal appeal was so sweeping that not even PDS voters could escape it.

There were good reasons for predicting that Genscher's electoral coattails for the FDP would be longer in the East than in West. Not only was he one of them, in a sense, but few East Germans were dyed-in-the-wool loyalists of either the CDU or the SPD. The August survey showed that even voters leaning toward the SPD liked Genscher more than Lafontaine; and those leaning toward the CDU gave Genscher the same high rating as Kohl. The Eastern FDP did outpoll its Western counterpart (13 percent against 11 percent) and did capture one constituency. But with Genscher's popularity being so sweeping in the East, one might have expected an even better electoral return for the FDP there.

We suspect that many Easterners failed to connect Genscher strongly enough with his party, or were plainly unaware of his partisanship. No matter how strongly a voter feels about a political leader, when that leader himself is not on the ballot, such feelings are not automatically channeled into votes for other candidates. Even among Easterners aware of Genscher's partisanship, it is likely that he was seen primarily as the foreign minister, and not as the leading figure of the FDP. In contrast, Chancellor Kohl stressed his partisan role and turned the Eastern CDU into the partisan vehicle of his electoral campaign.

Better than his competitors, Kohl managed to blend the three key ingredients of electoral success: party, personality, and policy. Whatever popular acclaim he had won for his success in delivering German unification he was able, in large measure, to transfer to his Eastern party. Among those who expressed support for Kohl's unification policy in August, eight out of ten said they would vote for the CDU. Kohl was thus able to deny his ally in government, the FDP, an equal share of the electoral reward for unification. At the same time, among voters who favored Lafontaine on unification, only one in two said they would vote for the SPD. Getting the voting support of so few when your side is already in the minority adds partisan insult to electoral injury.

Conclusions

The voting patterns in the first national election in almost 60 years revealed some striking similarities in the two parts of the newly unified Germany. Most remarkably, the newly enfranchised voters in the East gave the Christian Democratic and Free Democratic parties roughly the same majority support as did voters in the West. The SPD fared dismally in both parts, but particularly so in the East, where it was remembered by people with long memories as a party stronghold in free elections (Matthias and Morsey, 1979: 777) and not considered rich in electoral soil for CDU or FDP. Such traditions or handicaps count for little in the partisan choices of an electorate casting its first free ballot.

Except for some notable pockets of SED-PDS support, the partisan feelers of Easterners, just like their television antennaes, were turned toward the West. As long-time spectators, many were familiar with the cast of partisan characters over there. The CDU won the competition for the affections of Eastern voters largely because it was the leading party in a government that held the key to unification. First, by promising an aggressive policy toward unification, Kohl's party captured the lion's share of supporters of quick unification in March. Then, having delivered unity, it reaped its electoral reward in December.

In the electorate of the old Federal Republic, the unification issue also stamped electoral choices, though this process took longer and had to overcome bigger obstacles than in the East. For one thing, throughout the year in which the Wall toppled and until the middle of the election year, the Kohl government had to brave the winds of popular discontent over issues unrelated to unification. What is more, the sudden prospect of unification in early 1990 did remarkably little to brighten the electoral outlook of the CDU/CSU. Although public support for the idea of reunification in the Federal Republic was widespread, few were clamoring for a crash program to secure unity. Under these circumstances, advocating a policy of caution by no means condemned the SPD to its third straight defeat in the Western part of Germany.

It was the unpredictable breakthroughs on the road to unity that turned the partisan tide in favor of Chancellor Kohl in the minds of the West German public. Such events are known to generate "rally round the flag" effects that boost the popular standing of government leaders for a while. Recent examples of such an effect include Prime Minister Thatcher's popularity surge in the wake of the Falklands War (Norpoth, 1987), and that of President Bush after the Gulf War (Kagay, 1991). The political drama culminating in national unity with breathtaking speed placed the chancellor and the parties of his government in the center of public attention. In such situations it is the parties in office that get the popular applause, and the opposition gets, well, another chance next time.

There is no denying that, like Thatcher and Bush, Kohl pursued a risky course in securing his goal. One should not underestimate the uncertainties and electoral risks that this strategy faced, no matter how well it worked in the end. Had his strategy backfired, he may have earned little but rebuke for defying prudence and public opinion. Kohl took the lead, hoping voters would follow, rather than trying to pursue a policy that appealed to the median voter. It is an intriguing irony that had Kohl heeded the preference for a slow, cautious unification policy, he might not have won the support of most Western voters in the 1990 election. A gradual approach of action, in all likelihood, would not have led to the spectacular breakthroughs of the summer, without which, his government would have stayed in the somewhat unfavorable light that had fastened on it in Western opinion. In an odd way Helmut Kohl won the public's favor by going against its policy advice. As Bertolt Brecht once advised, he dissolved his people and chose another one.

Partisan votes cast at turning points in history may very well form the mold of lasting attachments to political parties. Most Eastern voters are not likely to forget how they voted for the first time in a year that brought them freedom. The CDU, and to some degree the FDP, may gain a long-standing advantage in the voters' minds as the parties of national union. At the same time, disappointments in the East coupled with resentments in the West are bound to stir up a pot of unfavorable feelings about those that brought about unity. It is at this moment that the opposition parties, as well as newcomers, may be able to successfully wage the kind of campaign denied them in the year of unification.

References

Berger, Manfred, Wolfgang G. Gibowski, Matthias Jung, and Dieter Roth. 1990. "Sieg Ohne Glanz: Eine Analyse der Bundestagswahl 1987," in *Wahlen und Wahler*, pp. 689–734, ed. Max Kaase and Hans-Dieter Klingemann. Opladen: Westdeutscher Verlag.

Campbell, Angus, Philip E. Converse, Warren E. Miller, and Donald E. Stokes 1960. *The American Voter*. New York: Wiley.

Converse, Philip E. and Georges Dupeux. 1966. "De Gaulle and Eisenhower: The Public Image of the Victorious General," in *Elections and the Political Order*, pp. 292–345, ed. Angus Campbell, Philip E. Converse, Warren E. Miller and Donald E. Stokes. New York: Wiley.

Downs, Anthony. 1957. *An Economic Theory of Democracy*. New York: Harper & Row.

Fiorina, Morris P. 1981. *Retrospective Voting in American Elections*. New Haven: Yale University Press.

Goergen, Christian and Helmut Norpoth. 1991. "Government Turnover and Economic Accountability," *Electoral Studies* 10: pp. 191–207.

Kagay, Michael. 1991. "Approval of Bush Soars," *New York Times*, 19 Jan.

Matthias, Erich and Rudolf Morsey, ed. 1979. *Das Ende der Parteien 1933*. Konigstein: Athenaeum.

Mueller, John E. 1973. *War, Presidents and Public Opinion*. New York: Wiley.

Norpoth, Helmut. 1987. "The Falklands War and Government Popularity in Britain: Rally without Consequence or Surge without Decline?" *Electoral Studies* 6: pp. 3–16.

Roth, Dieter. 1990a. "Schneller Aufstieg and tiefer Fall einer Protestpartei am rechten Rand," *Aus Politik und Zeitgeschehen*, Sept. 14, pp. 37–38.

______. 1990b. "Die Wahlen zur Volkskammer in der DDR: Der Versuch einer Erklarung," *Politische Vierteljahresschrift* 31: pp. 369–93.

Schmemann, Serge. 1990. "Kohl's Coalition Elected To Lead Unified Germany," *New York Times*, 3 Dec.

Teltschik, Horst. 1991. *329 Tage: Innenansichten der Einigung*. Berlin: Siedler.

IV. BEYOND THE ELECTION

10

The German Party System
and the Future

*Russell J. Dalton and Wilhelm Bürklin**

A N ELECTION IS NOT OVER once the ballots are counted. Helmut Kohl's coalition government emerged from the 1990 Bundestagswahl as the victor, albeit with only a modest return to show for the dramatic accomplishments of German unification. The CDU's modest showing, and the issues raised during the campaign, leave lingering questions about how to interpret the results in terms of the Federal Republic's political future. Events themselves have prompted further political developments since the election.

This chapter looks at the implications of the election and subsequent events for the German party system. Our most basic question is whether the 1990 Bundestagswahl results represent a pattern of continuity or political change for the Federal Republic. In the Western *Länder*, the new issues of German unification joined the established political controversies of past elections. What was the mix of both factors? In the new Eastern *Länder*, the party system was just being established, and the question was whether it would reflect Western patterns or introduce new forces into German electoral politics. Indeed, the chapters in this volume have described both elements of continuity and change in the 1990 Bundestagswahl.

One might claim that the 1990 Bundestagswahl was a "maintaining election" that basically continued the voting patterns of

*We would like to acknowledge the support of the Alexander von Humboldt Foundation, the Center for German and European Studies at the University of California, Berkeley, and the University of California, Irvine, for grants to conduct the research presented here.

recent elections – and extended this same system to the East.[1] Support for the governing parties among the Western electorate barely changed from 1987, returning the incumbent government to power. Moreover, many analysts claim that the expansion of the apparatus and personalities of the Western parties to East Germany in the March 1990 *Volkskammer* campaign already made this a Western election on Eastern soil. The December Bundestagswahl election results speak to this similarity: the CDU/CSU vote total in both regions was very similar (44.1 versus 43.4 percent), just as the result for the parties to the left of the spectrum (SPD and PDS) was almost identical (36.2 versus 33.5 percent).

Another perspective on the election stresses the elements of change. Several contributors to this volume describe the high levels of individual vote change that occurred in 1990 and the dramatically different patterns of party support in East and West. If not reaching the magnitude of a "realigning election," the 1990 Bundestagswahl may have been a "converting election" that changed the overall patterns of party alignment. For instance, the voting patterns of Easterners are different from the cleavage patterns that have structured partisan politics at least since the formation of the Federal Republic (Dalton, 1992, 1984). Thus, despite the similar vote shares in both West and East, and relative to the last Bundestagswahl, the composition of the parties' voting blocs in 1990 differed across regions and their traditional past. The perpetuation of these voting patterns might reshape the internal distribution of political power within the parties and alter their political identity.

A convincing argument can also be made that because of the unique historical circumstances surrounding unification, the 1990 election represents a temporary "deviation election" that might not be replicated in future contests. In the West, the unification issue overshadowed the older issues of economics and the welfare state (and the newer issues of the environment and women's rights). This was *not* a normal election fought on normal political

1. Angus Campbell (1966) proposed a typology of maintaining, realigning, and deviating elections, and Gerald Pomper (1967) extended this framework to include converting elections. Although theoretically useful, it is difficult to use these general labels for the 1990 Bundestagswahl, as there were essentially two elections: an established electoral system in the West and the new system of the East.

234

grounds. The political situation was even more tentative in the East, where political institutions and the entire democratic process were still being developed. For example, many of the basic socio-economic interest groups, such as business associations and labor unions, that will define democratic competition in the future were in the process of formation or transition (Fichter, 1991; Dalton, 1993, chap. 8). The political parties themselves lacked a firm organizational structure or membership base in the new *Länder*. Even more basic, Easterners are still learning about competitive democracy and the electoral process. The first elections may have had a determining influence in setting the political course of a new citizenry, but a course is also more easily changed early in the voyage.

Clearly, elements of both continuity and change exist in the current German party system. The following sections examine the level and sources of party support in an effort to judge the relative constancy or change in electoral alignments; we also examine the institutional base of the parties as another indicator of their present condition. By examining different features of the party system, we hope to assess how German unification has affected the political parties and the party system itself.

Shifting Levels of Party Support

Helmut Kohl and his government won the 1990 Bundestagswahl. Yet Kohl's reward for guiding the historic process of German unification was a 0.2 percent *decrease* in the CDU/CSU's vote share in the ten Western *Länder*, compared to the prior Bundestagswahl (Table 1.4). History will undoubtedly attribute Kohl's decisive actions as the key to German union, but the German voter seemed less impressed. Indeed, one of the surprising aspects of the 1990 election results was that so little had changed since 1987, and that the Eastern vote shares so closely approximated those in the West.[2]

It is also clear that Kohl's victory in 1990 represented a less than enthusiastic endorsement of him by the voters. Several of the analysts in this volume have noted that it was a lackluster campaign;

2. David Conradt (Chapter 3) even observes that the CDU/CSU's "victory" in 1990 was to regain its 1987 vote share, after having suffered in the 1989 European Parliament elections and state contests.

citizens seemingly voted for the government to acknowledge the accomplishments of German union, rather than to provide a policy mandate for the future. Moreover, as soon as the ballots were counted, the longer term costs of the election became apparent for the Christian Democrats and their Liberal party allies.

Kohl promised Eastern voters that no one would be worse off because of unification in the short term; reality has been different. Layoffs from Eastern firms continued through 1992, and the promised economic recovery has still not yet materialized. Throughout most of 1991 and 1992 nearly a third of the Eastern workforce was functionally unemployed. As they now will admit, the Kohl government initially overestimated the economic vitality of the East and the ability of Eastern industry and manufacturing to compete in a world market. The inefficient and undercapitalized nature of the Eastern economy made a transition to a Western market economy extremely dubious. As inefficiencies were corrected, the number of jobs in old state-owned industries decreased, and unemployment skyrocketed. Another economic blow came with the collapse of the Eastern trading bloc (COMECON), which ended most trade agreements with the nations of Eastern Europe and the former Soviet Union.

The critical problem for the East, however, has not been the loss of old jobs but the inability of the economic system to create productive new jobs in their place. A variety of factors have contributed to this economic failure. For example, the initial advantage of substantially lower labor costs in the East has evaporated as Eastern wages have risen to reflect the cost of Western-produced goods. The Kohl government has tried to create new investment incentives through grants and tax benefits, but this has not proved sufficient. Besides cost factors, the property restitution laws and the nebulous property titles on Eastern land have discouraged Western investment in the East. There are now more than one million individual claims to recover property confiscated illegally during the regimes of the Third Reich or German Democratic Republic. Until such claims are resolved, Western financiers are hesitant to invest in the East. The uncertain political and social situations in the East are additional disincentives to Western investors.

Thus, instead of a rapid integration of the two economies, economists are now extending the target date of economic parity between West and East until early in the next century. Moreover, Easterners have rapidly shifted their frame of reference from their former condition to the standards of the West. They are not asking if they are better off because of unification, but if they are as well off as Westerners. This was an inevitable development, and the East-West gap in living standards leaves Easterners feeling short-changed by unification.

Many Westerners also now believe they are suffering, at least economically, as a result of unification. Kohl had promised that German unification could be accomplished through a second Wirtschaftswunder and without new taxes. In January 1991, Kohl's government introduced legislation that called for a surcharge on income taxes (*Solidarbeitrag*) and increased other charges. The Social Democrats were quick to label this as Kohl's tax lie (*Steuerlüge*), and emphasized the costs of unification for the West.[3] Moreover, most of the funds going East were used for consumption rather than investment. In 1992, for instance, more than DM 200 billion in public funds were transferred from the Western *Länder* to the East, and two-thirds of these funds went towards social services and the basic operation of state and local governments. The crippling strike of the public employees union in mid-1992 signalled a level of economic discontent and conflict that was atypical of industrial relations in the West. Thus, Manfred Kuechler (Chapter 2) shows that Easterners became more critical of the unification process during 1991, while Westerners became more critical of Easterners' dissatisfactions.

Although the economic costs of German unification have been tremendous, a series of other political and social problems have arisen in the wake of German union. Even before unification, the Federal Republic was receiving a growing stream of individuals seeking to settle in Germany: ethnic Germans from Eastern Europe and asylum-seekers.[4] This stream of immigrants has

3. Ironically, although many people feel betrayed by Kohl's reneging on his promise of no new taxes, data from the Forschungsgruppe Wahlen show that most Westerners doubted the honesty of this promise when it was made in 1990 (Forschungsgruppe Wahlen, 1990).

4. The Federal Republic grants ethnic Germans the right to resettle in Germany and immediately attain citizenship. In addition, the Basic Law (Article 16) guarantees the right to asylum to individuals persecuted on political grounds. Individuals who claim asylum are allowed into the Federal Republic, and then supported by the state until their appeal is heard by the courts. In 1993 the CDU/CSU and SPD agreed to a revision of Article 16 that restricts the criteria for asylum.

grown because of the increasing instability in Eastern Europe and the rest of the world. The political and social tensions associated with these immigrants was a major factor behind the rise of the Republikaner party in 1989. The social and economic dislocations accompanying unification have intensified tensions over immigration issues in the new *Länder*. Starting with sporadic attacks against foreigners by small right-wing groups and youth gangs, there has been mounting opposition to foreigners in areas where they have been relocated in large numbers. Foreigners are criticized not because they are responsible for the situation in the East, but because they are vulnerable targets of attack for frustrated and worried Germans.

Unification also has revived debates about the structure of the Federal Republic's welfare system. Westerners are concerned about the high costs of social benefits being provided to Easterners; Germans on both sides of the border are criticizing the generosity provided to aslyum-seekers, who are viewed as economic-refugees rather than political refugees. Similarly, immigration into Germany and migration from Eastern to Western Germany have created severe housing shortages and worries about a new housing crisis of the 1990s (*Wohnungsnot*). Indeed, the present financial demands on the social welfare system are far greater than during the 1970s, when debates about the crisis of the welfare system were commonplace.

As these social and political problems have mounted, the governing parties have suffered losses in public support. State election results have signalled the declining fortunes of the CDU and FDP (Table 10.1). In January 1991, a small vote shift away from the governing CDU/FDP majority gave control of the Hesse state government to a new SPD-Green coalition (Schmitt-Beck, 1991). The results of this election were especially consoling for the Green party. Running under the leadership of the moderate Joschka Fischer, the party rose significantly above its recent Bundestag result.

An even more stunning loss for Kohl soon followed in Rhineland-Palatinate (Billing, 1991). This *Land* is a historic stronghold for the Christian Democrats; it is Helmut Kohl's home state and the CDU had ruled here since the first election in 1947. The April 1991 state election followed a series of tax increases from the federal government. The CDU also suffered because of an

Table 10.1. Election Results by State

	CDU	SPD	FDP	GREENS	REP	DVU	OTHER
Hesse							
Landtag 1991	40.2	40.8	7.4	8.8	1.7	—	
Bundestag 1990	41.3	38.0	10.9	5.6	2.1	—	2.1
Landtag 1987	42.1	40.2	7.8	9.4	—	—	0.5
Rhineland-Palatinate							
Landtag 1991	38.7	44.8	6.9	6.5	2.0	—	
Bundestag 1990	45.6	36.1	10.4	4.0	1.7	—	2.2
Landtag 1987	45.1	38.8	7.3	5.9	—	—	2.9
Hamburg							
City 1991	35.1	48.0	5.4	7.2	1.2	—	
Bundestag 1990	36.6	41.0	12.0	5.8	1.7	—	2.9
City 1987	40.5	45.0	6.5	7.0	—	—	1.0
Bremen							
City 1991	30.7	38.8	9.5	11.4	1.5	6.2	—
Bundestag 1990	30.9	42.5	12.8	8.3	2.1	—	3.4
City 1987	23.4	50.5	10.0	10.2	1.2	3.4	1.2
Baden-Württemberg							
Landtag 1992	39.6	29.4	5.9	9.5	10.9		
Bundestag 1990	46.5	29.1	12.3	5.7	3.2	—	3.2
Landtag 1988	49.0	32.0	5.9	7.9	1.0	—	4.2
Schleswig-Holstein							
Landtag 1992	33.8	46.2	5.6	4.9	—	6.0	
Bundestag 1990	43.5	38.5	11.4	4.0	1.2	—	1.4
Landtag 1988	33.3	54.8	4.4	2.9	—	—	4.6

internal battle over the leadership of the state party; as a result, the popular Bernhard Vogel was replaced by Hans-Otto Wilhelm at the top of the CDU ticket. The CDU and FDP both suffered major losses; together the two parties fell 10.4 percent short of their 1990 Bundestagswahl results. For the first time in the history of the state the CDU was forced onto the opposition benches; an SPD-FDP coalition took over the government.

The Hamburg and Bremen elections later in 1991 repeated this same general pattern (Bürklin, 1991; Roth, 1992). In these two elections both the CDU and FDP lost vote shares compared to their Bundestag results. The SPD retained control of the government in both city-states, either as a one-party government in Hamburg or as part of an *Ampelkoalition* in Bremen. These elections were also heartening for the Greens, who watched their vote totals increase significantly over their 1990 results. As Schoonmaker and Frankland suggest in their chapter (Chapter 6), voters apparently were rewarding the Greens' for moving to the center following their Neumönster conference.

The two state elections of 1992, in Baden-Württemberg and Schleswig-Holstein, continued this downward slide for the Christian Democrats. A CDU parliamentary majority had governed in Baden-Württtenberg, but local party scandals and the performance of the national party led to a sharp drop in Christian Democrat support (Sturm, 1992). Even more ominous was the sharp rise in support for the right-wing Republikaner party, up from 3.2 percent in 1990 to 10.9 percent in the 1992 Landtagswahl. The economic failures of the government and rising public concern over issues of immigration and East/West relations were polarizing the electorate, pushing formerly loyal CDU voters to the right (Republikaner) and left (SPD). With the Right divided, control of the government shifted to a Grand Coalition of the CDU and the SPD. The Schleswig-Holstein election compounded the damage (Bürklin and Layritz, 1992). In the previous *Land* election in 1988, the SPD had won control of the government by riding a popular backlash against the election dirty tricks scandal of the CDU. The Christian Democrats viewed this as a deviating election and rebounded in the 1990 Bundestag election. Yet, then the CDU lost resoundingly in the 1992 state elections. The CDU's vote total dropped 9.7 percent from its Bundestagswahl results and a far-right party, the German People's Union (DVU), siphoned off some of these conservative voters. The SPD retained control of the Schleswig-Holstein government.

These state election results have severely weakened the Christian Democrats. By mid-1982 there was not a single state among the ten Western *Länder* that was headed by a CDU-led government with the SPD in opposition. These losses mean that the CDU/CSU-FDP coalition no longer controls the Bundesrat, where SPD-led state governments are now a majority. Furthermore, the CDU/CSU's popularity continues to run low in the polls in both the Western and Eastern *Länder* (Figures 1.1 and 1.2). If elections had been held in 1992 in the East, the CDU might have been swept from office in all four states where it now holds power.

Helmut Kohl has been fairly sanguine about these developments. He calls this a period of difficult passage (*Durststrecke*) for the party, claiming that the Union's fortunes will improve with economic growth in the East; before the next election, it is hoped. These reassurances are unconvincing to many people, however. The CDU's commitment to free market principles helped the Federal Republic rebuild in the postwar period, but the same principles appear ill-suited to the problems of creating a functioning capitalist economy in the East (Smyser, 1992). The postwar Federal Republic already had a capitalist system in place, and the competition of the international marketplace is fiercer today. In addition, the social and political inequities between Western and Eastern Germany add an additional set of problems that were not present in the postwar Federal Republic. Beyond the economy, the CDU also has been ineffective is addressing the other social and political problems stemming from German union, such as health care reform. The government's commitment to stay the course it charted in 1990 further diminishes hopes that the situation will improve.

The Free Democrats share many of the CDU/CSU's problems because they are part of the governing coalition. The party and Foreign Minister Hans Dietrich Genscher were quick to take credit for the foreign policy accomplishments of achieving German union; yet they have been equally hesitant to address the social and economic problems flowing from unification. In addition, Genscher's resignation from the ministry in early 1992 robbed the party of its most visible and popular figure. Christian Søe (Chapter 5) stresses the problems that leadership succession poses for a small party. And like the CDU, the recent state elections have signaled the party's electoral decline since 1990.

The Social Democrats should be the natural benefactors of the electoral problems of the governing parties, but so far this has only partially been the case. Lafontaine had led the Social Democrats to an electoral disaster in 1990 by constantly criticizing the process of German unification under Kohl yet, ironically, Lafontaine's criticisms of Kohl's economic assumptions have often proven to be correct. Lafontaine's failure, however, was that he had no viable alternative – this is still the Social Democrats' problem. Björn Engholm, who replaced Lafontaine after the Bundestag election, was a more effective party representative. However, the party remains divided on how it should address the political challenges of unification. The SPD has criticized the costs of unification, but has not presented viable alternatives. Similarly, the SPD has openly struggled in defining its policy on asylum rights, redefining Germany's defense role, and other issues. The party was thrown in further disarray by Engholm's resignation under a cloud of scandal and his replacement by Rudolf Scharping. Even the SPD's support in the polls must be read with a note of caution. For example, Westerners voting against the tax increases introduced by the Kohl government do not really see the SPD as the anti-tax party. Voters worried about the influx of foreigners and the erosion of social order are unlikely to expect the SPD to take up these positions. Thus, the SPD's gains in state elections often reflect a negative vote against the CDU, rather than a positive endorsement of a Social Democratic alternative.

In short, the 1990 Bundestag campaign may have been a temporary respite for Kohl (a maintaining election), but events since the election have raised substantial questions about the public's confidence in any of the established parties to address the nation's pressing problems.

Correlates of Party Support

The parties' similar vote shares in the Western and Eastern *Länder* in the 1990 Bundestagswahl suggests a basic equivalency in their political appeals in both regions. Once one probes below the vote counts, however, there are signs that the nature of the election and the forces influencing voter choice are quite different.

For instance, Eastern voters generally lacked the social referent points that were important in structuring electoral choice in the West. It is difficult to apply Western notions of social class to the occupational structure inherited from the communist GDR. The economy was overwhelmingly comprised of state-owned enterprises; the GDR was ostensibly a state *of* and *for* the working class. Similarly, in place of the new middle class in the West, the East

242

had party functionaries, governmental appointees, and managers of state enterprises. Thus, the traditional contrast between the bourgeoisie and proletariat in a capitalist system was largely irrelevant in East Germany. Market-based class distinctions are starting to develop in the new *Länder*, but in 1990 they were still weakly defined. In addition, the intermediary institutions that could link the parties to class groups, such as the unions, business associations and church networks, were themselves still developing.

The impact of the religious cleavage on Eastern voters was also uncertain due to the GDR's political history. The GDR government had successfully promoted the secularization of society during its forty-year rule. For instance, a 1991 opinion poll found that 59 percent of Westerners never doubted the existence of God, compared to only 27 percent of Easterners (Times Mirror Center, 1991). Measures of church attendance and religious attachments show similar results. Among the minority of Easterners who express a religious preference, Protestants outnumber Catholics by a large margin, while the two denominations are roughly at parity in the West. Thus, unification has significantly shifted the religious composition of the new Germany.

The nature of the campaign debate in 1990 also made this an exceptional election. Dieter Roth, for instance, maintains that the March 1990 *Volkskammer* election was virtually a referendum on the single issue of unification (Roth, 1991; Schmitt, 1992). The dominance of the unification issue also carried over to the Bundestag election, temporarily eclipsing other political concerns. Debates on the course of unification overshadowed on-going public interests in the structure of social welfare programs, social benefits, issues of environmental quality, and many other topics (see Norpoth and Roth, Chapter 9). Holli Semetko and Klaus Schoenbach (Chapter 8) find that issues involving East Germany and unification were the most common themes of the campaign (also see Kaase and Schrott, 1991).

One of the most striking byproducts of these different electoral settings involves class-based voting (Table 10.2). Although the impact of social class on vote had waned in recent decades, class remains an important force structuring the Federal Republic's party system (Dalton, 1992, 1984). Class voting patterns were relatively unchanged for Western voters in 1990 (top panel). The SPD lost considerable overall support in the election, although

Table 10.2. Class Voting Patterns in 1990

Party	Working Class	Old Middle Class	New Middle Class	Combined Middle Class
Western Germany				
CDU/CSU	43.3	62.9	46.2	49.5
FDP	5.7	14.5	14.5	14.5
SPD	45.8	17.7	33.1	30.2
Greens	5.2	4.8	6.2	5.9
Total	100%	100%	100%	100%
(N)	(212)	(124)	(519)	(643)
Eastern Germany				
CDU/CSU	51.2	63.6	41.5	42.7
FDP	14.2	15.2	18.2	18.0
SPD	24.6	15.2	22.0	21.5
Greens/Alliance '90	5.3	3.0	10.0	9.5
PDS	4.7	3.0	6.7	7.9
Total	100%	100%	100%	100%
(N)	(338)	(33)	(460)	(494)

Source: December 1990 Election Study. Conducted by Forschungsgruppe Wahlen for the Zweites Deutsches Fernsehen (ZDF).

the party still polled a plurality of working class voters (46 percent). Conversely, most middle-class voters gave their support to the CDU/CSU, especially among members of the old middle class. If we simply calculate the difference between working-class and middle-class voters in the percentage of votes cast for leftist parties (the SPD and the Greens), the 12 percent gap in party support barely differs from voter gap in the two prior elections (Dalton, 1992).

While historical class-voting patterns continued in the West, the opposite pattern of class voting appeared among Easterners (lower panel of Table 10.2). The Eastern CDU won a majority of the working-class vote (51.2 percent), but fared less well among the middle class (42.7). Conversely, the leftist parties – SPD, Greens/Alliance '90, and PDS – garnered more votes among the middle class than among their "normal" constituency in the working class (see also Chapter 7 by Krisch). While the few self-employed professionals in the survey (only 33 voters out of 832) strongly support the CDU, white-collar salaried employees disproportionately endorse leftist parties.

Eastern voters thus began their political experience with the opposite of the class-voting patterns that exist in virtually all Western democracies. This may be a temporary occurrence, reflecting the dominance of the unification issue in shaping voting choices in 1990, yet now that they have formed these initial voting patterns may persist.

Because of the centrality of class to German politics and the political identity of the parties, these contrasting East-West patterns of class support for the parties may affect the future development of the party system. For example, an Eastern wing of the CDU that is oriented toward the ideal of christian socialism would strengthen the labor-oriented wing of the party (*Sozialausschüsse*), possibly creating new policy strains within the Union. The SPD is also confronting the question of establishing its identity among Easterners. A middle class-oriented SPD in the East might fit into the modernizing image of the current party leadership (see Hancock, Chapter 4), although this could also handicap the SPD's attempts to build up their working-class constituency in the East.

The patterns of religious voting might also create new intra-party tensions between West and East. On the one hand, religious voting patterns in the five new *Länder* closely parallel those found in the West (Dalton, 1992). The voting differences between secular and religious voters were very close to the Western pattern, as was the gap between Catholics and Protestants. On the other hand, the distinct religious composition of the East and the West are reshaping the parties' electoral coalitions. CDU voters in the new *Länder* are significantly less religious and less Catholic than their Western counterparts, and the different interests of Eastern CDU partisans was already apparent, for example, in the debate over abortion reform. In more general terms, the addition of nonreligious Eastern voters to the electorate will accelerate the general secularization process in German society and attenuate the importance of the religious cleavage. These new Eastern voters will also unbalance the historical parity between Protestants and Catholics in the Federal Republic.

In addition to the social bases of the vote, the dominant issue of 1990 – German unification – worked differently within the Western and Eastern electorates. While both publics endorsed German unification in principle, Easterners were much more likely to criticize the actual method in which the unification process has proceeded (Kuechler, Chapter 2). As the economic and social costs of unification have grown, Westerners are now expressing their own concerns. Thus, the issue of German unification takes on a different image, depending on whether one is looking from the West or East. Helmut Norpoth and Dieter Roth (Chapter 9) find that attitudes toward unification had a differential impact on Western and Eastern voters in 1990. Kohl won substantial support even among Easterners critical of the consequences of unification; it is unlikely that this pattern has continued beyond the 1990 celebrations of German union.

Electoral coalitions in 1990 thus consist of a series of anomalies, involving both the social and issue bases of voting choice. The crucial question is whether these divergent voting patterns are a short term deviation due to the unique political context of unification, or whether they reflect an enduring feature of electoral politics in the five new *Länder*.

There are many reasons to suspect that Eastern voting patterns will move toward the Western model. Even after only a brief period, the unique factors of the 1990 elections are beginning to change. Kohl's promises that no one would be worse off because of unification look less sincere in the face of 30 percent unemployment in the East, and rising taxes and inflation in the West. The economic costs of unification severely hurt the CDU's fortunes in subsequent state elections, and may stimulate traditional class reactions to these economic hardships. Moreover, economic interest groups are rapidly developing in the East, providing a formal means of intermediation between social groups and the parties. The parties, too, are changing. The Eastern SPD initially was a party of middle-class activists and middle-class goals; it is now reaching out to workers in the East. Many Easterners hold opinions on social equality, achievement, and the legitimate role of the state that could end up serving as the basis for a new social-democratic culture in the East (Bürklin, 1992). As the market economy spreads East, the ties between business and the CDU also are likely to strengthen. In short, as the political and social integration of Germany progresses, electoral alignments in the East may converge with the "normal" class voting patterns in the West.

There is, however, no reason why Eastern voters must follow Western patterns. The dramatic events of German union are the type of historical experience that can structure the formation of party alignments. For instance, the Civil War in the United States created a Southern party system that fundamentally differed from the North in its structure and patterns of voter support, and that endured in this anomalous situation for over a century. Thus, although public opinion surveys from 1991 show a convergence of class differences in partisanship among Easterners, the basic reversal of class lines remains. A continuation of such differences would generate the same type of intra-party conflict observed in the American case.

In summary, it is almost as though there were two elections in 1990, despite the similarity of vote totals between West and East. Eastern voting patterns represent a significant difference from the class and religious alignments that previously characterized electoral politics in the Federal Republic. These differing sources of party support between Western and Eastern publics contribute to the image that German unification is creating new strains on the German party system. This situation is like an earthquake fault, it might stimulate a major shift in electoral alignments or a continuing series of small, unsettling shocks to the electoral system. Future elections will begin to indicate which course is being followed. In either case, the inevitable result seems to be increased intra-party conflict and a continued weakening of the social forces that had historically structured electoral politics in the Federal Republic.

Building a New Party System

One of the major challenges of German unification involves the need to develop a system of party government in the East. Importing party experts and election paraphernalia from the

West can assist in this development, but the roots of the new system must establish themselves in Eastern soil if the party system is to be successful. More than voting results, the strength of the party system is measured by popular support for the parties and a commitment to the Federal Republic's system of party government.

One measure of the public's commitment to political parties involves feelings of identification with one's preferred party. Electoral scholars maintain that enduring party ties reflect the public's commitment to the party system and stabilize the workings of the electoral process (Converse, 1969; Baker *et al.*, 1981). Because the party system is new to the East, fewer voters should display these same feelings of party identification. At the same time, some early research suggested that many Easterners had latent affinities for specific parties in the Federal Republic formed by observing the party system from afar (Bluck and Kreikenbom, 1991). Moreover, 1990 provided a crash course in FRG electoral politics, with the Volkskammer election in March, followed by local elections in May, state elections in October, and the Bundestagswahl in December. The rate at which Easterners begin to identify with FRG parties thus will be an important indicator of the institutionalization of party politics in the new Länder.

The Forschungsgruppe Wahlen began asking survey questions about the strength of partisan ties in Eastern surveys in early-1991. As might be expected, these surveys find that Eastern voters are relatively hesitant to express party attachments (Dalton, 1992). Only 26 percent of Easterners declare strong party attachments; more Easterners say that they do not feel close to any party (37 percent). If partisanship is the tie that binds citizens to the party system, these ties are apparently still weakly formed in the East.

In general terms, one should expect Easterners' initially weak partisan attachments to strengthen as they acquire repeated electoral experience with the political parties of the Federal Republic. In this sense, the current situation in the East might be similar to the previous experience of the Federal Republic, where party ties strengthened as the party system took root. However, evidence from the Western electorate calls this assumption into question.

Over the past decade there has been an erosion in the strength of party attachments among Westerners (Dalton and Rohrschneider, 1990). The dealigning trend that began in the 1980s, under the onslaught of the Green party challenge and various party scandals, has continued downward in the 1990s. In 1972, for instance, 55 percent of the West German electorate felt strongly attached to their preferred party; by 1990 this group of strong partisans had declined to 40 percent of the public. In other terms, only 20 percent of Westerners defined themselves as complete independents in 1972; this percentage had increased to 27 percent by 1990.[5]

Thus, contemporary electoral experiences actually have weakened existing partisan attachments among Westerners. The political strains accompanying German unification that we have described in this volume seem unlikely to revive confidence in the parties among Easterners (or Westerners). Weak party ties thus mirror the image of weak parties that now exists in Germany.

The weak psychological partisan bonds of Easterners are also reflected in the stunted organizational development of the parties. The political parties in the East must attract new members, recruit candidates, and create a political infrastructure as the basis for democratic partisan politics. Some advice and expertise from the West is helpful, but the parties must develop this indigenous Eastern base on their own.

Despite initial claims of large Eastern memberships, citizens in the new *Länder* have been hesitant to join a political party. There is widespread evidence that early membership statistics were artificially inflated to increase a party's apparent stature among Easterners. For instance, the Eastern SPD initially claimed over 100,000 members; the actual figure for 1990 was probably closer to 10,000. Furthermore, Easterners have been leaving the parties in droves since the 1990 Bundestagswahl. The CDU has lost nearly 20,000 members in East and now counts fewer than 100,000 in its ranks. The FDP has suffered even greater losses, dropping from 114,000 in 1990 to 65,000 in 1992 (Søe, Chapter 5). In the new *Länder*, there are only 2,000 paid-up members of the Greens. Henry Krisch (Chapter 7) documents a similar loss in support for the SED/PDS.

To some extent, a hesitancy to join political parties is a natural legacy of the political experiences of Easterners with the party

---

5. Not only does the overall percentage of those expressing partisan attachments decrease over time, but the strength of partisanship within the various parties also decreases (Dalton and Rohrschneider, 1990).

politics of the GDR. Easterners are slow to become formal party members, since party membership had different connotations under the old regime. And yet, involvement in democratic parties provides a key means of participating in the democratic process. This was a goal of the peaceful revolution, and yet few people in the East have taken the additional step needed to become involved. Meanwhile, Easterners are joining other Western associations in large numbers, such as the labor unions.

Decreasing party membership might reflect the easing of the democratic euphoria that gripped the East in the wake of revolution and unification – except that similar downward trends are occurring in the West. Since the Bundestagswahl, all of the parties have lost members in the Western *Länder*. This reaffirms our general thesis that the parties' political position in the Federal Republic is weakening.

The problems of stunted institutional development confront the party organizations at other levels as well. For example, parties need candidates if they are to compete in elections. It is difficult to recruit good candidates in the East, however, because of their possible ties to the former communist regime. Virtually all of the parties have suffered embarrassments as top officials were exposed for former collaboration with the *Stasi* or secret work for the GDR government, ranging as high as Lothar de Maziere, the GDR Premier selected after the democratic *Volkskammer* elections in March 1990. Because of these difficulties, Westerners have assumed the position of minister president in three of the five new *Länder*. Large portions of the top administrative and judicial positions are similarly occupied by Westerners. The exposés of top party officials are only the tip of the iceberg. Thousands of candidates are required to staff the parties and represent it at the state and local levels. It is impossible to require the same level of scrutiny and credentials of these people, yet difficult for the democratic process if non-democrats are able to take shelter within the parties.

If one accepts the dictum that the Federal Republic is a party-state where political parties provide the machinery of democratic politics, then the present status of the parties is not an encouraging sign. A viable party system provides a method for integrating people into the political process and for aggregating political interests in making policy decisions. The parties' successful performance of these functions was crucial to the Federal Republic's first democratic transition, yet their present situation raises questions of whether they can perform these same functions during this second democratic transition.

The Challenge to the Parties

The 1990 Bundestagswahl was a celebration of German unification, at least for the governing parties that were returned to office. However, this chapter has argued that this was a temporary outcome. The 1990 election neither signaled the continuation of CDU electoral dominance (a maintaining election) nor the creation of a new party order uniting West and East (a realigning election). It was, instead, a respite from the fundamental political and economic problems that now face the Federal Republic as a result of unification. Now that the election was over, these longer term problems have come to the fore.

This chapter, and large parts of this volume, have recounted the story of a party system under stress. Many Germans on both sides of the former border are disturbed by the political and economic problems resulting from German unification, and they see the political parties as unable or unwilling to address these problems in an effective and convincing way.[6] The governing parties have lost substantial popular support since the 1990 Bundestag election, confirming the impression that the election results did not reflect a continuing pattern of conservative electoral dominance. The SPD has gained in the polls as the governing parties have suffered, but few voters believe the Social Democrats are offering workable solutions to the nation's problems; these are anti-CDU votes. Moreover, the growing strength of radical right-wing parties, such as the Republicans and German People's Union (DVU), when coupled with the revived strength of the Greens signals a fractionalization of the German party system that will severely complicate the processes of coalition formation and governing.

Germans' frustration with the parties also seems to be extend to the party system as a whole. Declining party attachments and

6. A national survey conducted for RTLplus in June 1993 found 39 percent favored the SPD, 33 percent the CDU/CSU, 11 percent for the Greens, 8 percent for the FDP, 5 percent for the Republicans, and 3 percent for the PDS.

party membership statistics document the general weakness of parties. In addition, turnout in the 1990 Bundestag election fell far below the average voting level of the last two decades, despite the historic nature of the first all-German democratic election since Weimar. This drop in electoral participation has continued into the state elections of 1991 and 1992. Similarly, a 1990 survey found that West Germans had the next-to-least confidence in political parties as general institutions among the nearly dozen social and political institutions included in the survey.[7] More recent data finds that Germans are increasingly likely to say that none of the political parties is competent to deal with the nation's problems (Gibowski, 1992). There is obviously a crisis in the German system of party government.

The problems of German union may have stimulated this crisis, but the present difficulties of the party system represent more profound problems in the workings of party government in the Federal Republic. Political parties are central institutions in the democratic process because they are the primary connecting link between the public and government. In the past year, however, a mounting chorus of critics claim that the parties have become more concerned about governing and protecting their political status than in representing the public. The most prominent voice has been the FRG president, Richard von Weizsäcker, who criticized the political parties as a whole for being obsessed with power (von Weizsäcker, 1992). Instead of pursuing the nation's interests, the parties are criticized as pursuing their own self interests. As the major parties became diffuse *Volksparteien*, a prior focus on ideological goals and problem-solving has been displaced by the simple goal of winning elections. The means of selecting governing parties (elections) have become the ends of party action. The established parties became fixated on attaining governing power, and this lessened their attention to interest aggregation and articulation functions (Haungs and Jesse, 1987). So powerful are these attractions that even the Greens have been drawn into this web of public campaign financing, public financing of party foundations, and other perquisites of office (Veen and Hoffmann, 1992).

The severe policy demands of German unification have exacer-

7. *Enmid Informationen.* 9/10 (1990): A 31ff.

bated these problems in the nature of party government. Instead of addressing the difficult problems that lay ahead in the unification process, the Kohl campaign focused on winning the election. Similarly, the SPD is now perceived as primarily concerned about how to position itself to win the next election, rather than as attempting solve the problems facing the nation. Little better can be said of the FDP or the Greens. In a similar vein, the initial growth of the Republicans and the DVU occurred because the established parties failed to respond to public concerns about asylum-seekers and the resettlement of ethnic Germans. Given this fragmentation of the party system, it becomes difficult to see how a consensus on governing can possibly develop.

In addition to these problems of German union, a series of party scandals has further undermined the parties' stature. For example, it was revealed that Oskar Lafontaine was receiving a government pension check as a former mayor on top of his salary as Saarland's minister-president. While not illegal, such a system of double-dipping from a top party leader distressed many citizens at a time of rising taxes and a falling economy. In mid-1992 Erwin and Ute Scheuch (1992) published a damning study of local party structures in Cologne, illustrating the self-centeredness of the parties and the collusion between parties to ensure their mutual access to government. Engholm's duplicity in the Barschel affair and his subsequent resignation from the SPD leadership reinforced distrust of the parties. Each case has its own mediating circumstances, but the combined impact is to increase public doubts about the efficacy of the present system of party government.

Certainly, the explanation for Germany's current political problems is more complex than simply a failure or crisis in the system of party government. The problems of German union, asylum-rights, and the redefinition of Germany's international role in a changing world are far greater than the normal demands placed upon political systems. Moreover, the parties are not the only institutions responsible for policy making. The policy-making process in the Federal Republic now involves a variety of overlapping policy networks that include interest groups, citizen action groups, the bureaucracy, individual political figures, as well as the political parties. The creation of a nonpartisan "Committee for Justice" to address the problems of Eastern Germany is one sign of the established parties' inability to resolve these issues, leading to extra-party action.[8]

The party system of the Federal Republic faces its greatest challenge since the Federal Republic's first democratic transition. This also presents a challenge for the parties themselves. The resolution of Germany's current political problems will require a renewal of political parties enabling them to focus their efforts on the goals of governing, rather than the perquisites of office. Like the unification process itself, we can be sanguine about the eventual outcome, but this process of renewal and resolution is essential if the Federal Republic's second democratic transition is to succeed.

8. The Committee was founded by Gregor Gysi, chairperson of the PDS, and Peter-Michael Diestel, a CDU deputy from Brandenberg. Its leadership includes a diverse group of Eastern politicians and social figures, such as Stefan Heym, former West Berlin mayor, Heinrich Albertz, the former president of Humboldt University, and several church figures. The stated goal of the committee is to provide an extra-parliamentary pressure group to represent the needs of Eastern Germany.

References

Baker, Kendall, Russell J. Dalton, and Kai Hildebrandt. 1981. *Germany Transformed: Political Culture and the New Politics.* Cambridge: Harvard University Press.

Billing, Werner. 1991. "Die rheinland-pfälzische Landtagswahl vom 21. April 1991: Machtwechsel in Mainz nach 44 Jahren," *Zeitschrift für Parlamentsfragen* 22: pp. 584–602.

Bluck, Carsten and Henry Kreikenbom. 1991. "Die Wähler in der DDR: nur issue- orientiert oder auch parteigegunden?" *Zeitschrift für Parlamentsfragen* 22: pp. 495–502.

Bürklin, Wilhelm. 1991. "Die Wahl zur Hamburger Bürgerschaft vom 2. Juni 1991: Neue SPD-Mehrheit im Wiedervereinigungsboom," *Zeitschrift für Parlamentsfragen* 22: pp. 602–19.

Bürklin, Wilhelm. 1992. "Perspektiven für das deutsche Pareiensystem," in Werner Weidenfeld, ed. *Deutschland: Eine Nation – zewi Gesellschaften – doppelte Geschichte.* Cologne: Verlag Wissenschaft und Politik.

Bürklin, Wilhelm, and Russell J. Dalton. 1993. "Das Ergrauen der Grünen," in Hans-Dieter Klingemann and Max Kaase, eds. *Wahlen und Wähler* Opladen: Westdeutscher Verlag.

Bürklin, Wilhelm, and Stephan Layritz. 1992. "Die schleswig-holsteinische Landtagswahl vom 5. April 1992," *Zeitschrift für Parlamentsfragen* 23: pp. 604–21.

Campbell, Angus. 1966. "A Classification of Presidential Elections," in Angus Campbell et al. *Elections and the Political Order.* New York: Wiley.

Converse, Phillip. 1969. "Of Time and Partisan Stability," *Comparative Political Studies* 2: pp. 139–71.

Dalton, Russell J. 1984. "The German Party System between Two Ages," in Russell Dalton, Scott Flanagan, and Paul Beck, eds. *Electoral Change in Advanced Industrial Democracies.* Princeton: Princeton University Press.

_______. 1992. "Two German Electorates," in Gordon Smith et al., *Developments in German Politics.* London: Macmillan.

_______. 1993. *Politics in Germany.* New York: Harper/Collins.

Dalton, Russell J., and Robert Rohrschneider. 1990. "Wählerwandel und die Abschwächung der Parteieigungen von 1972 bis 1987," in Max Kaase and H.- D. Klingemann (ed.), *Wahlen und Wähler*, Opladen: Westdeutscher Verlag.

Fichter, Michael. 1991. "From Transmission Belt to Social Partnership," *German Politics and Society* 23: pp. 21–39.

Gibowski, Wolfgang. 1992. "Political Communication and Public Opinion since the first All-German National Election," paper presented at the annual meeting of the American Political Science Association.

Haungs, Peter, and Eckhard Jesse. 1987. *Parteien in der Krise*. Cologne.

Kaase, Max, and Peter Schrott. 1991. "Media Coverage of the German 1990 National Election Campaign." Paper presented at the annual meeting of the American Political Science Association.

Kitschelt, Herbert. 1991. "The 1990 German Federal Election and the National Unification: A Watershed in German Electoral History?" *West European Politics* 14: pp. 121–48.

Pomper, Gerald. 1967. "Classification of Presidential Elections," *Journal of Politics* 29: pp. 535–66.

Roth, Dieter. 1990. "Die Wahlen zur Volkskammer in der DDR," *Politische Vierteljahresschrift* 31: pp. 369–93.

Roth, Reinhold. 1992. "Die Bremer Bürgerschaftswahl vom 29. September 1991: Ende der SPD-Alleinherrschaft durch eine Ampelkoalition," *Zeitschrift für Parlamentsfragen* 23: pp. 281–90.

Schmitt, Karl. 1992. "Politische Landschaften im Umbruch," in Oscar Gabriel and Klaus Troitzsch, eds. *Vor der Bundestagswahl 1990*. Frankfurt: Campus.

Schmitt-Beck, Rüdiger. 1991. "Die hessische Landtagswahl vom 20. Januar 1991: Im Schatten der Weltpolitik kleine Verschiebungen mit großer Wirkung," *Zeitschrift für Parlamentsfragen* 22: pp. 226–43.

Scheuch, Erwin, and Ute Scheuch. 1992. *Cliquen, Klüngel und Karrieren*. Reinbeck: Rowolt.

Smyser, W.R. 1992. *The Economy of United Germany: Colossus at the Crossroads*. New York: St. Martin's Press.

Sturm, Roland. 1992. "Die baden-württembergische Landtagswahl vom 5. April 1992." *Zeitschrift für Parlamentsfragen* 23: pp. 622–39.

Times Mirror Center. 1991. *The Pulse of Europe*. Washington, D.C.: Times Mirror Center for People & the Press, 1991.

Veen, Hans-Joachim, and Jügen Hoffmann. 1992. *Die Grünen zu Beginn der neunziger Jahre: Profil und Defizite einer fast etablierten Partei*. Bonn: Bouvier.

Weizsäcker, Richard von. 1992. *Richard von Weizsäcker im Gesprach mit Gunter Hofmann and Werner Perger*. Frankfurt: Eichborn.

Appendix

This appendix includes a summary of the 1990 Bundestag campaign platforms for each of the parties represented in the tenth Bundestag (1987–1990): Christian Democratic Union, Christian Social Union, Social Democratic party, Free Democratic party, and the Greens. This material is reprinted from: *Procedures, Programs, Profiles*, a special report by Inter Nationes, Bonn, December 1990.

Summary of the CDU's Election Manifesto

Foreign Policy

International politics is in a state of flux. Problems connected with maintaining world peace, developing world trade, protecting the environment, conserving energy and natural resources, closing the prosperity gap and safeguarding human rights make it increasingly clear that the only answer is close global cooperation. Germany has developed into a country with considerable international standing which implies a global responsibility. It is one of the leading trading and industrial nations and thus one of the guarantors of a stable world economic order. It is an important factor in the Western alliance, politically, economically and militarily, and it is a political motor of the European Community. Many nations expect Germany to contribute to the solution of common problems. Together with its Western partners it must help shape international policy.

Germany

The CDU considers it a moral duty and a national responsibility to help the people in the former German Democratic Republic accomplish their task of economic and political reconstruction.

This assistance will at the same time be an investment in our common future. The CDU's aim is an economically flourishing Germany. The economic and monetary union has introduced the social market economy to the former GDR. It has established a basis for successful investment by German companies.

The CDU wants a socially just Germany. The economic and monetary union also includes social union. Economic growth in the eastern part of the country will have to be supported by the country's overall social security system. In the transition period we must be prepared to help build up a system of unemployment, pension and health insurance. The unification of Germany offers many opportunities for the whole nation.

For the first time in history the Germans are united in a state which has a democratic constitution, which is conducive to a high level of prosperity and social security, and which lives in harmony with all its neighbors and is forging ever stronger bonds of friendship and cooperation with them. Precisely for young people who are ready to work and commit themselves, this Germany offers challenging and rewarding opportunities.

Europe

The timetable for the completion of the common internal market as from 1993 must be adhered to. The united Germany, too, will belong to that market. The CDU wants a European monetary union to follow from the single market. It will help to ensure that the European Community is developed into a social and environmental community, a research and technology community. The opening of frontiers must not diminish the Community's internal security, however. Consequently, cooperation among security agencies in combating organized crime, drug trafficking and terrorism must be intensified. A European federal police force is called for. The European Community must also standardize its laws on asylum so that those who are persecuted on political, racial or religious grounds can still claim asylum without its being open to abuse by others. The goal remains a united states of Europe embracing the nations of Central, Eastern and SouthEastern Europe. One of the European Community's new responsibilities, therefore, will be to support democracy and freedom in those countries and to give them access to the Community.

The Alliance

The Atlantic Alliance and the Bundeswehr will remain the pillars of German foreign and security policy in the 1990s. Precisely during a phase of transformation the Western community with their common values are a basic element of Europe's new security structure, which also embraces the United States and Canada. Through their presence the American forces will continue to safeguard peace in Europe. The goal must be to create a peaceful order spanning the whole of Europe in which a system of security linking the alliances of East and West will substitute cooperation for confrontation.

The military alliances will have to render an important political contribution towards the shaping of Europe's peaceful order, both in the East-West dialogue and in the disarmament process. In the future a minimum deterrent will suffice which will not depend on short-range nuclear systems and ground-based nuclear missiles in Germany. Alliance forces and strategy will have to be adapted to these new requirements. Every country's security must be guaranteed by means of defensive military systems and confidence-building measures. The CDU advocates the immediate conclusion of an agreement providing for the complete removal of all chemical weapons on a global scale.

The Third World

Our sense of Christian responsibility requires us to assist in the fight against hunger and poverty and to defend freedom, justice and human rights in the Third World. The CDU advocates help towards self-help as well as the promotion of education and training in order to release the people's creative energies. It promotes the development of a free market economy in the Third World which is committed to social justice and ecological conservation. It supports a development policy which gives priority to financial and technical assistance for the poorer countries and gives precedence to the poorest sections of the population.

The vicious circle of poverty, overpopulation and environmental destruction must be broken. The Federal Republic of Germany was the very first country to require all development cooperation projects to be screened to determine whether they are compatible with the environment. The CDU will energetically continue its efforts to ensure that development policy is consistent with environmental requirements. One of the most acute problems is that of international indebtedness. Ways and means will have to be found to ease the burden on the heavily indebted countries of the Third World.

Research

Germany is poor in terms of raw materials but rich where the inventiveness, diligence and skills of its people are concerned. Thus our economic opportunities lie in the export of high-quality products and services. Achievements in the field of research and in the development and use of modern technology are of increasing importance for a country's economic efficiency and its ability to compete on world markets. The CDU supports technological advancement, the introduction of micro-processors and new information, communication and environmental technology, which offer great opportunities for new jobs with safe prospects in the Federal Republic of Germany.

Industry and Finance

The renewal of the social market economy led Germany out of the crisis of 1982. The ground was prepared for the longest economic boom in the country's post-war history. This economic success of the past seven years not only bolsters the country's prosperity and social standards in the West but enables us precisely now to help achieve these benefits for our countrymen in the former German Democratic Republic as well. By dint of the social market economy the CDU is setting the stage for a second German economic miracle in a united Germany.

New jobs can only be created if our companies remain competitive on world markets. This applies especially in connection with the completion of the European internal market in 1993. There will be competition not only as far as products and companies are concerned but also with regard to locations. Companies themselves are responsible for the competitiveness of their products. In the Federal Republic of Germany the government and both sides of industry have a major responsibility for ensuring that it remains capable of competing for investment. In order to keep the Federal Republic competitive, therefore, a reform of company tax will be carried out in the next legislative term. Its purpose will be to stimulate growth, encourage new investment, and create new jobs.

The Environment

The CDU regards the social market economy as a model for enhancing environmental protection. It will therefore make greater use of that model's efficiency and innovative energy for the sake of the environment. The aim is to establish an ecological and social market economy. Environmental problems cannot be solved by individual countries. Global environmental partnership is required. The 1990s must become the decade of a global ecological awakening. An "environmental foreign policy" is called for to intensify international cooperation . The primary objective must be to prevent, reduce and recycle waste. With this policy the CDU aims to reform the "throw-away society". Waste must be disposed of in the countries of origin .

Laws are therefore necessary to ban exports of waste to Third World countries.

Social Policy

Economic and social policy are inseparably linked with one another. They mark each other's limits and are at the same time mutually complementary. An economic policy without social justice would be detrimental to social harmony and would weaken the national economy. On the other hand, a social policy pursued without consideration for economic efficiency and growth would be depriving the country of its own sources of revenue. The success of economic, financial and social policy depends on the extent to which it encourages individual initiative and a community spirit. The CDU wishes to develop a society which cares for families and children and a work environment which enables mothers and fathers to combine work and family responsibilities. Women must have better opportunities at work. Elderly people must receive adequate care and more humane nursing measures are needed to help them retain their independence so that they need not timidly accept poverty in old age. The health of the public must be maintained through more preventive care and by harnessing medical progress.

The Family

By introducing a child-raising allowance and leave from work for child-raising purposes, ensuring a more even distribution of family burdens and granting pension entitlements for child-raising periods, the CDU has not only improved the family's financial situation but reevaluated family activity. Child-raising allowances and child-raising leave make it easier for families to reconcile family and work responsibilities. They will have to be gradually improved. Those who take care of children need greater tax relief than people without children. The lower the family's income and the greater the number of children, the less tax they should have to pay.

The aim of Christian Democratic policy is to ensure freedom of choice for men and women. They should have equal opportunities for developing their way of life both at work, within the family, and within the community. Mothers rightly demand the right to work and to take part in public life. Fathers, too, want to live with children. Hence it must be made easier to reconcile gainful employment and life with children. This is not a problem which concerns parents alone but a responsibility of society as a whole.

Summary of the CSU's Election Manifesto

Foreign Policy, Germany

The CSU is aware that all ideas and proposals concerning the political and social life of the country and aimed at enabling the individual to live in freedom and bear responsibility for his own actions mean nothing unless the country's external security is guaranteed. Because freedom is indivisible internal freedom is not possible without that external security. With the support of the Christian Social Union the whole German nation has achieved freedom, self-determination and unity. This will make for equitable peace in Europe and throughout the world.

The CSU wants Germany to assume greater international responsibility, especially in relation to the developing countries, and to widen its own scope for action. Only thus will the Federal Republic of Germany be able, as a member of the European Community and of the free world, to meet the global challenges in all spheres. The building of a democratic federal state in Europe must receive high priority as a means of securing lasting peace and freedom in our continent.

Europe, the Alliance

In the opinion of the CSU, the nations of Europe will only continue to live in peace and freedom if they find the energy to unite. Only within a united Europe with a federal structure can the free nations of our continent preserve their independence and have a say in world affairs.

The security of the Federal Republic of Germany and Europe presupposes close cooperation with the United States. Hence our friendship and solidarity with the United States are the very foundation of German and European policy. There is still a need for the Atlantic Alliance.

The Third World

The Christian Social Union regards development policy as help towards self-help and thus as a contribution to peace in developing countries and in the world. In this process development assistance should be in harmony with our interests. Germany's development policy should be coordinated with that of the member states of the European Community.

Research, Education, Culture

Education, science and culture are fundamental to the CSU's policy for freedom. Education policy is one of the foundations of community life. Its purpose is to help the individual help himself, to remove social obstacles by providing equal opportunities, and to ensure the dissemination of culture and of the principles upon which a free society is based. Science and technology should be developed in order to safeguard the cultural and material existence and advancement of the nation. The aim of cultural policy is to help develop the individual's creative energies, to enhance the nation's cultural heritage, and to preserve an environment fit for human life. In the CSU's opinion, the autonomy of the federal states in matters of education and culture is one of the supports of the country's liberal, federal structure. Government must provide the financial support and the organizational framework for science and research. It must revitalize the universities so that they can fulfill their responsibilities.

A subdivided system of school education is the best way of monitoring each pupil's performance in terms of his individual needs and abilities.

Industry and Agriculture

The CSU upholds the social market economy. A socially just market economy forges individual freedom, social justice and economic efficiency into an effective social system. The social market economy also provides the best basis from which to pursue environmental objectives using means that are both ecologically and economically efficient. With no other economic system is it possible for producers and consumers to adapt to ecological requirements as quickly and as comprehensively as with the market economy. Only intensive competition produces economic efficiency, which in turn ensures a high level of supply with minimum waste of land, materials, commodities and energy, thus easing the burden on the environment. Ecology and economy must develop hand in hand.

Bavaria has advanced from a farming region to one of the most efficient industrial areas in Europe. Nonetheless it has retained its original features. Nearly 90% of Bavaria's total area is still forest and agricultural country. Legislation has been introduced to place the cultivation and preservation of the farming landscape on a par with food production. Agricultural policy has thus become part of a general social concept which continues to prove its value.

The Environment

The CSU has successfully coped with the challenge of environmental protection, having already made it one of the priorities of Bavarian policy at the beginning of the 1970s. It established its own ministry for landscape development and environmental questions, thus laying early foundations for a successful policy. Environmental protection has been a part of the CSU's basic policy program since 1976. In a document entitled "Environmental Policy in the 1980s" it updated that program and in 1984 proposed that a clause making environmental protection a responsibility of the state be incorporated in the Bavarian constitution. This progressive policy has produced measurable results. There are clear signs of improvement in many of the problem areas of environmental protection. The efforts of government and industry to ensure clean air and effluent and to improve waste disposal are bearing fruit.

The CSU sees man as a part of nature. He must make use of and shape nature, but he is also obliged to protect it. The most urgent ecological task of the present time is to develop a biotope network linking up ecological cells, thus providing an adequate habitat for local flora and fauna and ensuring the biological regeneration of the whole ecosystem. The CSU is playing an innovative role in the field of waste disposal. Where recycling is concerned, Bavaria heads the field in the Federal Republic.

Social Policy

The CSU identifies itself with the welfare state, which is required to help the individual lead an independent life and be responsible for his own actions, to ensure social justice for all, and to provide assistance especially for the poor and weak.

In a modern industrial society genuine freedom can only prevail if the democratic state also perceives itself as a welfare state. The CSU must ensure that the welfare state protects itself from abuse. Those who make increasing demands on the rest of the community without accepting responsibility are reminded that this leads to higher taxes and contributions which they themselves have to pay. This places an irresponsible restriction on the freedom of future generations. In the CSU's opinion, a government's quality lies not in its ability to develop ever more bureaucratic procedures for ever more financial services. Its main responsibility is to organize society in accordance with the principles of freedom, solidarity and subsidiarity and to show itself capable of acting in the interests of the country's internal and external security.

Foreign employees in Germany have the same rights and responsibilities as their German colleagues. The Christian Social Union considers that during their sojourn in the Federal Republic of Germany they should be assured of equal living conditions and be enabled to integrate with the community.

Family Policy

The CSU visualizes a society in which every man and woman, young or old, healthy or sick, is able to lead his or her life freely and has his place and responsibilities in the community. The family performs a special function as the most important unit in that community. The problems confronting the individual and society as a whole must be solved on the basis of solidarity. Promotion of the family, including the partial family, is the most effective form of social policy because the family renders an indispensable service to society and provides the best basis for the individual's upbringing.

In law, women already have equal status with men. The CSU's main aim is to ensure that they can enjoy that status in their daily lives.

The CSU seeks the best possible protection for unborn life. It is the responsibility of government to afford that protection.

Summary of the SPD's Election Manifesto

Foreign Policy

The international community must give itself a system which will make it possible to safeguard world peace, to ensure political control of economic power, to distribute commodities, technology and know-how fairly, and to protect our natural sources of life. The United Nations can bring us closer to this goal. It must therefore play a larger role. It must become an instrument of peaceful global domestic policy. We intend to support it, politically and financially, in this role.

Germany

Our aim now must be to shape the modern Germany, a Germany from which peace will emanate. A Germany which has its place in a united Europe and fosters the coalescence of the nations of the world. A Germany of prosperity and social justice, of humane working conditions and social security for all. A Germany which will create a better environment for ourselves and coming generations. A Germany in which men and women have equal status, a society based on the principle of justice, with no privileges, discrimination or isolation. A Germany with a modern, efficient government supported by the people.

Europe

On account of our own history and our strong position in Europe, it is very important, especially now that the country is united, that we Germans do not lose sight of the great aim of European union. In the European Community the fundamental decisions with a view to expanding the Community to the whole of Europe now have to be taken. The SPD wants a United States of Europe. The concept of a "European Confederation" is consistent with that aim. One of the major tasks of the future is to integrate Central and Eastern Europe. It is thus a primary objective of SPD policy to strengthen the Community and at the same time to make it accessible to the EFTA countries and the new democracies of Central and Eastern Europe.

The Alliance

The ending of the division of Germany has not removed all sources of world conflict – as palpably shown by the Gulf crisis – but it has made Germany and Europe safer. Now, at long last, consequences have to be drawn from the process of détente. The SPD will seize the opportunities for drastic disarmament by reducing the personnel strength of the German forces by half; by stopping production of the Jäger '90 combat aircraft and other major weapon systems; by discontinuing low-flying exercises and significantly reducing maneuvers; and by substantially reducing military installations and effectively banning exports of arms to developing countries, areas of tension, military dictators or countries where human rights are violated. The immorality of economic crime in this sector has been made shockingly clear by the Gulf crisis. The military blocs are losing their function. The SPD continues to advocate an agreement setting up a European security system within the framework of the CSCE which would absorb the present military alliances. If Germany is to enjoy equal status in NATO, the forces of third states may not have any other status in Germany than that enjoyed in other NATO countries.

The Third World

A modern Germany must live up to its responsibility as a member of the international community and play an active part in helping the world's economically weak countries. The SPD will make an international plea for the cancellation of the debts of the poorest countries and will take the initiative. It will channel some of the savings from the defense budget to development cooperation. It will press for a modification of the general financial and monetary conditions as well as the terms of trade in favor of Third World countries in order to achieve progress towards a socially and ecologically viable world economy. It will call for sound UN programs to contain population growth and provide political and financial support. It will urge an ecological reformation of the industrial society so that developing countries too will receive new opportunities to run their economies in a manner compatible with the environment. And in an all-German government it will ensure that all decisions are reviewed as to their compatibility with development cooperation policy.

Research

Research will be more strongly oriented to the ecological transformation of the industrial society. The aim in particular will be to concentrate research less on nuclear energy and more on alternative sources of energy and potential methods of energy conservation. The research project "humanization of the work environment" will be revived.

Industry and Finance

Germany is very attractive to international investors. In the medium term that attractiveness will grow as a result of unification, provided the necessary steps are taken to help the former German Democratic Republic make up the leeway. The SPD therefore proposes that all efforts now be concentrated on developing a sound infrastructure in eastern Germany. It is especially necessary to establish legal clarity with regard to ownership of land and property, to improve the telecommunications system, to boost housing construction, to improve transport and communications, and to clean up the environment.

Such an ecology-oriented infrastructure program will create many new jobs. Regardless of the policies implemented in the former German Democratic Republic, it must not be forgotten that ecological investment programs are imperative in the Federal Republic as well. They should be concentrated on relieving the housing shortage, especially by promoting publicly subsidized building programs, improving local public transport and the federal railways, and on energy conservation in manufacturing establishments and private households. With regard to financial policy, the SPD's maxim will be reliability and stability. If tax increases are to be avoided, public spending will have to be extremely cautious in the next few years, in spite of increased revenue resulting from the favorable economic situation. The SPD sees no room for global tax cuts for companies and people on top salaries. There must above all be drastic cuts in defense spending.

The Environment

The ecological transformation of the industrial society is a basic element of the SPD's policy for the environment. On assuming the responsibility of government the SPD will take decisive steps to safeguard the natural sources of life. Ever more citizens recognize that prosperity depends on a healthy environment. Investment in the environment makes us richer not poorer. It ensures our survival and creates jobs. An ecology-oriented social market economy must be the nucleus of the modern Germany. The ecological transformation concept presupposes the fulfillment of three requirements. First, taxes on energy will have to be increased. The extra revenue will be plowed back in the form of greater basic wage and income tax relief, better allowances for travel to and from work, the abolition of the motor vehicle tax, and tax relief for investment in energy conservation measures. The second requirement covers an environment levy to reduce the incidence of waste, special refuse, air and water pollutants. And the third is to tighten up environmental protection regulations. This will include, for instance, the introduction of limits on petrol consumption and lower speed limits.

Social Policy

Apart from introducing basic changes in the field of family policy, the SPD intends to introduce a basic old-age and invalidity pension entitlement for all. It abides by the compromise on pensions but intends, during the next legislative term, to review the raised pensionable ages and to look at the question of old age security for women when it amends the legislation governing employment capability. The need to offset the nursing risk faced by elderly people assumes growing importance. The SPD therefore intends to introduce a new and separate branch of social security known as "statutory nursing insurance." It will carry out a health reform program worthy of the name, that is to say, there will be a free choice of health insurance fund for all and health insurance institutions will have more rights. The drugs and medicine market will be overhauled by an independent institute which will prepare a list of prescribable preparations.

Family

It is wrong that people in the higher income brackets have much greater tax relief in the form of child allowances than average earners. The injustices inherent in the present equalization of family burdens legislation must be removed. To achieve this aim the SPD will introduce a higher, standard child allowance of at least DM 200 per month for each child, thus also including the first child (which usually imposes the biggest financial burden on the family) . There will be a supplementary family allowance of DM 100 per month and child as from the fourth child.

Working conditions will be made more family-friendly. This will include the urgent expansion of child-care facilities, such as kindergartens, all-day schools, children's creches, etc. The first step will be to establish in the Youth Assistance Act a legal claim to child-care for all children in the appropriate age groups. The SPD intends to legislate on termination of pregnancy, with emphasis on the protection of unborn life and the woman's right to decide for herself on her own responsibility. Should a woman opt for abortion then it should be performed within the first three months and be free from criminal prosecution.

Summary of the F.D.P.'s Election Manifesto

Foreign Policy

For more than 20 years liberal foreign ministers have been at the helm of German foreign policy, a policy of reason aimed at peace, freedom and progress. The F.D.P. will continue the successful policy of Walter Scheel and Hans-Dietrich Genscher. A united Germany, a democratic and economically efficient state, must render a major contribution to stability, progress and prosperity throughout Europe and the world. Cooperation instead of rivalry, equality instead of hegemony, must be the catchwords of the 1990s. A policy of responsibility must supersede power politics.

For Europe this means that the progression and integration of the European Community must become the model for and component of pan-European unification. The nations of Central and Eastern Europe, including the Soviet Union, require comprehensive assistance to ensure that the ideological causes of tensions in Europe are not followed by economic causes. The Conference on Security and Cooperation in Europe must become the mainstay of a peaceful order in Europe. It is the aim of the F.D.P., within the framework of the CSCE, for instance, to achieve cooperative security through comprehensive disarmament and by using the alliances, whose function will have been changed, mainly as political guarantors of security. But progress in Europe must not be achieved at the expense of the Third World. The Liberals intend to increase Germany's contribution to development in the Third World with a view to overcoming famine, disease and ignorance all over the globe. A united Germany must become a partner for the people in the developing countries.

Germany

In order that the new federal states in Germany will be able to compete on equal terms, it will be necessary, during the difficult adaptation phase, to generate strong impulses which will result in new jobs and preserve existing ones. Support is required for the development of an efficient infrastructure and the promotion of private investment. But a new outlook on life and new job prospects presume that the liberal principle of help towards self-help is respected. Hence it is necessary to apply as quickly as possible the well-tried instruments of regional assistance and promotion of local infrastructure in the new federal states. Encouragement of private investment must be oriented first and foremost to the conditions affecting small and medium-sized companies. Their ability to adapt and their vigorous development will accelerate the process of adopting the free market system in the new states.

The terms of such assistance must allow for the exceptional need for restructuring in those regions. For a limited period, therefore, investment must be given priority. Both sides of industry must bear their responsibility for improving the employment situation. Wages which rise faster than productivity destroy jobs. Pay differentials are required. It must be possible for the works council and management to agree on modifications of collective wage agreements. A shorter working week does not come into consideration at the present time. That would hamper the harmonization of working conditions throughout the country and minimize the opportunities for quickly bringing living conditions in the new federal states up to the level of those in the rest of the country.

Europe

The F.D.P. advocates the development of the European Community into a European union, that is to say, a federation with a democratic constitution. The European Community should be given comprehensive legislative powers. The European Commission should become the European government elected by the European Parliament. The European internal market must be completed by 31 December 1991 according to plan. The F.D.P. is strongly in favor of a European monetary union in which an independent European central bank committed to monetary stability will effectively support a common economic and monetary policy. The European Community must be open to all European nations who share its goals and values and meet the political and socioeconomic requirements. The Community must play an active part in shaping a world economy based on free market principles. There must be no "Fortress Europe".

The Alliance

The F.D.P. calls for a peaceful order in Europe ranging from the Atlantic to the Urals and serving as a common area for democracy, rule of law, industry, environmental protection and military security. The United States and Canada, and the Soviet Union, have a firm place in this European framework. The Conference on Security and Cooperation in Europe must feature prominently in the creation of Europe's peaceful order. It must be developed as the mainstay of a new system of stability in Europe based on cooperation. The F.D.P. wants a united Germany to be an active member of the North Atlantic Alliance. It cannot imagine a neutralized Germany. NATO and the Warsaw Pact must redefine their strategy, their weaponry, their respective roles, and their relationship with one another. NATO's political character must be strengthened. The F.D.P. calls for further rapid progress in the disarmament negotiations, for instance by holding a second round of Vienna talks on conventional forces in Europe.

The Third World

Cooperation on development policy must facilitate the main task of Third World countries, which is to help establish favorable general conditions for their private sector and also to help the poorer sections of the population help themselves. In doing so greater consideration should be given to the positive effects of a market economy based on social justice and to eliminate trade barriers and restraints on competition, especially in the industrial countries. GATT's principles must also govern free trade in the agricultural sector. The F.D.P. would use the savings resulting from disarmament to increase official German financial assistance to developing countries.

Cooperation with developing countries should focus on environmental protection, that is to say, policies aimed at conserving resources and securing energy supply in the Third World without damaging the environment. Special efforts are also required to limit population growth in the Third World. An effective debt cancellation policy is needed to help the developing countries build up a productive economy. In pursuing this aim the F.D.P. prefers carefully considered individual solutions to blanket debt cancellation for Third World countries. The F.D.P. advocates the adoption of a common position by the members of the European Community to restrict the export of arms. Future disarmament agreements should contain a clause requiring contracting parties to refrain from exporting weapons they no longer need to Third World countries.

Research and Technology

The aim of the F.D.P. 's research and technology policy is to establish and maintain good living conditions in Europe and throughout the world. These aims should be achieved by protecting the environment, reducing the North-South gap, providing a suitable basis for structural change, and making companies more competitive. Liberal scientific, research and technology policy guarantees free, creative and independent research, on condition that scientists are committed to the principles of humanity and the task of safeguarding the vital interests of present and future generations. It gives priority to private research but considers that where it is a question of safeguarding and improving living conditions the government should take the initiative if it is not possible to make up for shortcomings by other means or in time. The promotion of research and technology also embraces effective support for environmental research and technology, to be backed up by effective European and other international programs. Nonmembers of the European Community should be involved in order to provide the broadest possible basis for joint action.

Industry and Finance

The aim of liberal economic policy is to secure maximum individual freedom. Achievement, creativity and an active way of life are prerequisites for social progress, economic growth and greater environmental protection. All policy must focus on the individual, hence the F.D.P. would strengthen the fundamental elements of the market economy. It would establish a monetary constitution with an independent central bank unequivocally committed to monetary stability. This would apply in the united Germany and in the context of a common European currency. There should be a system of open markets and free competition . This would involve deregulation and the development of an outward-looking single European market.

The F.D.P. would give preference to private ownership. Precisely in view of the new challenges resulting from the integration of the world economy and from environmental problems, the country requires the inventive capacity of many individual citizens to find solutions to these problems within the framework of an ecology oriented social market economy. In this process private ownership and profit are the main generators of growth. They provide the energy with which to combat unemployment, environmental damage and poverty. The F.D.P. advocates a policy of continuity so that the people will have sufficient confidence in government planning. This is particularly important with regard to tax and financial policy. Lower taxes mean less state involvement. For instance, the corporation and income tax rates should be reduced to a standard 46%.

The F.D.P. is opposed to tax increases to finance joint expenditure by the central government and the states. It recommends instead cuts in subsidies, deregulation and privatization. The housing problem cannot be solved by price controls, since they would be unsocial. Supply-oriented housing programs and assistance for people with low incomes should be introduced to inject more free enterprise into the housing market.

The Environment

The Liberals are aware of but see no reason to be pessimistic about the future or to oppose progress. In fact, the F.D.P. thinks it is possible to finance environmental protection measures through the purposeful use of free market instruments and without ruining the economy. In the 1990s it will resort increasingly to economic instruments to reward companies who keep emissions below the permissible levels and to create incentives for environment-friendly conduct. They will also make it possible to achieve environmental objectives at lower cost. The precious assets of soil, water and air can no longer be made available free of charge but must be taken into account in production and consumption costing.

The production system regenerates itself faster when the economy is in growth. The best economic instrument with which to protect the environment is a policy that is conducive to dynamic, quality-oriented growth and thus to technological advancement. It should include, as specific measures, a Europe-wide tax on fossil sources of energy to protect the environment, an emission tax on cars instead of the present car tax based on cylinder capacity. The amount of tax should depend on the type of vehicle. The F.D.P. would also introduce a product-related levy on special types of waste, as well as a dual system of waste collection and utilization which would be organized and financed by the private sector. There should also be a residue contamination levy in order to reduce air and water pollution.

Social Policy

The aim of liberal social policy is to enable the individual to enjoy life with the maximum amount of freedom and dignity. The limits of the welfare state lie where industriousness and efficiency are hampered by the financial burden of the social security system and the individual is, moreover, relieved of his social responsibility. The F.D.P. therefore abides by a liberal policy based on social justice, solidarity and subsidiarity. Social policy is intended to protect the individual's freedom and dignity to enable him to take care of himself on his own responsibility, to provide a safe financial foundation for the social security system and thus create the basis for further economic growth and continuing prosperity for all.

Society needs more citizens whose standing in the community derives more from direct social commitment. Hence the F. D. P. supports proposals for neighborhood help and private initiative since they help to make the welfare state more flexible. It wants older people to be fully incorporated in the social life of the community and advocates comprehensive support to enable them to lead an active and full life in old age. The F.D.P. sees self-care as the third element of provision for old age, in addition to the statutory old-age pension and works insurance schemes. Priority should be given to home nursing and out-patient treatment rather than hospitalization. Young people should be given better opportunities for development by encouraging them to show initiative, to cooperate with others, and to accept responsibility for their actions. Men and women should have equal opportunities to divide their time between work and family. This requires financial and other support for families, who should have a legal right to a place in a kindergarten for their children. It is also necessary to provide many more day nurseries and creches. The F.D.P. attaches great importance to the fight against AIDS and drug abuse.

Summary of the Green's Election Platform

Foreign Policy

The Greens' foreign policy is aimed at demilitarizing relations between countries. We consequently support the dissolution of military blocs, particularly NATO. Our strategy of unilateral disarmament steps, which we propose for the Federal Republic of Germany, is to be a contribution to this end. A pan-European order of peace, a system of collective security should replace NATO and the disintegrating Warsaw Pact. On the other hand, we reject an EC federation of states since this would merely create a further superpower. The Greens' foreign policy is aimed at a reduction in the Federal Republic's enormous export surpluses. The exploitative relations between industrialized and developing countries can only be brought to an end if the latter receive fair prices for their raw materials and their debts are forgiven – which they cannot repay anyway.

German Policy

The Greens' German (domestic) policy, following the unification of the two German states, is aimed, on the one hand, at limiting the harm suffered by the (former) GDR population in the economic and social sectors. On the other hand, the Greens' German policy together with women's movements, is intent on replacing the Basic Law with a constitution legitimized by the people – in line with the mandate in the Basic Law. This – on the basis of the Basic Law and the draft constitution by the Central Roundtable in the (former) GDR – should establish the rights and regulative mechanisms which provide the answers to present day problems: ecological, informative, social, basic rights; the supplementation of representative democracy through direct democracy (grass-roots democracy); democracy in all societal sectors; prevention or control of societal power; emancipation of women, demilitarization; ecological and solidary order of world economy. To preserve the earth, society must change – that is the motto of the Greens' German policy.

European Policy

The Greens champion a democratic Europe. The Greens favor the democratization and decentralization of EC decision structures. Europe, for the Greens, is more than a European Community. Cooperation and solidarity must not stop at the (bloc) borders. A humane future must be striven for, internationally and globally. International solidarity is more than development aid, in our view. It means worldwide opposition to many an industrial nation's policy of suppression and exploitation, to the policy of dictators and power elites.

The Greens demand that environmental conservation be a priority objective of European policy. The trend towards the concentration of economic power must be brought to an end through decentralization and regionalization of industry and a strict control of mergers.

Alliances

The Greens advocate a civil, non-violent, foreign and security policy. They are against all superpower policies with hegemonic claims, against military alliances which are designed to safeguard this power policy regionally. The aim of the Greens' policy is the dissolution of military blocs in Europe, a non-military, pan-European order of peace. Since their establishment, the two opposing military blocs have engaged in an arms race without peer worldwide and concentrated on Europe – which took the world to the brink of World War II on several occasions. The continuation of military-policy logic, of outward-looking bloc policy to safeguard every form of supremacy vis-à-vis the underdeveloped countries of the "Third World" cannot be the answer to the end of the East-West conflict.

Third World

A responsible shaping of our common earth calls for political emancipation of all peoples from economic dependence and political tutelage. Instead of the currently predominant agreements from north to south, the Greens propose a global "round table" on the basis of international law: There is no alternative to the United Nations (UN) as a multilateral, regulative body for a solidary world society. The UN must be strengthened through the removal of bureaucracy and through democratization, the participation of non-governmental organizations and the dissolution of the current power cartels (such as "World Economic Summit").

A world ecology council and a world economic council should be established – in which all groups of countries should be involved – within the framework of the UN. Here, the guidelines for an ecologically solidary world society must be elaborated and controlled. The Greens support the emancipatory forces in the "Third World" which are fighting against suppression and corrupt regimes. The Greens demand: all arms exports and every form of police or military help must be stopped. This also includes atomic technology.

Science and Research

Science and research must bear a large share of the responsibility for the destruction of the ecological foundations of life on our planet, as testified by the development of atomic energy and genetic technology. Research budgets in all industrial nations are mainly devoted to private enterprise, military and high-risk technological projects. Research projects of an ecological or social nature, on the other hand, lead a shadowy existence.

The Greens want to break with this situation, pledging their support for the expansion of higher education research. Only 12 percent of total research funds in the Federal Republic are available to higher education institutions; many projects at these institutions are nothing more than appendages to industrial research. If higher education institutions are to be effective as a corrective, for industrial, technological and social defective developments, they need far larger research capacities than they have at present, more autonomy vis-à-vis the state and private economy, as well as representation of ecological-social interests in leading democratic bodies.

Industry and Finance

The Greens champion an ecological, social and democratic, economic system which is oriented on the vital requirements of this and future generations, on the conservation of nature and economical exploitation of nature's riches.

Both capitalist and "real-socialist" industrialized nations have shown themselves incapable of realizing an ecological, social and democratic economy. An ecological economy does not view social wealth in the boundless expansion of the commodities world, but in the preservation and reclaiming of natural means. This means that manufacturing processes and products should be adapted to natural cycles without impairing the natural foundations. Long-life consumer goods are to replace throw-away products. A social economy guarantees an adequate income for all and humane working conditions. It calls for the abolition of the sex-specific division of labor.

A democratic economy demands maximum democratic control of "what, how and where" in production. The Greens support all movements favoring decentralized and readily comprehensible production units. Large combines should be broken up into comprehensible businesses. A regional-specific, mixed economy should be promoted. The population must be given political authorization needed to be able to keep a check on and influence enterprises.

Environmental Conservation

If the earth is to be saved, society must change. The ozone hole and the climatic catastrophe are alarm signals; so are the pollution of the soil and ground water, the imminent, biological death of rivers and seas, the disappearance of more and more plants and animals species. Planet earth's endurance limits have been exceeded. The question as to whether the human race will find a life-sustaining environment in the future will be answered in the future. If we do not summon up enough strength now for a turn-around along democratic lines, we shall be heading for an ecological, emergency administration.

If an ecological turnaround is to succeed, the primacy of ecology must take priority over the currently predominant, economic interests.

The destruction of the environment is a global problem. The burdens of an ecological turnaround must be borne by those mainly responsible, according to the principle of "polluter pays": the rich, industrialized nations of the north.

There must be a turnaround in energy and transport; there must be an ecological disposal of waste. In this context, the main points are: the departure from motorcars as a means of mass transport, the promotion of local, regional and long distance transport; the immediate withdrawal from atomic energy; a reduction in energy consumption and an increase in energy prices; the switch-over of production to low-waste products which can be returned to the natural cycle, the avoidance and utilization – instead of the incineration and depositing – of refuse.

Social Policy

Many persons in the Federal Republic are suffering social distress, many are poor. Following unification, the number of poor people has grown. The Greens are striving for a society in which everyone has the right to an existence worthy of humans. For the Greens, the means to this end are:

– a requirement-oriented, basic security of (currently) DM 1200;

– a radical reduction in working hours; a 6-hour day;

– a quota system; at least half of all training and work places must be preferentially offered to women and occupied by women.

The Greens advocate a democratization of labor relations and an expansion of trade-union rights.

Notes on Contributors

Wilhelm Bürklin holds the Lehrstuhl für politische Wissenschaft at the University of Potsdam. His major research interests are party systems, voting behavior, democratic theory, and policy implementation in Southeast Asia. He is now working on comparative studies of political culture and party formation in West and East Europe. He is the author of *Grüne Politik* (1984) and *Wählerverhalten und Wertwandel* (1988).

Alexandra Cole is a graduate student in the political science doctoral program at the University of California, Irvine. Her research interests include political-psychological theories of political behavior and electoral politics in Germany and other industrial democracies. She has recently worked on a study of the role of talk radio in American politics.

David Conradt is professor of political science at Eastern Carolina University. He is the author of *The West German Party System* (1972), *The German Polity* (5th edition, 1993), and co-author of *Comparative Politics* (1983) and *Politics in Western Europe* (1992) in addition to numerous articles in professional journals. His research has focused on political culture, public opinion, elections, and parties. He has been a visiting professor at the Universities of Mannheim, Konstanz, and Dresden.

Russell J. Dalton is professor and department chair of politics and society at the University of California, Irvine, and Director of the UCI Research Program on Democratization. His scholarly interests include comparative political behavior, political parties, and political change in advanced industrial societies. He is author of *The Green Rainbow* (1993), *Politics in Germany* (1992), and *Citizen Politics in Western Democracies* (1988); co-author of *Germany Transformed* (1981); and editor of *Electoral Change in Advanced Industrial Democracies* (1984), and *Challenging the Political Order: New Social and Political Movements in Western Democracies* (1990). He is now working on a comparative study of citizen information processing and voting choice.

E. Gene Frankland is professor of political science at Ball State University. His primary teaching and research interests are comparative politics and environmental policy. He has written numerous articles on Green parties. Most recently, he has co-authored (with Donald Schoonmaker) *Between Protest and Power: The Green Party in Germany* (1993).

Donald Hancock is professor of political science and Director of the Center for European Studies at Vanderbilt University. He is a specialist in comparative politics and public policy, with research interests in Germany, the United Kingdom, Scandinavia, and the European Community. Professor Hancock is author of *West Germany: The Politics of Democratic Corporatism* (1989), co-author of *Managing Modern Capitalism: Industrial Renewal and Workplace Reform in the United States and Western Europe* (1991), and editor of *Politics in Western Europe* (1993). He has served as president of the Conference Group on German Politics, co-chair of the Council for European Studies, and president of the Society for the Advancement of Scandianavian Studies.

Henry Krisch is professor of political science at the University of Connecticut, Storrs, and currently President of the GDR Studies Association. He is the author of *German Politics under Soviet Occupation* (1974), *The German Democratic Republic: The Search for Identity* (1985), as well as articles and book chapters on GDR politics. He is currently working on the relationship between political culture and political change in the GDR, particularly within the SED.

Manfred Kuechler is professor of sociology at Hunter College and the Graduate Center for the City University of New York (CUNY). Before he took residence in the United States in 1985, he was a professor at the University of Frankfurt, Germany. His numerous articles in scholarly journals and contributions to edited volumes are in the areas of voting behavior, social movements, and research methodology. He is co-editor and contributor to *Challenging the Political Order* (1990).

Helmut Norpoth is professor of political science at the State University of New York at Stony Brook. He has published numerous articles on German elections and is co-author of *Politics and Government in Europe Today* (1990). His most recent publication is *Confidence Regained: Economics, Mrs. Thatcher and the British Voter* (1992). He was president of the Conference Group on German Politics in 1988–1990.

Dieter Roth is a co-director of the Forschungsgruppe Wahlen and a lecturer at the University of Heidelberg. He is one of the leading analysts of electoral behavior in Germany, and co-host of the monthly Politibarometer program on the Second German Television Network (ZDF). Roth has written extensively on the development of the German party system over the past twenty years, based on the extensive public opinion surveys of the Forschungsgruppe.

Klaus Schoenbach is professor of journalism and mass communication research at the Academy for Music and Theater in Hannover. He has published widely on political communication and media effects. His most recent English-language book, co-authored with Lee B. Becker, is *Coping with Plenty: Audience Responses to Media Diversification* (1989). He received his Ph.D. in communication research in 1975 at the University of Mainz and his Habilitation in 1982 from the University of Münster.

Donald Schoonmaker is a professor of politics at Wake Forest University. He writes about German political culture and political parties. His articles focus on the changing party system, the development of the political culture, and the relationship of literature and politics in Germany. He has written several essays about the Greens of West Germany, and a book that he co-authored with Gene Frankland, *Between Protest and Power: The Green Party in Germany* (1992). He is currently working on the problems of cooperation between East and West in the formation of an all-German Green party.

Holli A. Semetko is assistant professor of communication and adjunct assistant professor of political science at the University of Michigan, where she is also a faculty associate in the Research Program on Media and Politics at the Center for Political Studies, Institute for Social Research. She is first author of *The Formation of Campaign Agendas: A Comparative Analysis of Party and Media Roles in Recent American and British Elections* (1991), which is co-authored with Jay Blumler, Michael Gurevitch and David Weaver. She received her Ph.D. in political science from The London School of Economics and Political Science, and received the 1988 Samuel Beer Prize for the best dissertation on British politics.

Christian Søe was born in Denmark and studied at the University of Michigan and University of British Columbia before receiving his doctoral degree in political science from the Free University of Berlin. He is professor of comparative politics and contemporary political theory at California State University, Long Beach. His publications include articles on German party politics. He is editor of the annual series, *Comparative Politics*, and is co-editor (with Dirk Verheyen) of *The Germans and Their Neighbors* (1993).

Index